To

The Roadmap to the American Dream

The Roadmap to the American Dream

How to Reach Financial Prosperity in a Changing World

Joshua Cadillac with Timothy Paul Cadillac
and Cody Shaw Lampariello

Copyright © 2017 Joshua Cadillac with Timothy Paul Cadillac and Cody Shaw Lampariello
All rights reserved.

ISBN: 1542769493
ISBN 13: 9781542769495
Library of Congress Control Number: 2017901249
CreateSpace Independent Publishing Platform
North Charleston, South Carolina

Table of Contents

	Preface	vii
Part 1	The Dream	1
Chapter 1	Where did the American Dream come from?	3
Chapter 2	Has the American Dream always been the same or has it changed with time?	10
Chapter 3	Is it really getting harder to achieve the American Dream?	22
Chapter 4	If the American Dream is so great how does one get it? What tools do I need?	29
Chapter 5	Objections to the American Dream	35
Part 2	The Concepts	59
Chapter 6	The things you should understand before you invest	61
Chapter 7	Debt	77
Chapter 8	Common types of debt and how they work	85
Chapter 9	A little detail on methods to avoid risk	107
Chapter 10	The markets	131

Part 3	The Math	155
Chapter 11	The basics	157
Chapter 12	The basics when adding debt	161
Chapter 13	Advanced investment ideas and the math to use them	169
Chapter 14	Where this math matters in your life	179
Chapter 15	Taxes	187
Chapter 16	Basic things to know when buying real estate	198
Chapter 17	Buying Securities	206
Chapter 18	Caution!	215
Part 4	Becoming an Investor	223
Chapter 19	Setting yourself up to invest	225
Chapter 20	Go get it! Achieving your American Dream	237
	Suggested Reading List	243

Preface

The first thing you are probably thinking is why am I reading a book written by a guy named Cadillac? It sounds like he should be selling cars or maybe performing in a Vegas act. While my last name seems like a weird place to start a book, bear with me and it will make sense soon, I hope.

The story of my last name follows the tale of a young Italian man named Johnny. He arrived with his parents at Ellis Island in the year 1900 when he was only two. He lived with them above their restaurant in Little Italy in lower Manhattan, and there he learned from them that if he worked hard he could achieve anything in this land of opportunity. He decided as a young man that he was gonna "make it" in America and one day be his own boss. In the early 1920s he saved enough money to start a small taxi business using only Cadillac taxicabs. To stay in business, he developed an amazing talent for fixing his cars to keep them running. This allowed him to be successful and eventually he got a great reputation for being able to fix any car.

So, you have an Italian, in New York, in the 1920s, with a reputation; it is pretty much a forgone conclusion that this story had to end in a nickname. Sure enough, with his success came the nickname Johnny (you guessed it) "Cadillac". If you had a car that no one could figure out how to fix, people would say, "You couldn't get your car fixed? Take it to Johnny Cadillac."

Unfortunately for Johnny, the Great Depression came along in 1929 and wiped him out. He lost his cars and his cab business. While he lost that company, he did not lose his nickname, or the desire to be his own boss. In fact, over the course of the next few years he would start nine other companies, all of which failed—that is, all but the last one.

This last company formed in 1938 was an export packaging business that boxed things for shipment overseas. They would disassemble and box things like vehicles, farming equipment, and heavy machinery. A few years later, there was this little world war going on (WWII) and Johnny, along with just about everyone else, was doing his part converting the business and his factory to work exclusively for the war effort. One day, however, the FBI came in and said to Johnny, "We have a problem. We are at war with Germany, Italy, and Japan. You are Italian and our records show you are married to a German woman. That is two thirds of who we are fighting in this war, and you are operating your business under an alias."

Johnny was shocked. While it was true that everyone knew him as Johnny Cadillac, he always used his legal name to sign all his documents. He was also doing all he could to support the war effort. Regardless of the facts, the FBI told him, "You have to choose one name or the other or else there will be problems." So, my grandfather legally changed his name to Cadillac without a second thought.

I asked my father why Grandpa gave up his family name so easily? (It was obviously not to help his grandson sell this book or to give my Vegas act a leg up.) My dad told me he did it because he loved his adopted country and the opportunities it offered. He came from a place where he never would have had the chance to achieve what he did here. With will power, determination, and through hunger he was able to build something he could be proud of. He was able to provide for his family and create a business to pass on to his children. (By the way, although Grandpa has long since passed away, that company he fought so hard to build in 1938 is still in business today.) He gave his family a good life and set his children up to be even more successful than he was. He believed wholeheartedly in the American Dream, and he achieved it.

That is a brief snapshot of the path that one person took to achieve his dreams and leave a legacy that outlasted him. I have written this book to help you identify and attain *your* American Dream.

The American Dream is a thing we often hear about. It involves something like 2.3 cars or kids, or maybe it was a dog and 1.3 cats and a half of a hot dog. Whatever it is, it seems to be really important, and from what people are saying in the news, it sounds like it is getting harder to achieve. So what exactly is it? And has it changed with time? Is it really getting harder to get? Or are they just saying that? If it is so great, how does one get it?

As we go forward, we are going to try to track this down, give you the answers to these questions, help you with the skills you need to make the American Dream a reality for you. A word of warning, to go forward in the pursuit of this dream, we have to reach back into history to understand what it is and where it came from.

It starts with "society." It is a funny thing when you think about it. Society passes ideas on to you so subtly that you don't even realize it. We are completely immersed in our own culture. We assimilate complex ideas without realizing it, ideas which may have evolved over thousands of years of societal change. We do this without any conscious effort simply because it's what we see modeled everywhere. This can be a good thing. We pick up ideas like not punching people we don't like, shaking hands, teamwork, manners, and not passing gas in an elevator (unless it is full of your friends, or you can reasonably blame it on someone else who is of more questionable "hygienic persuasion" in the elevator.)

One serious problem with cultural immersion is that often you have no basis for context. So, you don't even notice that what you might be doing is silly, crazy, or just plain wrong. It's like walking into someone's house that has several cats. The owners are immersed in the experience of being a pet owner and do not recognize the "lovely" bouquet of au de fuzz ball that overwhelms you when you walk into the room. Yet, for the pet owner, they smell nothing amiss. They have been exposed to it so much that they have lost the ability to sense what an outside observer can easily smell, and do not recognize their obvious need—to be added to the scented candle of the month club.

Then what are some ideas that our society embraces that we may be blind to? More importantly, what are some of the ideas that may not be entirely accurate (bad ideas); ideas which society tells us are indeed the way to go? That is a topic for a different book. The thing that matters here is that the American Dream itself is a societal construct. Folks who are doing well are told that they are "living the dream". Let's look now at how society tells us to get this dream.

One thing that our society has embraced strongly is the idea that education, especially higher education, is *the* critical steppingstone on the pathway to success. This idea permeates our society. It seems that is all they talk about in middle and high school, never far from any politicians' top talking points, and something every parent wants for their kids—right? Degrees and advanced degrees are a verifiable necessity to most of the truly high paying careers that exist in our economy. That is a fact. Moreover, there is an existential benefit experienced with the "expansion of one's view of the world" during the college years that is often a paradigm-shifting event in young people's lives. There is the added benefit of kids being on their own and learning to cope in "the real world". You would have to have lived under a rock to not hear of these benefits.

Society makes it seem like if you just go to college and get your degree, the American Dream is waiting for you with dinner on the table, your fuzzy slippers in one hand, and your newspaper in the other (read iPod for those who don't know what a newspaper is). Is that true? Is college truly a turnkey prep course to achieve success? Does the current higher education system really give young people *everything* they need to go out and take the world by storm? Considering the tremendous debt—much of it college debt, the high number of loan defaults, and vast number of college grads moving back home to live with their parents, it would seem that some key components to successfully "launch into life" must be missing.

This is a book about figuring out what is missing, and how in today's society, it is still possible to achieve the American Dream (or I really should have come up with a different title for this book I suppose). So, let's focus only on those things that affect it.

In the last several years, the only group to really experience any major growth of wealth in the U.S. is the investor class.

It is my contention that the missing pieces of the educational puzzle are: Understanding money, the capitalist economy in which we live, and how those things affect reaching financial goals.

This book is about the ideas that drive investment. We start with the idea of the American Dream because achieving some level of financial prosperity is essential to it, and without some knowledge of investing it is very hard to actually reach that goal. The idea that you just put your head down and work as hard as you can, don't spend too much, and save a lot; then eventually everything will work itself out is prolific in our society. The working and lower classes have stagnant wages, something we find out in later chapters means they are actually losing money and not just "treading water". So rather than taking the "pie in the sky when you die" approach and considering that we live in a capitalist society, which thrives on the availability of capital, it would seem wise to have the tools necessary to take advantage of this system.

You might figure that these basic financial skills would be taught in high school or at the very least in the first couple of years of college—right? Not so much. In fact, unless you are taking a degree specific to finance or economics, much of the basic tools we discuss won't even be alluded to during your entire college experience. The cynical person might say, "they do not want you running a time value of money calculation on that $100,000 plus degree they are selling you," and to some extent that argument may have value. A financial analysis of the prospects for a certain degree would probably be a good tool in determining how much debt a certain career could reasonably sustain. In fact, one would hope that a student's ability to pay back these loans would be taken into account when these loans are given (in fact, that sounds eerily reminiscent of something they were saying after the housing crisis). This is not in any way to pick on the information gained in school, but to make us question why basic investment education does not make the roster of most colleges' first two years of available courses. Yet, so many other "really important" classes, like art history, bowling, gardening, weightlifting, and French literature are all classes that earn you credits. *Really?*

I know some people are ready to toss this book across the room: How dare anyone speak an ill word against French literature or gardening. Yes, I could make the case that bowling (at least the way I do it) teaches humility, and yes smashing pins can be cathartic I suppose (I wouldn't know much about that as my bowling ball, much like my mind, spends way too much time in the gutter). All of the courses above have value, but as an investor, it is important to weigh carefully all investments, and that includes your time. These classes might provide a lot in the way of self-fulfillment, but they do not do a whole lot to help you actually pay for college, or buy a house, or get married and have kids, or send them to college—and by the way, forget about retirement. That is pretty much a list of many of the things by which most people measure success, and it is not addressed. A large part of what motivated the writing of this book is to fill in this gap in the conventional educational curriculums.

So, is the cynic above correct? Is the education establishment knowingly keeping these skills from students? Probably not. The reality is that most of the educators who are not specifically in the field of finance do not understand these principals themselves. I know this may come off like an attack on higher education, and if this behavior is malicious on their part, it probably would be. Truthfully though, educators are often the ones in financial trouble. Being an educator, especially in the realm of higher education, requires skill and dedication usually in one field. It is unrealistic to expect someone who is a specialist in one field to be a master of them all. You can have a great attorney, but it is not reasonable to expect him to give you a colonoscopy—although it sometimes feels that way.

People have areas of specialty and educators are no different. One effect of specializing is that you do not know what you do not know in other fields. This puts one in the dangerous position of potentially flying a kite made of tin foil in a thunderstorm, while standing in the pool and wearing a sheet metal bathing suit, having no idea this might not meet OSHA standards. Especially in the first two years, a college education gives you a smattering of many fields and you start to feel like you know a lot. You think you know what you are doing, but you have no idea how dangerous a little bit of learning can be.

None of this in any way removes an individual's responsibility for their own financial education. Individual responsibility is another idea our society gives us, and we have tended more and more to the idea of external responsibility for our lot in life. A "victim mentality" is prevalent in our society. We look for reasons why society, circumstance, upbringing, or other people have conspired to keep us from achieving our goals. Successful people can list those reasons too; however, they realize that they can waste time complaining about the problem or start fixing it.

Our society has often become fascinated with wasting time and assigning blame anywhere but on one's self, instead of getting stuff done. Some people complain that the Oreo commercial made the cookies irresistible, and now they are fat or have to go get their butt on the treadmill. Understanding investment ideas and strategies is something that you need to take responsibility for by adding these to your knowledge portfolio. Buying this book is a good step toward making that happen. Knowledge is invaluable. My father used to tell me as a kid, "Once you learn something son, no one can ever take that from you. It is yours forever." You have the greatest ability to affect your life, and that does not necessarily mean for the better. Bad thinking leads to bad results.

It is problematic that these ideas are not taught to a greater extent, and they usually have to be sought out because they are not widely available. The part that really hurts, however, is the financial destruction you see strewn about. That damage ranges from people in their twenties buried in debt and considering bankruptcy all the way to eighty-year-olds who do not have the funds to retire, and perhaps forced to take a job handing out stickers at Wal-Mart or eat cat food to survive. These individuals may be victims of circumstance, but most often they simply let opportunities pass them by through lack of knowledge. People are being hurt by these ideas because they are not widely proliferated (distributed), and this is something that this book hopefully helps with.

There is another reason for this book: To give people a way forward, and encourage you, the reader, to be a person of action. I want to help you take your financial future into your own hands instead of hoping for some "happy occurrence," or political legislation to secure it for you I want this book to give you the tools you need to achieve the level of prosperity that generations before you enjoyed.

The goal here is ambitious. I want to give you a robust understanding of this subject. This is where many other types of books on this subject tend to fall short. They put forth areticent perfect set of circumstances and tell you what to do in the panacea or ideal world— that is their model they are assuming. But as soon as something goes wrong, you get hurt, learn a painful lesson, and move on; or worse yet, stop investing all together.

It is not always easy to understand the underlying mechanics of what is happening. Yes, you make mistakes along the way (just like my Grandpa did), but with a deeper understanding of the why things work the way they do you can limit those mistakes and respond to them in a better way. It's kind of like an understanding of cars. Most people understand that when they put the gas in one end, the car goes. As soon as that process breaks down, however, some people only know the number for AAA. On the other hand, others possess a more complete knowledge of the car's systems and can resolve the issue for themselves. The more depth there is to your knowledge, the easier it is for you to figure out how to properly respond.

The way we are going to go about building this knowledge base may seem counterintuitive, much like building a house. When you want to put *up* a house, the first thing you do typically is go *down*. The foundation usually requires going the exact opposite direction you eventually do want to go, but the strength of your house is most largely determined by how well and how deeply you do go down. For this reason, we are first going to go into the history of the American Dream and address some of the ethical issues that people may have. Then we look at the actual ideas that drive investing, give you some tools you can use to analyze where to put your money, and finish up with some tips on how to put your money to work. This is a how-to-understand investing book, not a book on doing a specific type of investment or transaction. We go into some detail, but you need to add other knowledge specific to the type of investment you decide you want to do. This is the place to begin your education before delving into a specific deal type. Think of this book as the general anatomy textbook you need to read before deciding to be a neurosurgeon.

Some of the ideas expressed may be hard to grasp. Initially, we try to go slowly and give good examples to clarify the ideas being discussed. We are going to write this in a very informal and conversational tone because reading this information is tough and you don't need me trying to impress you with my literary prowess. Some humor will probably work its way in here too so that we can have some fun along this journey together. Hopefully, we can track down that pesky American Dream.

Part 1

The Dream

Chapter 1

Where did the American Dream come from?

*Those who do not remember the past
are condemned to repeat it.*

-George Santayana

To find the basis of the idea of the American Dream, we must go back well before the founding of the United States of America. In order to fully grasp all that it entails, we need to look in on Europe in the 1600s to 1700s. So, let's hop into our "way back machine" and see how things looked in those days.

Europe was going through significant changes at the time, and these changes were causing people to revisit how they thought about themselves and their place in the world. For a very long time, people were led to believe they were born into their state and position in life. They were told since birth that they were created by God to inhabit a particular position and there was nothing they could do about it. So, if you were born a king, it was because God had created you better equipped than anyone else for this position. Not so bad if you're the king, right? On the other hand, if you were born into a family of pig farmers you were doomed to smell like pig for the rest of your life (and not the good bacon kind of pig smell). The next generation followed in the footsteps of the previous one. If your name was Smith, then you were a blacksmith, as was your father and his father, and so will your children be for that matter.

The leaders, whether they be barons, lords, kings, etc., were actually supposed to take paternal (parent-like) interest for the people under them. Remember, in their mind God put them into a place of authority because they possessed the skill and intelligence to match their position in life. So, if someone on an estate was ill, the person who owned the estate was responsible for making sure their children were cared for and that nothing happened to their subjects' property.

You could argue that this was just a way of protecting their interests, and it seems very oppressive and wrong. But remember, although this system seems like it would be rife with corruption, it was actually carried out by God-fearing people that more often than not did their best with the concepts they had at the time. Also, this system was far less oppressive than some of the modern methods we have tried in our infinite wisdom, for example, think Communism.

"Hold on," you say, "Is this wacko expressing a desire to go back to feudalism"? No, not at all. I am trying to set the scene for the times as well as provide some balance in order to understand the feudal period of history that often gets nothing but bad press.

> **Tip:** *Let me pause here to say that balance in perspective and in life are both difficult to maintain. It is like a pendulum with one kind of crazy on one side and the opposite type of crazy on the other, with sanity right smack in the middle of the pendulum's swing. Guess when the pendulum is moving fastest? If you guessed, "as it is flying by sanity on its way to crazy" you would be correct. This does not mean that some things are just plain wrong and should be fought. It does mean, however, that a lot fewer things than we think actually fall into that category. We should probably be very hesitant to put something there. A very wise man once said "Any story sounds true until someone tells the other side and sets the record straight." (Proverbs 18:17.)*

So back to feudalism—this idea meant basically that people in the lower classes were not equipped to handle anything more than their lot in life. These were deeply rooted beliefs by both the people in power and the under classes. This meant that it was pointless to educate the poor. Funds used for educating the under classes would simply be squandered, and any sort of cross training or change of fields would simply be a waste. This, of course, meant that the underclasses did not possess the tools necessary to actually prove the system wrong: "You can't be a land owner Johnny, because you can't read. So, can't I go to school to learn to read? That's crazy talk Johnny every fool knows you must be the child of a land owner to learn to read. You're such a kooky kid Johnny!" Don't you just love a vicious circle?

Now enter the Dutch. The Dutch actually looked back to an ancient form of government and decided in the year 1581 to form a modern republic. Their inspiration came over two thousand years before the above example from the Greeks, those who came up with the idea of people actually governing themselves. The Greeks used this system for centuries, and eventually it was adopted by the Romans. It was not a true government by the people because the votes of the landed always counted for more, and bribes were used to get the plebes (poor people) to vote the way the powerful wanted them to vote. Also, these were huge slave owning cultures where the vast majority of the people that actually inhabited an area were slaves and did not have the right to vote.

This Dutch republic was very important to history because the Dutch were a major maritime power during the age of exploration. This meant that they exposed vast parts of the world to their culture and ideas. Did the Dutch get everything right? No, they were one of the foremost slave trading nations of the time and known to be especially brutal. That does not mean they did not get some things right. There is some sayings involving babies and bathwater that would be appropriate here.

The Dutch, however, elevated the position of the common man to a place where he could, by his own efforts, rise above the station in his life where he was born. (Yes, I am using masculine pronouns. It was the 1600s, women's suffrage still had a couple of hundred years for people to become that progressive.) The Dutch were also major advocates of personal and religious freedom. In fact, for those that remember their American history unusually well, you

Where did the American Dream come from?

may remember that Holland, in the Dutch Republic, is where the Pilgrims fled to, from England, after religious persecution forced them to leave.

The Dutch did a lot of spice trading and therefore focused much of their exploration in the tropical islands where the rarer spices grew. They also took time in their travels to found a little settlement called New Amsterdam. New Amsterdam was a small settlement in a port city with one of the greatest natural harbors in the world. Because of its natural maritime features, much of the "New World" trade went through there, and it was often where new settlers would arrive. For that reason, many people became exposed to the ideas of the republic because of those early Dutch settlers.

Take a moment to think back on what it must have been like in those days when people never traveled much further than five to ten miles from their homes, and ideas from a country far away were not easy to hear about. Imagine a world with no transportation other than horses and wagons, poor streets, and no real means of communication other than letters and word of mouth. It would be hard to know about what is going on a couple of cities away let alone in another country. For those sports fans out there, think about how long it would take to get the results of away games—not pretty huh? Yet there was opportunity in the New World. People started following that opportunity, and they became exposed to the thought that they could actually improve their station in life.

Flash forward a little way. Although the Dutch they continued to do well with their spice and slave trades in general, they lost interest in that New Amsterdam place when it didn't measure up to their expectations. So when the Governor of New Amsterdam sent them reports that the English were planning on laying siege to the city, the Dutch leadership decided not to send help. The English took over, and in order to eradicate what they could of the Dutch influence, they changed the name of that city to New York.

They could not, however, erase all of the Dutch flavor. One Dutch word we have and still use is very telling of how their influence persisted. The Dutch word "boss" actually means that a person is over you by your choice. That was a paradigm shift at the time when most people still thought the person above them was there by divine right (God's will). The idea that people could choose their leaders soon led to a place where people realized they could be their own leaders.

There were a lot of other factors that went into the creating the idea of an American Dream, for example, the writings of John Locke, and others were huge influencers. But history talks about these people all the time. I'm here to tell you stuff you don't know—that the Dutch were major influencers of how people in the U.S. began to think of themselves and their station in life.

Okay, we get it. All men are created equal, but what does that have to do with the American Dream? The American dream most simply is: *A person can achieve whatever the limits of their talents and abilities allow them to.* This type of system is called a meritocracy, a place where people are promoted in life based upon their merits regardless of their station in life. So, stated another way, the American Dream means that without anyone else's help, by the fruits of my own labor I can succeed and prosper if I put forth the effort. This idea was championed by the founding fathers that challenged the leaders in England; the very leaders who looked down on them and would not treat them as equals by giving them adequate legal and political standing.

The movement away from limited voting rights and slavery was fueled by the idea that men were actually created in the image of God and are therefore equal. It took quite a while for the last vestiges of paternalism and feudalism to work their way out of the systems of the U.S., but rather than focus on what they got wrong, let's look at what they did well. Our history gave us a system that, for the time, was very radical and allowed for the ability to grow and change to address the systems' shortcomings. We possess choices every single day that we take for granted; these options were never available to our ancestors. By those choices and our efforts, we can largely decide the course of our life.

Putting it all in perspective

The system we inherited still stands. We still live in a meritocracy, but the merits that allow us to succeed are not always apparent. There are some merits that have great value at some points in history, and now—not so much. There

Where did the American Dream come from?

was a time where the witch doctor made a really good living hexing people for their disgruntled customers. These guys were rock stars of their day, yet you don't really see Willie the Witch Doctor nowadays on an episode of *Cribs* or driving his Bentley around town. Why? Because the things that made them successful then are not as valuable now. Things change. Living in the system we do grants us unmatched potential for success, but we are responsible for what becomes of this potential. We were given a gift: An American Dream, which allows us to be the captain of our own ship. But with that position, there is responsibility to actually work to achieve the dream.

As captain of our own ship, our choices have consequences. So, if we make good choices and work hard we win, right? Is that true? Well yes and no. It's possible to make a good choice and not a wise one. Here's an example for the gamers out there: If you are going to buy gold for your MMO gaming character (which no one ever does, right?), it is a good decision to buy gold from a less expensive source. Although spending real money on fake money is really hard to explain in any way that is even slightly credible, despite the extra D.P.S. the gear you bought might add (you gamers know what I'm talking about). This is a good choice but not a wise one. It does not get you closer to long term success. Not an analogy that you get? Wait, there's more. Let's say you want to buy a designer purse because it is just sooooooo cute, and typically, it costs $5,000. But you make a good choice and find it at an outlet store on sale for $2,500. Now you can make everyone envious for the next fifteen seconds while that bag is still cool, and then it is on to the next one. This would be another example of a good choice, but not a wise one.

You need to check what is important in the long term. Unless the way you measure success are things such as how many weeks a night you can party like a rock star, have a reputation as the best raiding guild on your server, or own the latest iPad, BMW, or smartphone, you may need to consider if these goals will still be important to you twenty years from now. Will the fact that you stayed awake for forty hours straight to pay $200 more for the latest smartphone still seem like a good idea when you realize you can't retire? I know what you're going to say, "Oh but I will always have the experience of having done something wild and crazy." You know what else is a wild and crazy experience? Having to be the guy tearing movie tickets in half at a theater when you're eighty because you were so wild and crazy when you were younger. On the bright side, you will have your stories, and the other people in the retirement home can shake their head about what a party animal you were "back in the day".

Look around you at all of the older people. Most made a lot of good choices and probably followed the rules. Yet so many are barely getting by.

Reality Check: *That will be you when you are their age if you do not start actively planning to avoid that fate. So we have been given the freedom to be captain of our ship, but do we have the responsibility to steer our ship wisely? Can we look ahead to see where best to steer our ship? Yes, and no.*

Wow! This books a big help, huh? Hang in there. What is required to achieve the financial prosperity implicit in the American Dream has actually changed with time.

Oh great, a moving target. Any more good news for us?

Yes, there is some good news. We can look back and see how this moving target has changed to anticipate what we can do in order to be in the right place at the right time. It is kind of like trying to run through an area where the sprinklers are on when you don't want to get wet. You look and see the spray pattern of the sprinklers and make your move (run like crazy, usually) when the time is right. If you did your research right, you come through the irrigating gauntlet dry as a bone, or at least less wet. If not—you get wet, followed most likely by some really colorful language. So, where have the sprinklers been, and what does that mean for where they are going? For that answer we turn to chapter two.

Chapter 2

Has the American Dream always been the same or has it changed with time?

A people without the knowledge of their past history, origin and culture is like a tree without roots.

-M̲ᴀʀᴄᴜs G̲ᴀʀᴠᴇʏ

The American Dream has two main parts to it, and these have changed significantly over time. These two parts stem from the right of "the pursuit of happiness". The first part is the freedom to enjoy any prosperity we can achieve; the second maybe even more important part is the freedom to take advantage of opportunities as they came up. This is important because it actually allows us to achieve the prosperity in the first place.

> **Note:** *This idea of the pursuit of happiness, as meant by the founders, is a little different from what most people think it means today. To the founders it meant something along the lines of: The joy one gets from a life well lived. This means there is not just a bowl of candy, but instead, a fence that needs painting and then a bowl of candy. You get the candy and also to admire the*

work you did on the fence. To them the joy of having painted the fence well actually exceeded the pleasure of eating the candy.

Also, this right never gave the guarantee of happiness only the freedom to chase it. This right never promised you a job, only the freedom to hustle to get one. It would be nice if we lived in a world where everyone got the job they wanted and was paid tons of money to do it. It would also be great to live in a world where fried butter wrapped in maple bacon à la mode served on a bed of cheesecake was a healthy snack. That world is not our world so let's deal with what we have.

The shift in prosperity and opportunity are closely correlated. These changes occurred because of world events, technology, and supply and demand. So, what caused the American Dream to change? It occurred for two reasons. The first is a perception thing: What we think of as success now, is different than what our ancestors thought. The second is a market thing: Remember our buddy Willie, the Witch Doctor from chapter one? His skills were valued in his day, but society has moved away from using his trade, leaving him with no market demand for his formerly valuable talents.

Note: *This is a very good example of a market (supply and demand.) People often think of supply and demand with things like oil, but not as much with things like labor. Supply and demand applies to any market, and learning to recognize them in the world around you can open your eyes to opportunities. We discuss this more in a later chapter.*

Now let's look at the same U.S. historical events from chapter one, but draw different conclusions based upon the set of glasses we use. As consumers, we look at what we feel we need to "have" in order to consider ourselves successful; and as employee/competitors in the workforce, we can see how what we needed to "do" to have access to the opportunities for success changed with these same events. We need to know both: What it is we need to "have" in order to feel we have achieved the American Dream, and then what work we need to "do" to allow us to earn it.

The perception thing

Most of the early settlers in the U.S. came from Western Europe and had agricultural backgrounds. In other words, they were farmers. Most never had the experience of owning their own land. They were vassals or serfs. They worked land that did not belong to them and were allowed to keep a portion of what they made for themselves. This portion typically was never enough to afford them any real excess or bounty from their production. If these folks remained in Europe, they would have worked their entire lives and never been able to get ahead.

Along comes this new place where all the cool kids are going to, a place called America. It was possible there to own your own land and not have to share the fruits of your toil with anyone. Let's put this in perspective because these early immigrants do not get nearly enough credit: These folks left everything they ever knew, got into glorified wooden bathtubs (the sailing vessels of the day), and came to a place they had never seen before—all for the *chance* to just work hard and succeed. Talk about guts. Makes you realize how soft and comfortable we really are. We don't even want to get up to reach the channel changer for the TV, but would prefer to download an app to our phone to save the effort. These folks risked everything for just a shot to fight like crazy to make a life for themselves. For these early settlers, just having a farm and being able to say that it was "their land" was the culmination of the American Dream.

This idea was held by many of the early U.S. Presidents who were farmers in their own right. Thomas Jefferson thought that this country should be a nation of farmers, and he distrusted all banks, business, and industry. Folks like Alexander Hamilton (the guy on the $10 bill and yes, the Broadway play too) thought that America could be more. They thought America could be an economic powerhouse of industry and business. In fact, there was an early battle for the destiny of this country waged between Hamilton and Jefferson. It turns out that Hamilton's vision for this country eventually came to fruition, and with that industrial vision came changes to people's desires.

As America grew, it began to change from a bread basket, food-producing power house of export, to a manufacturer as well. Strong intellectual property rights encouraged innovators to come up with ideas and innovations to make people's lives better. Things like the cotton gin are examples of this. It allowed for increased farm production, which meant fewer workers were needed to produce the same amount of materials. This meant that there was extra labor (farmers who were no longer needed for farming) now available for manufacturing. This extra labor could be used to create finished products like clothes or steel instead of simply selling the raw materials to another nation, which would then produce the clothes or steel. This was hard physical work, but it allowed a path to a reasonable level of prosperity.

By the mid 1800s, people became even more enamored with the idea of the self-made, manly man. It was no longer enough to own a farm to qualify as being successful, you also needed to rise above your birth. The American dream moved from ownership to ownership plus growth. This was a major shift, and it was evidenced throughout the culture of the time. For example, from the time of Abraham Lincoln (1860) on to Woodrow Wilson (1912), nearly all of the Presidents of the U.S. were from the frontier portion of the country, and therefore, rocked some serious facial hair. Only two presidents did not have major facial plumage in that time: Andrew Johnson who congress impeached (they say for other reasons, but conspiracy theorists suspect that it was due to resentment for his refusal to grow mutton chops), and William McKinley, who was assassinated (probably for his baby smooth skin). The point here isn't to draw attention to presidential shaving practices, but to point out the importance for the American people to have a President who looked the part of a "frontier man".

The idea of these self-made men on the frontier forging their way in an unsettled country was a cultural ideal. Before you go saying how crazy those ideals are (and the folks who follow them), let's just remember some of the "super cool" fads we had like *The Macarena* (a song and dance that possesses the ability to stick in your head like the Barney song with the added benefit of making you look simultaneously stupid while dancing it), the original Volkswagen Beetle (with a slightly worse ride than a Model T), and anything involving clothing from the 1980s.

In the mid to late 1800s, basic schooling was considered important, but higher education was looked down upon. People were valued for what they could make and not so much for book knowledge. This meant that in order to achieve the American Dream you needed more physical skills and hands on innovation. The growth of industry was driven by people with little in the way of formal education but instead possessing a trailblazing mindset. They were undaunted by problems, and instead, sought to find solutions.

Another component that altered the American dream during this time was the growth of transport. How does that change things you may ask? (You really don't have to ask, you know we're writing a book so we kinda have to tell you.) The answer is: Lots of ways. With the introduction of man-made canals, goods were able to be transported longer distances at cheaper prices. This meant people could afford more. Also, these canals made the land along them more valuable because people who lived on or near them could save time and labor in transporting their goods to market. Improvements in ship building made travel much safer and more accessible to people. Now people actually could think about travel as a leisure activity as opposed to nautical Russian roulette. This became another way people began to measure achievement: The ability to travel for leisure.

Finally, in the latter half of the 1800s railroads really began picking up steam (get it? the pun's so bad it is almost funny). The introduction of railroads meant that landlocked places could be easily and readily accessed without the need for costly canals, or labor and animal intensive transport. People now had access to markets to sell their excess goods (more than what they needed for basic survival), which increased the opportunity to produce to their maximum potential. By producing more and having a place to sell the excess production, people could actually accumulate a surplus. Because rail transport was so much less expensive per mile than alternative overland routes, goods from greater distances could be accessed. This competition was encouraged and made the cost of goods significantly lower.

With the availability of these new and much less expensive (than the imported items) manufactured goods, lots of previously prohibitively expensive items became affordable. The result: People started to want more things. They felt they needed to have more "things" to feel like they had reached the same level of prosperity as before. As that happened, Americans needed larger homes to put these new things into. This meant that the hundred-foot square home that used to be their castle rapidly turned into a storage shed.

Moving into the late 1800s and into the early 1900s, better farming equipment and techniques continued to make many farmers obsolete, but the need for workers in other trades continued to grow. Former farmers had to move themselves and their families into cities. People started living much closer to each other than they used to, and proximity breeds comparison. Once again, innovation drove prices down and things that were once luxury items got to the point where the common person could afford them. These things were quickly added to the idea of what constituted prosperity. In no case is this more evident than the car. In the early 1900s, if you had a car you had really "arrived". You knew what everyone on your block drove, and the car they drove was a major indicator of your success. Hard manual work was still what people expected to do, some people went to college but not most, and families would often live together into adulthood to save money.

Moving into the post WWII era and the mid part of the twentieth century, the jobs that tended to provide the better pay and could be found in quantity were white collar "office jobs". These jobs required more in the way of book knowledge than just street smarts and elbow grease. Parents that wanted their children to achieve more than they had realized they needed to send their children to school. This moved the emphasis away from the long-standing practice of apprenticeships, and more toward the idea of actually completing high school and maybe even figuring out where the local college was on a map. Formal education became necessary for children to be successful. Parents also needed the economic prosperity necessary to afford their children's education in order to feel that they, as parents, had achieved their dreams for their kids. By this time, owning a car was commonplace, but if you had a Cadillac, you were living the dream. People started realizing that two cars were better than one, and this too was adapted as a means of measuring success.

One more major change throughout the mid and later 1900s was medicine. How does that affect the American dream you may ask? Well, it introduced this idea into the American psyche of not dying at, on your way to, or from work. The idea of actually surviving long enough where you might not have to work is a fairly modern idea—enter retirement into the log book of things required to achieve the American Dream. People wanted not only to earn enough to survive, but also enough to hang up their cleats and chillax for their later years. How they retired also became a big issue. Would it be in "Stinky Acres" old age home, on your yacht just off of your winter home in Fiji, or some place in between.

Where we are now has not changed much, has it? All we want is our own land, to do better than our parents, to travel, own a bigger house, lots of stuff, a couple of cars, obtain college education (for us and our kids), and of course, retire well. Insurance would be great too, an investment portfolio, perhaps that new smartphone, the latest laptop every three years, a master's degree, a vacation home, a time share in Disney, a purse-size dog with a complete wardrobe of K-9 clothes, and on and on and on. The American Dream has changed, and continues to morph. We want more than ever, so what we have to know and do to achieve this has to be more than ever.

Before we get into that let's look at one more way the American Dream has changed.

The Market thing

The skills employers value change with time. This happens because fads change. People used to love jukeboxes, and so if you were a jukebox repairman (back then they were not "technicians" yet), you had great job security. But societies' tastes changed, and what was once a secure job is now obsolete. On the other hand, positions like computer programmer did not exist in the 1930s. New fields come into being and old fields become obsolete. Anticipating these changes is not an easy thing to do, but we can look at what has happened in order to at least be as prepared as possible to make educated decisions (as opposed to a blind guess).

In the 1700s, the U.S. started out as primarily a nation of farmers. Yes, there were other fields, but farming was top dog back in the early years. Better transportation and farming innovations made it possible for farmers to produce more food per farmer, while also giving them access to larger markets. This meant that there were food surpluses. These surpluses drove down the price of food, as food was abundant, and this forced many people out of the fields and into alternative employment. People who had other skills besides farming were more readily able to find jobs. In order to have employment opportunities, it became a good idea to spend some time apprenticing (and you would want your children to know a trade, right?) So now what was needed to be successful were alternative skills to farming. You did not need any formal education, just a strong back and you would be just fine.

As we start looking more toward the early to mid-1800s, design, transport, and manufacturing rapidly became more and more a part of the U.S. economy. Much of this innovation involved farming, which once again eliminated the need for many more farmers. The now out-of-work farmers needed to learn new skills in order to take advantage of the rapidly growing fields of manufacturing work, transportation, and innovating. All of this required very different skills than farming, but the most room for employment was in one of these places. Once again, people needed to change to meet the opportunities. Basic education was needed—still a strong back—as well as the ability to learn and innovate on the job. These things would allow you to achieve the cultural ideal of the time, which was "the self-made man".

In the later 1800s and into the early twentieth century, one had to learn more specialized skills in burgeoning fields, like automated manufacturing, electricity, and plumbing. These fields did not exist fifty years before, and they rapidly became indispensable parts of the economy. The advent of automated manufacturing (assembly line) meant that instead of doing all the work, it was often the person monitoring a machine that was doing most of the work, or simply doing a repetitive, but often mind-numbing job. This required specialized knowledge of the machines being used, and a change in the basic temperament and discipline of the individual. Jobs like these once again required people to work very hard, but also required training and skills for employment. People had to not only be able to read, but also be able to read and understand technical data. They also needed to work in the same spot all day as opposed to roaming the fields. This was a very different experience for most people, and took some serious getting used to. There still was little emphasis on higher education, but there was a higher premium paid for being smart. People that had jobs in fields like electrical were on the cutting edge of modern science.

Into the mid and later part of the twentieth century, white collar management type jobs became more prevalent, and were typically were better compensated. The people in these jobs were expected to know how to handle people, be innovative, and have a broad base of knowledge. Formal education became more and more coveted by employers, and as the level of education went up, so did their expectations. This meant that higher and higher levels of education became mandatory for the same jobs. In order to achieve the American Dream, you would probably need these skills at a minimum. Gone were the days of a high school education being enough. A college degree was almost a prerequisite for achieving the American Dream. In fact, paying for college is part of most parents' American Dream. This is a response to a market demand for a college-educated population.

Where are we today?

Right now, the competition among employees in most white collar job markets is strong, and this has forced workers to acquire higher and higher levels of very expensive education in order to be competitive in getting these jobs. The competition for the available positions has gotten tougher and tougher. "Experience in the field" is the main filter employers often use to weed through the glut of applications they receive. For people just coming out of decades of schooling, nothing can be more frustrating. They need to get the job to get the experience they need in order to get the job in the first place. Sound circular? That's because it is.

Markets with high unemployment allow employers to be more selective, and when they are, it is frustrating. Many people are pursuing careers in what have been historically high paying jobs like law, only to find out that most major firms are telling new attorneys that they have no chance of making partner. If they don't like that response, then maybe they will enjoy the gentle thud on their back half as the door smacks them in the butt on the way out. Law firms can do this because of the huge numbers of lawyers graduating from law school. They have a need to pay their loans, and so they have no ability to hold out for better terms. If they try to negotiate, the firm can simply hire someone else that will work under those terms. Labor is a supply and demand market. A glut of supply causes a lowering of wages.

As a society, we tend to look down on what was once honorable, blue collar work, and we tend to think of people that do that type of work as not being able to handle the schooling to get a better job. We have nearly eliminated all shop classes in schools anymore lest we tempt any student to think of any career that does not take them on a four-year detour through a university campus. Yet, college student dropout rates are at an all-time high, as are tuitions. So when students realize college may not be right for them, they not only have a sense of failure, but also a huge bill to go with it. Talk about kicking someone when they are down, right? We have almost arrived at the point of having contempt for those folks that don't quite make the college cut, that is, until our toilet backs up and the "you know what" quite literally hits the fan. In summary: We are glad to have a plumber, but we do not want our kid to grow up to be one.

Conclusions

Let's quickly look at a couple of ways this information allows us potentially to "track the sprinklers" and anticipate some things that might help us. It would appear that a fresh emphasis on broadening one's skills through internships or apprenticeships might be a good idea to meet the employer demand for experience. Schools that offer such programs would be able to show higher employment levels for their graduates (who would leave with experience on their resumes), while providing free labor to firms providing the apprenticeships. The obvious downside would be employers reluctance to train temporary employees, but the opportunity to test drive and recruit from outstanding performers may counteract this initial reaction.

Another potential market shift may come from a lack of people going into the trades. This trend has caused a shortage of supply in many of the skilled trades (plumbers, electricians, carpenters, etc.), which has resulted in very high wages for people in these fields. As compensation rises, these fields have more potential opportunities for young people seeking a career without the burden of huge college debt. The lack of jobs paying enough to compensate for the college debt of students and providing a reasonable subsistence could easily cause an increase in college loan defaults. This in turn may make lenders for these types of loans more selective about who gets student loans. Couple this with rising tuitions and you could begin to see the number of students attending universities shrink. In other words, the college bubble could burst, or at least noticeably shrink.

An example of fields that would seem to be in need of college educated grads would be—wait, let me get my captain obvious super hero costume on—jobs in developing technologies that have strong social demand like green energy and show promise for long term growth and implementation. Obviously, computer and programing-related fields are the current high demand industries, and with no real signs of let up. This is probably the place where large numbers of new jobs need to come from, as more new technologies replace jobs from other fields. An example of this is the self-driving beer delivery trucks now being built. Many of my friends used to think, "Hey, if this doesn't work out I can always drive a truck!" Not so much in the near future. So what happens to those beer truck drivers? The same thing that happened to the farmers in the late 1800s and the early 1900s. They are going to need to start working in industries where the country's economy has greater need. Back then it was industrial work and management, now it is going to be in technology and technology related fields.

Nobody thought there would ever be enough work for all of those farmers, but that is because they didn't realize all of the additional industries created from the industrialization of our nation. Will those self-driving trucks have new systems that need maintenance? Will they need specialized parts to allow the computer to drive the truck? Who is going to work on the programing for that? Will there be some automated way to refuel the trucks? How will that work, and who will build the infrastructure? Will there need to be more vigilant painting of the streets so computers can sense what lanes they are in? Is a new type of paint for roadways needed to make these trucks safer? What happens when the truck reaches its destination? How is it unloaded? With no driver there to represent the company's interest, who checks what comes off of the truck? These are just a few examples, but they highlight one thing—the obvious need for technological training.

On the other hand, an example of over supply would be that four-year business degree. There are too many graduates with this degree for the jobs that require it. This makes the cost versus the return of the degree work against the degree-holder's favor. To be competitive, some supplemental skills should be acquired to help separate you from the herd. This is not to say there is anything wrong with having a degree in business, but it has almost reached to the point where employers expect to see that as often as they expect you to wear a shirt to the interview.

There is a lot more that can be gleaned from the history of the American Dream, but the purpose of this overview is simply to establish that it is not a fixed concept. Both the prosperity needed to achieve the American Dream and the skills needed to earn it are a moving target. If you are aware of these factors, you can check your perceptions, make sure they are realistic, and have a better idea of what opportunities may be coming down the pike.

We are now tracking the sprinklers and ready to prepare our path through them.

Chapter 3

• • •

Is it really getting harder to achieve the American Dream?

"Unfortunately, the real minimum wage is always zero, regardless of the laws, and that is the wage that many workers receive in the wake of the creation or escalation of a government-mandated minimum wage, because they lose their jobs or fail to find jobs when they enter the labor force. Making it illegal to pay less than a given amount does not make a worker's productivity worth that amount— and, if it is not, that worker is unlikely to be employed."

- THOMAS SOWELL

Labor is a market in which employees compete to earn the employment they want. They do this with things like education, experience, professional designations, etc. The competition over time tends to get tougher, and what was outstanding before becomes the minimum standard as more and more people vie for better jobs. It is similar to how things are with cars. It used to be that features like air conditioning, power steering, and electric turn signals were special options (pay extra) on cars. Because of competition, however, these same items are standard on almost all cars now. Manufacturers began including them to separate themselves from the other cars on the market, and as their competition responded in kind, the market began to expect these things. In this same way, a college degree used to separate someone from the majority of the workforce, and now it has become "standard equipment". This is a good thing for employers as it makes the overall labor pool better, but a bad thing at the same time because many of these expected "standard equipment" items are time consuming and costly to acquire for the actual workers.

So would you say it is harder to make cars than it used to be? Well, it is and it is not. Taking out of the picture any regulation changes and other peripheral items that would affect manufacturing a car, the reality is this: Cars are always forced to be on the cutting edge and constantly trying to outdo their competition. So it has always been hard to make cars, but the things that make it hard change over time. We as consumers are the beneficiaries of this. Today's cars do lots more for lots less (adjusted for inflation) than older models. Labor is much like this. People are expected to know lots of things their predecessors didn't, along with many of the things that they did. So each generation has gone through the same struggle of not being able to follow the same steps their forbearers did to succeed. In order to impress the employer market, they must find the "power windows" or "navigation system" of job skills.

Jobs, jobs, jobs

The importance of employable skills is most evident during an economy in recession. When labor markets are tight, there are jobs for just about everyone. Employers must pay more to retain quality help. When an economy is in recession, even very qualified, educated, and experienced people often can't find work. Also, because jobs are harder to find, employers can ask for more from their employees as the employees have fewer options. Don't start feeling too bad for the employees though, as they tend to "get their pound of flesh" from the employers when labor is tight. With high unemployment, employers can have people work longer shifts, receive lower wages, give fewer benefits, and layoff high paid employees to replace them with cheaper options. Add to all of this a demand for people seeking employment to have more and more education and consider the rising costs of education. You now can see how a tight economy makes this very tough. All of this puts tremendous strain on employees, and can make them feel that success is impossible.

Americans often cannot financially survive any sort of prolonged unemployment because in general, we tend to spend too much and have so much debt. This puts a ton of pressure on people today, and it is downright depressing when you can't find a freaking job. This is not a new thing. It is something that just about every generation went through in our country's history. Prolonged recessions have been seen at least once each generation since the 1930s. This means that similar set backs are not unique to this generation or this economy.

Does this mean it isn't as hard as you may think? In some ways, it is not harder. Huge numbers of people from past downturns have been successful even though they've been through very similar circumstances as we see today. Yes, the housing crisis was a fairly unique occurrence in size, scope, and from the standpoint of how many otherwise stable households were financially damaged by it. But there have been many booms and busts throughout the history of this country, and nothing has exceeded the resilience of Americans ability to overcome and adapt. The U.S. suffered a five-year recession at the end of the Civil War where 640,000 Americans lost their lives and half of the country was destroyed. During fifteen years of the Great Depression, unemployment rose as high as 25 percent, yet none of these things stopped Americans from coming roaring back. In fact, times of great prosperity tended to follow these dark days. That gives everybody something to look forward to (almost as much as the end of this chapter).

Were they really the "good ol' days"?

We have discussed some of the common areas where people believe achieving the American Dream has become harder. These things change, but at the same time remain the same. What do I mean by that? I mean that while attitudes such as employer expectations have changed and are more challenging, previous generations also had to put up with change and challenges in their time. Change is never easy. So while it is possible to say that it has become tougher to attain the American Dream because of this or that change, it is also possible to say that the same type of adapting was required by previous generations. The challenge remains the same. Did previous generations have seemingly all-downhill path on roller skates to success? Did they leave us with an Everest climb with some industrial dental floss and a half of a box of rusty finishing nails for our climbing equipment?

There are some differences, however, that we can look at that definitely seem to make it tougher today. Two are the cost of the higher education and the age at which people can enter the workforce. A college education, which many companies have made a prerequisite for employment, should give people the ability to produce higher wages, but a college education puts a serious financial burden on them that was not widely experienced by previous generations. Also, it takes time to earn these degrees. So instead of starting work at age eighteen, or if you go back even further, thirteen or fourteen, we are now in our mid or even later twenties when we get started—and with a nice heaping side order of debt.

Lest you start feeling too bad for yourselves though, *past generations were working at thirteen freaking years old!* They had to grow up much faster than kids do today. In some ways, previous generations were more naïve than the current one, but when it came to taking on responsibility, they did so at much at a younger age. So we now have to spend more time and money on education, but they had to take on responsibility much sooner. Which is tougher? That's a matter of opinion.

Another factor that has an effect on the achievement of American Dream has been a shift in society in our perception of work. Many people tend to look at work as something you have to suffer through in order to do the things you want to do. This is very different from the views held by many of our forbearers. They thought of their work as a reflection of themselves, and therefore, enjoyed and took fulfillment from their work much more than

Is it really getting harder to achieve the American Dream?

contemporary Americans. This may seem like something small, but we are talking about the American Dream and this is an idea reflecting a perception of success. It is hard to feel like you have succeeded if you hate what you do for forty plus hours a week.

On that note, personal anecdote time: When I was a little boy, my Daddy told me something I never forgot. He told me, "Son, I don't care if you are a floor sweeper, but you be the best damn floor sweeper there is. That is your floor son." He would say, "All work deserves to be done well." My Dad was born in 1930. His idea of work was common place for his era. That is a major shift from the way people now perceive their employment. Most people in my father's generation would work at one or maybe two different jobs their entire life. This is largely due to the how much of themselves they invested in their work. It was not just about getting the work done for them it was personal. The current generation changes jobs much more frequently. Millennials stay at jobs for less than three years as compared to 4.4 for the workforce in general.

Yes, lower job security is a factor, but lower employee loyalty must be a major contributor as well. If employees only look at their jobs as a meal ticket, then it becomes much easier for employers to show little loyalty when it comes to "firing time". This is sort of a chicken and egg situation. Did employers stop showing loyalty first or did the employees? There are good arguments for both sides, and the reality is, it doesn't matter. The important idea is that this shift in the perception of what part work plays in finding fulfillment in life is culturally different than it once was. We have to look at it because it affects how we feel regarding our own success.

Earlier we touched on the change in the American Dream that has us wanting more things in order to feel like we have "made it". We live in a consumer society where things that push our "I want" button are everywhere. Advertisers are masters at making us feel like a pile of dog poo if we don't have the latest and greatest_____ (fill in the blank with just about anything).

Note: *They are not wrong for doing this. Sellers tend to think their products are pretty freaking awesome and they want the world to know it. Advertisers fill this need in society. If you question this, think about what life would be like if you had a great product. This item is absolutely wonderful. The* *product would allow you to sit on the couch and have your body burn one hundred calories a minute. It regrows hair where you want it, while removing it where you don't, all the while making you better looking. It would make your significant other treat you nicer, and make you smell like lavender-washed linen with a hint of vanilla. All of that for the low, low price of $19.95, and it actually works. Getting the word out about a product like this would be in the best interest of a lot of people. As the seller, of course, you would profit but also for the consumers would benefit from its use. It is easy to think of advertisers and sellers as charlatans, but most are not. To some extent, sellers feel their products are superior and the consumers' need to hear it. Advertisers see the sellers' need, and then try to meet it.*

Back to what we want—wanting more things has an added cost of paying to buy those things. If we can't afford these things, we feel like we are not successful, but in order to buy them, we need to generate additional income necessary to afford them. So the more things we want, the more we have to spend, and therefore, the more we have to earn. Because we want more, it is harder for us to feel successful than it was for previous generations. There are two ways to handle this: One, adjust your expectations downward. Nobody wants to hear that but it is a viable answer. Or two, make more money so you can afford more of what you want. Luckily for you, I'm giving you the tools to do that; it is why I wrote this book. We get into that later.

Summary

To conclude, some of the things that make achieving the American Dream seem so hard now have been problems every generation has gone through. It therefore requires us to adapt in a similar way to those who went before us (so stop whining). Other things are based upon a labor market that favors employers, and these things tend to even out in an economy that more favors employees (seriously, stop whining again). Lastly, there are things that genuinely do make success more difficult, like prerequisite skills or education that competition in the labor market has made so common place that they have become expected. The costs of these things are borne by those that want to even be considered for many corporate jobs (okay, you can whine a little bit on that one).

Looking at work as simply a paycheck instead of something to enjoy also makes success much more difficult. In other words, if you look at your job as something you receive fulfillment from it is much easier to feel fulfilled (so get your head on straight and stop whining). Also, allowing yourself to lust after "things" makes being content and feeling successful harder (so adjust your expectations and stop whining, or finish reading this book and earn more and you won't have anything to whine about).

We have touched briefly on some tools to help you achieve the American Dream, but are there others? If that feels like a segue to chapter four—it is.

Chapter 4

If the American Dream is so great how does one get it? What tools do I need?

I can make just such ones if I had tools, and I could make tools if I had tools to make them with.

-Eli Whitney

To get the American Dream you need to know where to look. Surprisingly enough, it is not stocked at Walmart or on Amazon (which really bums me out as I am Amazon Prime). Do they sell the tools at least? Yes, they do sell some tools that can help you to get ahead in the race. So what tools do we need? The most important tools we need are a willingness to invest (expending resources with no guarantee of return), the grey matter between your ears (your brain is the one true natural resource), ambition, under-consumption, time management, the ability to recognize and minimize risks, and the skills to allocate your resources wisely enough to achieve the American dream. Wait, didn't you say they sold some of these tools at the above mentioned retail sites? I did. Well, what isle is that "risk to allocate" thing on because I spend lots of time at Walmart and I've never seen it. Luckily, the paragraph below answers this question.

Investing in the grey matter between your ears, and time management

Tool one: You can buy books at the places mentioned above, allowing you to invest time to learn a skill that might be a help when opportunity strikes. That is actually an investment in your grey matter. Tool two: You have a finite amount of time, and how you use it determines the skills and tools you have to navigate life with. It also determines at what point in your life you have those skills. It is probably better to have a skill at age twenty than at age thirty because you would have ten years of additional use of the skill acquired at age twenty. Looking at time as an investment is critical to really using it well.

You can choose to invest young and have the greatest opportunity for success, or squander your asset (time) and have to try to make it up later. In other words, you can choose to read that romance novel and maybe learn the skill of not blushing when reading the details of the lengths a certain fireman would go in building good community relations with a certain lovely, lonely and very athletic lady in her shower, or you could read a book on how money works. Don't get me wrong; I love some quality fiction. It is a great way to unplug (blushing is still a bit of an issue and rest is important), but buying the other book is a much better investment. One life skill pays much better dividends than the other.

Not a fan of romance novels? Substitute in sports, video games, hanging out at the mall, etc. All of those things are *way* more fun when you actually can afford to do them, and when you do not have to worry about money and success because you already have them. They can wait.

> **Tip:** *Statistically speaking, wealthy people read more than non-wealthy folk. If you don't like to physically read books, audiobooks are a fantastic alternative. So be like the cool kids, grab your headphones and listen to a great book.*

You are your best asset. Taking the time to not only invest in the particular field you are choosing to enter, but also surrounding fields gives you a huge leg up when working with people and building relationships. If you had been a shipping clerk and then had moved up to managing the shipping department, you would have an excellent idea of what problems the shipping clerks have and what things would actually help make them more efficient. This can be applied not only to moving up in a job vertically, but moving in related fields horizontally. A mortgage broker that used to be a real estate agent has a much better idea of how to serve their real estate agents and their customers than someone that did not have this experience. I am not saying you should have fifty different jobs. I *am* saying; be curious and ask people in various field's question about how they do what they do. Volunteer to work with them and help. Build your data base of experience.

How many people ever asked their teacher in school how long it takes them to make their lesson plan or grade homework? If I wind up working in a field related to schools, perhaps editing a text book or running a cafeteria, that information would give me a leg up in trying to earn business, relating to my customers, and making decisions that will be helpful to them. If I am editing the text book, making the questions at the end of the chapter multiple choice so they can be graded more quickly would probably be appreciated. Or if I ran the cafeteria, I could try to remove the need for the teacher to stay with the class when lunches are handed out so they can enjoy the full lunch period. In all these examples, investing your time to build data from people and books gives you more data to make better decisions.

Tip: As said earlier: *My Daddy used to tell me: "Once you learn something son it is yours. No one can ever take it away from you." Investing in the right kind of knowledge is a very wise use of time.*

Ambition/work ethic

You must not only want success, but you also must be willing to make the sacrifices and take on the risk to make it happen. Ambition is the driving force behind this, and work ethic is what puts that force into effect. If you are unhappy with where you are in life, you have two options: Stay unhappy, or change your circumstances. The willingness to do the uncomfortable work that is involved with changing your circumstances is a life skill. This means it can be learned as well as honed. Ambition does not mean you have to be "gunning" for the person above you. It does mean taking everything you do very personally and trying to figure out how to do it better. Also, you want to constantly be looking for better opportunities outside of what you do. You need to prepare and prepare so when opportunity comes, you are ready.

Personal Anecdote Time: *This is from a time when I actually got it right in life (I got it wrong plenty of times too). I was about fourteen and wound up being volunteered for cooking pancakes at a men's breakfast. I was shown by the person in charge how to use the very tiny grill (about 18"x24"), and told that we could make six pancakes at a time. I had about two minutes of downtime waiting for the first pancake to be ready to be flipped, and then another two minutes before it could be taken off. I had never made a pancake in my life, and so I deferred to the boss lady.*

After a while as I was making the pancakes, I noticed that if I spaced them differently I could get eight on the grill instead of six and if I turned the heat up a little higher, I would only have about a minute break in between turning and taking the pancakes off the heat. Turns out it was a really popular pancake breakfast, but the one place they didn't have issues was with pancakes. You see, I didn't stop with getting eight pancakes on the grill. I eventually realized that I could fit twelve with no space to spare, and with the heat turned up just right as soon as I ladled out the last pancake the first one was ready to flip. I wound up with zero down time and more than quadrupled the previously-thought max production for that tiny little grill.

Did I become president of IHOP for my display of flap jack prowess? Sadly no, but it helped me to define myself (not only to my boss but more importantly to myself) as someone that would always be looking for a better way. I won't just rest on the knowledge that something could be done better, but instead, actually go in and do it better.

Plenty of ambitious people stand by critiquing the jobs their bosses do while trying to sabotage them at every chance, or they just do the bare minimum in order to skate by. Having a good work ethic makes you stand out for doing more than required. The trick is not to work hard just because you want something. You work hard because that's how you roll. If you recall from earlier when my father told me how to handle sweeping a floor; just imagine how seriously everything else should be taken if that is your standard. You always want to be the person that is not content with the status quo. You make people's lives better by doing that. My pancake customers didn't have to wait as long to get those "coronary" cakes because I was working hard and being ambitious.

Find a problem and figure out a way to fix it. The way we live today is largely shaped by people that embraced this idea and made our lives better. Ambitious folks can do a lot of bad things as well, and this is something to be aware of and avoid. From making fire to smartphones, ambitious people are the ones that solve problems (fire, so we wouldn't be cold and smartphones, so we could trip more often while walking and texting). Capitalism gets the bad rap for being built on greed, but in reality, the best way to succeed is to consider the needs of your fellow man, and then find a better or cheaper way to meet that need. The folks that do this make a resounding impact on our world, and by emulating them, you are better positioned to achieve the American Dream. Yes, ambition can be a very good thing.

A willingness to accept risk and invest

People can be very funny when it comes to risk. There are some who can't wait to jump out of a perfectly good airplane wearing a parachute, but are terrified to put their money to work. This would lead you to conclude they are obviously more worried about losing money than their life. Does that make sense? We all have our inconsistencies, but this seems a wee bit more strange than most. Often, however, people engage in risky behavior that gives a temporary thrill but does not do anything to help them in the long run. When you invest, there is risk, but the benefit can be much longer lasting than a simple adrenaline high.

We all are risk takers in one way or another. We do things all the time that have risk associated with them. We cross the street, drive cars, dine at fast food restaurants, go on dates, and even eat candy and red meat—just to name a few. We are risk-taking machines. Talk about living on the edge!

An example of risk people don't normally think of would be when you commit to a four-year degree. Now this is an investment with risks. The investment doesn't always work out. You run the risk that the market won't be there for your skills when you leave. You take on that risk when you chose what you study and commit to paying for it. We take the risk of getting a degree because we analyze the cost benefit ratio and feel the rewards justify it. If we want to be really smart, we would try to find ways to minimize that risk. How would you mitigate (minimize) that risk? You could research the demand for your chosen degree, and then talk to others in the field, speak to recent grads in the field to see what their job hunt experience was like.

This is an example of the type of risk and reward we face all the time whether it be in the career we chose or walking across the street. The ability and willingness to accept these risks allow us to achieve nearly all we do. Investment risk is everywhere. Those that are willing to understand the risk and study how best to mitigate it are the ones with the greatest chance of achieving success.

Here is another example: Should I invest more in a relationship with my lovable but under-motivated friends? Pros: They are a lot of fun, we have a good time, and maybe I can help them be more motivated. Risks: My friends keep me from investing my time in other more productive endeavors, an opportunity comes along and I miss it or lose it because of them, and perhaps eventually I become more like them. Would I not be better served with investing in more ambitious friends? True they are probably less likely to own a gas mask equipped with a bong attachment, but they may help me get to the place where I want to actually be.

Looking at most things in life as investments and analyzing if the reward is worth the risk is often a much more effective method of decision-making. We discuss risk a lot more in a later chapter.

> **Tip:** *All the money in the world is no good if you don't have anyone with you to enjoy it. Don't lose sight of what is important. Make the money to have the flexibility to build the relationships that make it all worth it.*

So, now we have looked at the ideas of labor as a competitive market and the tools that help us achieve success. This hopefully helps us survey the landscape for the opportunities that we can use in order to prosper. For the most part, this is what achieving the American Dream really is: Seeing an opportunity and having the timing and skills to exploit it. Let's jump to some of the objections people sometimes have to the system we use that allows us to prosper.

Chapter 5

Objections to the American Dream

*"Democracy is the worst form of government,
except for all the others."*

SIR. WINSTON CHURCHILL

There are a lot of concerns that people have about success. Is success based on exploitation? Do others have to lose for me to win? These are just a couple of questions people often think about and ask. The morality of business and profit is an important topic. So, let's take a look at a few questions and see where profit and business fit into the world.

Is profit a dirty word?
Many believe that profit is at the heart of nearly every evil in the world, it should be a four-letter word, and is an activity one should never undertake with their mother. If this is true, we should want nothing to do with profit and perhaps move to Manitou Springs, Colorado and become hippies. But before you start packing your tie-dyed t-shirt, let us rethink what profit is and what it is not, in order to see if it really is the spawn of Satan, as so many claim.

Profit and greed are not synonyms

If I had a dollar for every movie or TV show that talked about greed and profit as synonyms, I would have a lot less in student loan debt, but I wouldn't necessarily get a visit from three ghosts this Christmas. Why? Because greed is an unhealthy attitude towards acquiring wealth, while profit is actually the money that is made. To say that the two mean the same thing is like saying gluttony (an attitude toward food) is the same thing as food itself. (If you have this attitude towards food, please see a doctor because you're anorexic.) A profit, even a substantial one, can be made without having an unhealthy attitude towards it.

Profit is moral but greed is not

Yes, Gordon Gekko is wrong, Greed is *not* good. Greed is a sign of a life out of balance. It assumes that the only thing, or the most important thing in life, is making more money. The problem is life is not that simple. We have lots of important things going on in our lives, many of which have equal or greater weight that need to be given to them than making money. A good example of such an important responsibility includes being a loving, intentional parent to your children. A bad example of an important responsibility is playing WOW (World of Warcraft) all night, and as a result, not being ready for work. We must maintain a balance between making money and our other obligations in life.

Making money is important because it allows us to care for many of our other important needs, but if those needs did not exist, making money wouldn't be that important. Think about it, if you found a magic lamp and asked the genie to make it so that everything you wanted or needed was free, what value would making money have to you? Almost none. This is because money is really a means to getting other things. It is only valuable to the extent that it allows you to do so.

Money really is worthless in and of itself. This is easy to see in countries where hyper inflation has occurred and money is worth almost nothing. People burn it to keep warm and use it as toilet paper. In other words, they use it as a poor substitute for the things they cannot buy, such as wood and toilet paper. On the bright side, they *do* get to enjoy the knowledge that the fastest growing brand of toilet paper in their country bears the portrait of the person probably responsible for their economic misfortune on every single piece.

> *Inflation hasn't ruined everything. A dime can still be used as a screwdriver.*
>
> -Quoted in P.S. I Love You, compiled by H. Jackson Brown, Jr.

Making a profit, however, without being overly consumed with doing so, is good. Why? For one thing, people rightly assume being wasteful is wrong. Think about that talented and capable brother-in-law or cousin you have who has dedicated his life to ensuring companies like Blizzard®, Domino's® and LazyBoy® stay in business? How do you think about this person—positively or negatively? You probably think he or she is a lazy screw-up and deserves to get their butt kicked for being a "loser". When we say someone is lazy, what we really mean to say is that they are wasting their ability to work. Being wasteful simply is wrong. When you are not putting your money to work, you are making your money lazy. Your money has the potential to produce more money through investment, but instead, it is sitting on the couch—which is your bank account—watching Sportcenter® and drinking a beer with potato-chip crumbs all over Ben Franklin's face. We could even go so far as to say that not making money, to the extent that it is wasteful, is morally wrong.

For those who still think it is morally wrong to make a profit, consider someone that religiously goes to the gym. They spend hours working on their body. Do we begrudge them the six-pack they now have, as opposed to the Buddha-pack they started with? No, they earned the profit of a better physique. If you are not willing to get upset over their six-pack, why are you mad at people who turn their $1,000 in savings into $6,000 through investments? You might say "Yes, but when you work out, you are not hurting anyone else, whereas the only way you can make a profit is to exploit other people." First of all, for those of you that think no one gets hurt when you work out, call me two days after you did ten sets of squats in the gym (#MyButtHurts). Second, we directly address profit's effect later in this chapter.

Profit is necessary and not arbitrary

The human body produces blood. The body needs blood to survive, but the body does not exist for the purpose of making blood. (Contrary to what the vampire lobby would have us believe.) Profit is like blood to a business. Much like the body, a business needs blood, that is profit, to continue. As an example, imagine you had a million dollars (I know, you like this example already). As a wise investor, you want to put this money to work in the best way possible. You have a choice, you could put the money in a mutual fund that averages seven percent annualized return, or you could start your own business—let's say a restaurant because that's a business with which I am familiar. If you put the money in a restaurant, you have to be there all the time, watch everything like a hawk, and deal with both employees and customers' needs all the time. If that restaurant only returns an annualized profit of seven percent, you would be crazy to take on all that extra trouble associated with the restaurant when you could be sitting at home eating take-out, earning the same 7 percent with your mutual fund. The truth is, profit is a necessary operating expense for a business. If a business does not make enough profit to justify all the work that comes along with it, then it either needs to change so it does make enough, or close down.

You might be thinking about the body analogy I gave and be saying to yourself, "Well, bodies do not exist to make blood, but business sure exists to make money." This is true and it is not. Can a business exist solely for the purpose of making money? Sure. Is that the popular understanding of the function of business or investing? Yes. However, we shouldn't have such a shallow view of people putting their money to work. For example, when I look at my father's generation, which some have called the greatest generation—the generation that created some of the world's greatest businesses—I see a very different understanding of the purpose of business and investing. My father

The Roadmap to the American Dream

was one of the perhaps largest exporters of motor vehicles in the world during the 1950s and 1960s. In his plant hung a sign that said. "Quality and Service are Our Only Products." This sign was not for his customers benefit, but for his and his employees. The reason: His generation saw the businesses they owned as extensions of themselves. Was my father concerned with making money? Absolutely, because he understood that making money was necessary for the life and growth of his company, and to provide for his and his family's needs. However, he would not want to be in a business that made money but produced crap.

In the same way, not only is it possible, but there also is ample historical evidence to show that many of the most successful business ever created have been driven by their owners' pursuit of a bigger dream than money. This is evident from the decisions they made when choosing to follow their mission over the path that would maximize profits in the short term. One of the clearest example of this today is grocery giant Whole Foods. Just read their motto:

> *Whole Foods, Whole People, Whole Planet* emphasizes that our vision reaches beyond food retailing. Our success in fulfilling our vision is measured by customer satisfaction, team member happiness and excellence, return on capital investment, improvement in the state of the environment and local and larger community support.[1]

The other day I went to a Whole Foods with my wife and wanted a Coke. (Surely I am not the only not-so-health-conscious hubby who has reluctantly gone shopping with his wife at this store while wandering around aimlessly, waiting for this experience to be over, and then went in search of that delicious, brown, fizzy, sugar water.) My point is, if Whole Foods wanted to sell Coke, they could, because there is a market of lost hubbies' who would buy it. When I asked the clerk where to attain this liquid delight, he said they did not carry Coke at all. Coke does not fit with their mission, and therefore they do not carry it, even if it they can make money selling it.

---

[1] "Declaration of Interdependence," *Wholefoods.com*, accessed July 11, 2016, http://www.wholefoodsmarket.com/mission-values/core-values/declaration-interdependence.

Objections to the American Dream

Microsoft®, Apple®, Google® and many extremely successful companies have made similar decisions. As a matter of fact, Jim Collins, author of the best-selling business and leadership book, *Good to Great*, found that one of the main difference between good companies and truly great—that is, wildly successful companies—is that good companies were chiefly concerned with making money, while great companies were committed to a mission[2]. Part of the reason for this is the fact that there is no doubt, people want their work and their investments to have more significance than only making money. They are willing to work harder and be more attentive to a mission that they are passionate about. Mission-driven businesses and investing have shown themselves to be more profitable, and have resulted in tremendous good to their customers, employees, and communities.

Also, many people have the view that how much profit a business makes is determined by whatever they feel like charging for their product. That is, they believe that profit is arbitrary. However, if we think about this for a second, it is fairly easy to see this is not the case for the vast majority of businesses. Imagine, for a moment, you had the power to make whatever laws you wanted. After you undoubtedly outlawed the TV show, *The View,* and possibly put a body fat limit on the purchase of spandex; let's say for whatever reason, you wanted to help Domino's (formerly Domino's Pizza) make more money. So you decide to pass a law that wherever Domino's Pizza is sold, it cannot be sold for less than $1000 a pie. The hope is that Domino's will do really well because they are making such a big profit on their pizza because it costs around $990 more than a pie would normally cost. The truth is, you have just caused Domino's to go out of the pizza business. Why? Because nobody is going to by a Domino's Pizza for $1,000. (Just like no one, besides your mom, and even she is fifty/fifty on the decision, is going buy your karaoke version of Whitney Houston's *I Will Always Love You*.) Pizza lovers are going to buy their pizza somewhere else with reasonable prices.[3]

---

[2] Jim Collins, "Building Companies to Last," *Jimcollins.com*, 1995, accessed July 11, 2016, http://www.jimcollins.com/article_topics/articles/building-companies.html.
[3] Michael Bauman, "Dangerous Samaritan: Poverty in America," *Summit Ministries*, Summit.org, recorded November 8, 2009, accessed July 9, 2016, http://www.summit.org/resources/summit-lecture-series/dangerous-samaritans-poverty-in-america/.

Nearly all companies (with the exception of monopolies, which are extremely rare), cannot just charge whatever they want to increase their profit. Businesses are limited in what they can charge by lots of factors, the three most important being: How rare or costly is the service or product they are selling (supply); how many customers want it; and how much are they willing to pay for it (demand). Demand is then affected by; what is the lowest price that a business' competitors are willing to accept for the same product or service. Just like you cannot charge $1,000,000 for your latest karaoke creation and expect to have lots of sales (unless, of course, mom is really rich), a business cannot charge whatever they want for a product just to make lots of profit. It just doesn't work that way.

Will children in some Third World Country starve because making a profit inevitably leads to exploitation?

Many people think about economics like they think about the board game *Monopoly*®. The only way for one a person to get more money is for someone else to lose money. (The only difference: In real life, nobody gets money for passing "GO." As a matter of fact, in real life everybody lands on "Income Tax" every time they go around the board.) People believe that like *Monopoly*, life—at least as it concerns money—is a "zero-sum-game". That is, in order for someone to be winning, someone else, perhaps everyone else, must be losing. (Now you remember why you hate playing *Monopoly*—that, and your older brothers always took the battleship and race car, leaving you with the boot or the iron, both of which you imagined sticking somewhere where the sun don't shine. Now that's free parking!)

This zero-sum view is based on an assumption that the amount of wealth in the world is fixed. In order words, an assumption that the total amount of wealth in the world does not change. If this assumption is right, then the only way for you to increase your profit is for you to take what someone else has. Think of it in terms of a pie chart:

Imagine the world only had two people in it, Bob and Larry. The pie represents all the wealth in the world. Bob has 25 percent and Larry has 75 percent. Bob is poor relative to Larry. However, on the zero-sum view, the only way for Bob to gain one percent of the wealth in the world is for him to take some of Larry's wealth. Moreover, the only way for Larry, who is wealthy compared to Bob, to get any richer is do the same and take from Bob. So taking the zero-sum view, the only way to improve one's own way of life is to take advantage of someone else. The problem with this view is that it wrongly assumes that the amount of wealth in the world stays the same.

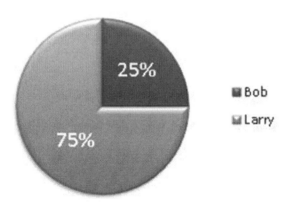

The fact is, economies grow and shrink, and the amount of wealth in the world has drastically increased in the last thirty years. According to the Barna Group, "Over the last 30 years, the percentage of the world's population living in extreme poverty has decreased from 52 percent to 21 percent.... "

And further, in a recent Barna Group survey, done in partnership with Compassion International, and the new book *Hope Rising* by Dr. Scott Todd:

"...more than eight in 10 Americans (84 percent) are unaware global poverty has reduced so drastically. More than two-thirds (67 percent) say they thought global poverty was on the rise over the past three decades...."

Despite the very real good news, more than two-thirds of US adults (68 percent) say they do not believe it's possible to end extreme global poverty within the next twenty-five years. Sadly, concern about extreme global poverty—defined in this study as the estimated 1.4 billion people in countries outside the US who do not have access to clean water, enough food, sufficient clothing and shelter, or basic medicine like antibiotics—has declined from 21 percent in 2011 to 16 percent in 2013[4].

If world poverty is decreasing, does it mean that poor countries are becoming wealthier? And if the amount of wealth in the world remains the same, then we would expect the wealthy countries to be getting poorer (remember the Bob and Larry pie chart). For Bob to get richer, Larry has to get poorer. Yet, when we look at wealthy countries' economies over the last thirty years, we see that the economies have grown, not shrunk. This means that somehow Bob (representing the poor) and Larry (representing the wealthy) both got richer. That is, they both made a profit and nobody got screwed. How is this possible? (I assure you David Copperfield, Penn and Teller, and Chris Angel had nothing to do with it.) No, what happened is that the pie got bigger. That is, the overall amount of wealth in the world grew.

For the most part, business and investors make profits by growing the amount of wealth in the world *not* by taking advantage of someone else. Here is how it works: Imagine Bob owns a tree farm and Larry owns a furniture business. Larry knows he can sell handcrafted rocking chairs for $300 a piece. All Larry needs is some fine cedar lumber to start making his chairs. Bob sells cedars. Bob knows he can sell Larry the lumber he needs to build his rocking chairs at an average cost of $50 per chair's worth of lumber. If he does this, Bob can make $30 dollars for each chair's worth of lumber he sells to Larry. Larry buys one hundred chairs worth of lumber from Bob. This means that Larry paid Bob $5,000 ($50 x 100) for lumber and Bob made $3,000 ($30 x $100).

Now Larry takes the lumber and adds $150 dollars for his labor to each chair to carve them and putting them together. This means that Larry's cost for making the chair is $50 for lumber plus $150 for labor, totaling $200 per chair. Since he can sell the chair for $300, he now makes $100 per chair. If he

---

4 "Global Poverty Is on the Decline, But Almost No One Believes It," *Barna.org*, April 28, 2014, accessed July 5, 2016, https://www.barna.org/barna-update/culture/668-global-poverty-is-on-the-decline-but-almost-no-one-believes-it, #.V3yEbDUnJ2C.

sells all one hundred chairs he will make $10,000 ($300 - $50 - $150 = $100 x 100). Not only that, but the person who willingly bought the chair now has the use of a $300 chair. So Bob made money. Larry made money, and the customer who got the chair now owns a $300 asset. No one lost wealth and at least two people gained wealth.

The above example shows that it is not only possible but also likely you can make money without hurting any else. Also, it is important to consider that many of Larry's customers could never or would never make their own handcrafted rocking chair. (Part of the reason for this is some people should not be allowed to use power tools, and I am not just talking about babies.) Nonetheless, Larry, and others like him, gave all these customers a chance to own something that they could not have enjoyed without the skill of carpenters in this world.

There is more. You might actually help other people get richer by buying their products and services, as Larry did, when he bought Bob's lumber. You also aid your customers by providing them with things they need or might not get if you were not trying to make a buck. As Robert Sirico points out:

> Here is the simple reality: the past 200 years have seen the astounding rise of billions of the world's population out of abject poverty. But that in itself is not the astonishing thing. The amazing fact is that this has been accomplished not by charitable endeavors, much less by governmental aid programs. What rescued hundreds of millions of people from the direst poverty? Simple, humdrum business.[5]

The reason that business has been so successful in raising people out of poverty is two-fold. First, for the vast majority of people who are poor are still capable of work. Charity is meant to be a temporary solution, whereas a job is meant to be a long-lasting one. If you receive a handout when you are down on your luck, the purpose of the handout is to get you by until you can care for yourself, that is, until you can find work. If things were as they should

---

5 Robert A. Sirico, *Defending the Free Market: The Moral Case for a Free Economy* (Washington DC: Regnery Publishing, 2012), 48, Kindle.

be, everyone that can work would be able to work to care for themselves, and hundreds of thousands would not be receiving charity.

The second reason is that human beings seem to be made for work. Consequently, business does not rob them of the dignity that comes with doing that for which we are made. A job gives a person the ability to meet the responsibility to care for themselves and their family. When this duty is shirked, particularly over long periods of time, it seems to be harmful to the human psyche. Moreover, when one is unable to work—not because of lack of desire but because of lack of opportunity—it is common to feel a sense of loss of purpose and to experience depression. This is why business is such a powerful antidote to poverty. It is meant to be a more permanent solution, which provides a sense of dignity and pride that charity cannot.

Let's jump back to the pie example for a moment. If you are wondering what makes it possible for the pie to get bigger, much of the answer lies in the fact that human ingenuity and work have the potential to create wealth that did not exist before. Consider oil. Oil prior to three to four hundred years ago was black stuff that most considered a nuisance. It was only human ingenuity that turned this annoyance into one of the most valuable commodities in the world. Silicon is another example, somehow humans took what is basically sand and turned it into the key components in one the most revolutionary products in the last hundred years—the computer.

The pie also grows because when human beings work in the areas they are good at, more can happen that when one person tries to do everything themselves. Imagine if you had to grow your own food, make your own car, find fuel to power your electricity, etc. In such a scenario, you would get very little done and probably just provide enough to maintain your family, never mind getting rich. Human beings prosper more as a group during times when people focus on what they are good at, and pay others do what they are not good at. (For example, the world would probably not be a better place if Danny DeVito and Shaq had switched careers in their prime. Then again, DeVito might have a better free-throw average.)

Is capitalism evil?

Many people think capitalism is based on greed, and therefore, is evil. However, the father of capitalism, Adam Smith, does not see it this way. First, he notices that humans cannot help but to partake in commerce with each other. Smith believes there exists:

> ...a certain propensity in human nature...to truck, barter and exchange one thing for another.... It is common to all men, and to be found in no other race of animals, which seem to know neither this nor any other species of contracts. Two greyhounds, in running down the same hare, have sometimes the appearance of acting in some sort of concert. Each turns her towards his companion, or endeavours to intercept her when his companion turns her towards himself. This, however, is not the effect of any contract, but of the accidental concurrence of their passions in the same object at that particular time. Nobody ever saw a dog make a fair and deliberate exchange of one bone for another with another dog.[6]

What Smith is saying is that human beings seem to want to make deals with each other all the time. They just seem to do it without being taught to do it. However, humans are the only species we know of that does this. Dogs don't make deals. They make poop. Fido and Rover don't decide to go halvesies on that extremely lucrative bone-making scheme. (If you have a dog that makes deals, you should get him to appear as a contestant on *The Apprentice*. Ratings goldmine right there.)

Second, man seems driven not only to buy and sell, but to consider what his neighbor needs, not out of interest for his neighbor, but out of interest for himself. By determining what his neighbor needs and providing that good or service, he is ensuring his own financial well-being. It is this "invisible hand" of self-interest, which drives economic activity[7]. As Smith says, "It is not from the benevolence [good will] of the butcher, the brewer, or the baker, that we

---

6 Adam Smith, *An Inquiry into the Nature and Causes of the Wealth of Nations: Books I, II, III, IV and V*, *Ibiblio.org*, digital edition, *MetaLibri*, accessed November 20, 2015, http://www.ibiblio.org/ml/libri/s/SmithA_WealthNations_p.pdf, 2007, 15.

7 Adam Smith, The Wealth of Nations, page 349

expect our dinner, but their regard to their own interest.[8]" Nonetheless, it would be wrong to assume that Smith believes self-interest is, or should be, the only motivator for economic action. Smith does not believe people should be selfish and not care about how their actions affect others. Rather, he says:

> That to feel much for others and little for ourselves, that to restrain our selfishness, and to indulge our benevolent affections, constitutes the perfection of human nature; and can alone produce among mankind that harmony of sentiments and passions in which consists their whole grace and propriety.[9]

In plain English, to be the best people we can be and make the most out of ourselves, we should control our selfishness and be concerned with the needs of others. This is how the father of capitalism views his economic system.

Capitalism does not begin with the idea that I must get as much as I can and screw anyone who gets in my way. (However, this is how Monopoly and Mario Kart seem to go. Darn you spiny shell!) Rather, capitalism begins with the idea that *if you do something good for me I will do something good for you*. For example, if you give me that gum, I will give you some of my money. If you paint my house, I will give you some of my money. (If you scratch my back, you will get hair under your finger nails. Oh, I mean— I will scratch yours.)

For you to do well in a capitalist system, it requires you think of others. For example, if you own a restaurant, then to do well you are going to have to think about what your customers want to eat; what kind of place do people want to eat in (the correct answer for all you nerds out there is *not* you grandmama's basement); how do they want to be treated, and the list goes on. Not only that, but capitalism requires you to treat people well. For example, let us suppose you are an obnoxious jerk who is verbally and physically abusive to his wife and children. What is going to happen if you treat your customers at your restaurant like your family? Assuming you don't go to jail, you are going

---

8 Adam Smith, The Wealth of Nations, page 16
9 Adam Smith, *The Theory of Moral Sentiments*, sixth edition, *MetaLibri*, accessed December 29, 2015, http://www.ibiblio.org/ml/libri/s/SmithA_Moralsentiments_p.pdf, 1790, 94.

out of business. The fact is very few businesses can survive if they treat people poorly in a capitalist system.[10]

On the other hand, this idea that one needs to consider the needs of others to succeed definitely does not apply in a socialist system. Socialism, at least as its creator, Karl Marx, thought of it, is a system where for the most part the government owns all businesses. Think about when you go to government agencies. Do you anticipate receiving good customer service or bad customer service? (It is only a guess, but I am sure many people have died waiting in line at the Driver Motor Vehicle office (DMV) and the US Post Office. I know a little part my soul died when I went to get my license renewed.) The reason for this poor customer service is that the government has a whole different set of incentives than private business.

Let us consider the different incentives that a business person might face versus those which a politician might face in the same situation. Remember, socialism involves government run business, so politicians are ultimately in charge of these corporations. Let's say you own a bus company. Your current fares sit at 25 cents a ride. As time goes by, you recognize that at the current fares, you will not have the money needed in five to ten years to repair and replace busses when they break down. If you raise fares to 35 cents, you will be able to maintain your fleet of buses into the future. This makes your investors happy because you are insuring the continued success of the business. If your investors become unhappy, they will remove their money and you go out of business. It also protects you as the owner from the likelihood of your business failing in five to ten years when you can no longer provide a bus service because you are unable to pay for a working fleet.

The incentives here are investor satisfaction, which insures they keep funding your business and you are able to stay in business after five to ten years. The disincentives are that your customers will not be happy about paying the higher fares. However, since repairs and replacement are a fixed cost for all bus companies, it is likely that your customers will be paying similar fares to your competitors. Even though the customers may get upset, it should

---

10 Bauman, "Dangerous Samaritan," 2009.

not result in much lost business. Upon weighing your options, it is clear our incentives will push you to raise prices.

Now consider the same scenario, but instead of a private bus company it is a public (government owned) one. You are the politician in charge of the committee over city transportation. You know that if you do not raise fares, the transportation system will lack the funds to repair and replace buses as they break down over the next five to ten years. You have an election coming up. As a publicly-elected official, you have no investors to satisfy just constituents. If you raise prices, then your constituents who ride the bus will be unhappy, as will environmentalist groups who advocate for more public transit. This decreases the number of cars on the road as well as those who lobby for the rights and privileges of the poor —those are most likely to take advantage of the bus system.

If you upset enough voters, you lose your next election. On the other hand, the public transit system will be in bad shape five to ten years from now if you do not raise prices. But you will not be in this office five to ten years from now, and even if you are, you can simply blame it on the other party. The incentives are to keep voters happy and get re-elected. Your disincentives are that someone else will have a huge public transit problem to figure out in five to ten years. Also, note that there is no risk consideration that the government will cease to be in business. Clearly the rational choice, from the perspective of the politician, is to keep fares the same in order to win the election and leave the problem for someone else to solve.

In these two scenarios, we see that the threat of going out of business forces the capitalist business owner to consider what is best for everyone involved. This includes the customers who won't have to ride in a crappy bus in a few years, and has the capitalist company as option to provide a service they need. Whereas in the politician's case, the public official did not actually have to consider what was in the best interest of voters in the long run, only what they cared about in the short term (which allowed him to get elected). The point is not to say that politicians are horrible human beings (there are good and horrible human beings in every profession), but the capitalist, whether he is a horrible human being or not, has an incentive to think about other people's needs in a way that someone in a socialist-based environment does not.

This is why someone starts with a full head of hair and is bald by the time they reach the front of the DMV line, only to find out that they filled out the wrong form and must go back to the end of the line. The DMV will be in business regardless of whether it gives good service. The DMV, unless there is a revolution, doesn't answer to the people and does not receive their funds because the people standing in line are making a conscious choice to pay them. The people at the DMV answer to politicians and those politicians decide how much funding they get. The DMV knows they have a monopoly on issuing and renewing driver's licenses. You have to come see them if you want to legally drive; there is nowhere else to go. Consequently, there is no incentive to provide good customer service.

Under socialism, all business is owned by the government so all business effectively becomes a monopoly. Under capitalism, competition is encouraged because the moment someone gets a monopoly and starts treating their customers badly, for the most part, some other business person is ready to swoop in and steal the monopoly's customers. They do so by providing the same product with good customer service. This is why few monopolies can be maintained in a capitalist system. They almost always naturally start to break apart.

The most fundamental difference between capitalism and socialism really boils down to the difference between how they exchange goods and services. Capitalism, as we have already seen, has a means of exchange based on the principle: *"If you do something good for me, I will do something good for you."* For example, I give $1.50 to Walmart and Walmart gives me that Coke. We call this the "peaceful means of exchange". On the other hand, socialism starts with the principle: *"If you do not do something good for me, I will do something bad to you."* An example of this coercive means of exchange that we see in our capitalist system would be, if you do not pay your taxes, the government takes your house. We call this the "coercive (or violent) means of exchange".

The Roadmap to the American Dream

PEACEFUL

COERCIVE/VIOLENT

I know many of you reading this are probably overflowing with objections to capitalism and examples of where it has run amok. However, before you burn this book and light a bag of poop on my doorstep, remember that people are messy creatures that tend to foul-up even the best systems. Voltaire said, "Perfect is the enemy of good." That is, even if you have found something that works fairly well, you can always point to the ideal and show how it falls short.

Capitalism is not a perfect economic system, but often when I ask people about other real world economic systems compared to capitalism, their idea turns out to be some perfect system that they have created in their mind rather than some other economic system proven to work in the real world. We should consider the words of William Shakespeare, "Striving to better, oft we mar what's well (King Lear, Act 1, Scene 4)." Put another way, sometimes by trying to reach perfection, we make what is good, seem bad. It's like not eating Thanksgiving dinner because there are no cranberries, even though you have everything else. If we stop and ask the question, "Which flawed, imperfect economic system works the best and leads to people being treated the best, especially the poor," our answer would not be socialism or feudalism. It would have to be capitalism.

That said, I will now briefly answer perhaps the main objection to capitalism in response to what has been written. Even if capitalism is not based on greed, it inevitably leads to greed. I have four answers to this objection.

First, if we compare the sheer amount of poverty resulting from greed due to socialism and feudalism throughout history to that of capitalism, we would have to conclude even if there is more greed, the poor actually do much better.

For example, one of the first things that the former leader of Soviet Union, Mikhail Gorbachev, said to President Ronald Regan when he came to visit the U.S. was, "My how rich are your poor."[11]

Second, if we compare the U.S. to the USSR in its prime and ask, "Where was there more corruption and greed?" we would have to answer, "in the USSR". Third, not every capitalist is consumed by greed. Most of you who are reading this book live as capitalist, even though ideologically you might embrace a different economic philosophy. Many of you are probably not consumed with making money. You might be rightly concerned with making money, but that does not mean that you are uncontrollably driven by that concern. If this is true, then capitalism does not inevitably lead to greed.

Lastly, just because people misuse a system, does not mean that the system, in itself, is bad. It could just mean there are bad practitioners of that system who violate its intended purpose. (For example, I have played basketball a time or two. Let's just say the Harlem Globe Trotters will not be knocking on my door any time soon to offer me a contract. No one would seriously say that because I'm terrible at basketball, basketball as a sport is also terrible. You might think it is terrible but for different reasons.) We have already seen that Adam Smith does not consider greed to have a proper place in the capitalist system. Condemning capitalism because some capitalists are greedy is like condemning parenting because some parents are neglectful. It is throwing the baby out with bathwater. (This is yet another reason to thank God for indoor plumbing. I am sure it has saved many a baby's life.)

Are corporations the spawn of Satan?

By this we mean, on a bad day, straight from the pit of hell, after not being able to sleep the night before because of the five-alarm chili Satan ate?) Corporations are groups of people pursuing a common goal together. Like any single person or group of persons pursuing a goal, whether they are good or bad corporations depend on what their goals are and how they go about reaching them. If a goal is bad, say creating a game that consumes

---
11 Bauman, "Dangerous Samaritan," 2009.

every waking moment of your life away, causing you to lose your job and your girlfriend, and then move back in with your parents, then you are Blizzard® and your company may be evil. (Actually, that is probably not Blizzard's true goal but you get the idea.) Or if your goal is to transport baby seals but the way you go about achieving that goal is loading as many as can fit into the back of a pick-up truck, with a pitch fork, then you are evil. If a company or person has relatively good goals and pursues them by relatively good means, then that company or person is relatively good. I say relatively because no person or group of persons is perfect, so we can only judge them relative to other persons and groups.

Broadly speaking, when we consider the track records of companies, even though people scream the loudest about the bad they have done, business has done a tremendous amount of good that people rarely consider. Take John D. Rockefeller, owner of the Standard Oil Company, perhaps one of the most notorious businessmen in all of history. As recorded by the *Foundation for Economic Education*, in 1885, John D. Rockefeller wrote one of his partners:

> "Let the good work go on. We must ever remember we are refining oil for the poor man and he must have it cheap and good."

Or as he put it to another partner: "Hope we can continue to hold out with the best illuminator in the world at the lowest price."

Even after twenty years in the oil business, "the best . . . at the lowest price" was still Rockefeller's goal; his Standard Oil Company had already captured ninety per cent of America's oil refining market, and had pushed the price down from 58 cents to eight cents a gallon.

Consider how much good Standard Oil did for all the people that depended on oil for light and heat. It would be like gasoline, which is at about $2.50 where I am now, going down to about 35 cents. Imagine how much that actually would help people struggling to make ends meet. Now, Rockefeller was no sweetheart to his competitor, and did not always achieve his goals by good means. Even so, if we ask how his company did in helping people rather than hurting people we have to give him at least a C-plus.

Objections to the American Dream

Many companies have done the same thing as Rockefeller, lowering the prices of goods and raising their quality for consumers because they realized their interests were tied to the interest of their customers. Furthermore, many of these businesses not only benefitted their patrons but also did so by much better means than Rockefeller. There are also companies, like Enron, that lied to investors and really hurt a lot of people. However, Enron is the exception. For the most part, companies do more good than harm by allowing us to live in the relative comfort we currently experience.

Consider the good McDonalds and Wendy's have done, particularly for the poor in America. According to Michael Bauman, they have helped the poor in two significant ways, as consumers and as workers. Prior to companies like McDonalds and Wendy's, going out to eat was a privilege to which the poor did not have access to on a regular basis. My wife and I had very little money when I was in college, and if it was not for Wendy's dollar menu, we would not have been able to get out of the house to have our date night once a month.

Second, these companies have helped countless people start their careers,[12] According to Bauman :

> "They gave the poor a chance to step onto the first rung of the ladder of success. You can't make a career out of flipping hamburgers. You can't. But you can start a career by flipping hamburgers. Because you can get those important marketplace skills, things like: punctuality, teamwork, appearance, deference accuracy [and] dependability. All those things you need to be a good worker in the marketplace not matter where you work, you can get at a job like that. And along the way you will get a recommendation for your next job and a little bit of money to boot. Now if you think that's not realistic, let me tell you something and write this down because *12 percent, almost 1/8, of the entire American workforce has worked for McDonalds or Wendy's at one time or another.* You got that? If you throw in Taco Bell and Arby's and all that, the percentage is enormous. You can't make a career

---

12 Ibid.

flipping hamburgers but you can start one and literally millions of people have done exactly that, millions.[13]

Corporations, largely speaking, do far more good than most people realize. However, just like every institution, or person for that matter, they are subject to corruption. Nonetheless, consider what would happen if every corporation shut down tomorrow. What would life be like? For most of us, it would mean we better get our boots on and go milk a cow, slaughter a pig, and start grinding the grain. We would have a potentially even bigger problem with what to do next: Where do we get the cow to milk, the pig to slaughter, or the wheat fields to harvest the grain we are going to grind. Let's not forget about electricity, water, garbage, sewage and gas, all which at some level depend on private corporations. The fact is; these "evil" corporations allow us to live in relative comfort. The alternative is to go back to living in the Wild West and having to go to the outhouse to do our business, aka go to the original not-so-portable porta potty.

Is a world with debt a worse world?

Ever since the housing crash of 2008, there has been a movement to avoid debt at all cost. For many, debt has become a four-letter word both in number and vulgarity. Unfortunately, this may be another case of a freshly cleaned baby flying out the window with its bathwater. Not all loans are bad. On the contrary, Peruvian economist Hernando de Soto in his milestone book, *The Mystery of Capital,* presents powerful evidence that it is precisely *because* people in Third World countries lack the ability to take out loans on their assets that most them will never be able to escape poverty.

According to the extensive studies done in the year 2000 conducted by De Soto and his team:

> ...the total value of the real estate held but not legally owned by the poor of the Third World and former communist nations is at least

---
13 Ibid.

Objections to the American Dream

$9.3 trillion. This is a number worth pondering: $9.3 trillion is about twice as much as the total circulating U.S. money supply. It is very nearly as much as the total value of all the companies listed on the main stock exchanges of the world's twenty most developed countries: New York, Tokyo, London, Frankfurt, Toronto, Paris, Milan, the NASDAQ, and a dozen others. It is more than twenty times the total direct foreign investment into all Third World and former communist countries in the ten years after 1989, forty-six times as much as all the World Bank loans of the past three decades, and ninety-three times as much as all development assistance from all advanced countries to the Third World in the same period[14].

Why can't the poor in these countries get this money out of their property? According to De Soto, it is difficult to get legal title of your property in these places, and the countries lack the infrastructure to sufficiently track the title of these properties so they can be used as collateral for a loan.

In many countries, when it comes to owning a property, it is much like the Wild West. You own the property not because you have a legal deed showing it is yours, but because your great granddaddy settled on this land sixty years ago and your family has lived there ever since. People do not seek legal title of their property because it is often tremendously difficult to get a deed. Here are just two of the many examples De Soto gives showing the time and red tape one must wade through to legally own their property:

> [It takes] as many as fourteen years and seventy-seven bureaucratic procedures at thirty-one public and private agencies in Egypt, and nineteen years and 176 bureaucratic steps to legalize the purchase of private land in Haiti.[15]

---

14 Hernando, De Soto, *The Mystery of Capital: Why Capitalism Triumphs in the West and Fails Everywhere Else* (New York; Basic Books, 2000), Kindle Locations 544-550.
15 Ibid page 1223-1223

(And you thought your condo closing was awful.) Consequently, because most of the poor people in Third World countries that own land cannot legally prove they own their land, they are unable to take out a loan on that property.

Some of you might be thinking, thank God they cannot take out a loan. They're already poor and now you want to put them in debt besides. (Gosh, what are you trying to do, turn these people into student loan recipients?) On the contrary, despite the bad press mortgages get, the truth is, even in America, "The single most important source of funds for new businesses in the United States is a mortgage on the entrepreneur's house.[16]

Third World poor people do not have access to this capital, and as a result, most are unable to escape poverty despite having the assets they need to start a successful business. For example, many poor people own far more land than they can farm. Take Bob, who owns ten acres of land, but he and his family can only harvest one acre's worth of crops before what is not harvested goes bad. This is just enough food for Bob and his family to avoid starving. Despite having the land to grow ten times the food he normally does, Bob only plants on one acre of his property a year.

Now imagine that Bob can legally prove he owns his land and he takes out a loan on it to buy a tractor. The tractor allows Bob to harvest all ten acres of his land. The money from selling four acres worth of crops covers the mortgage payment and all the expense associated with the tractor. Instead of keeping one acre's worth of food for his family and barely surviving, Bob keeps two acres and they eat like kings. That leaves him with four acres of profit, which he can use to accelerate the payment of his loan (making Dave Ramsey happy), or save it (have to watch out for inflation though), or blow it (after all, it is important to have a Mercedes for every day of the week), or reinvest it, perhaps buying another acre or two so next year Bob has an even greater crop. Who knows, maybe Bob will hire a few more people to work for him who can begin raising themselves out of poverty? (Now you know what Kenny Chesney was singing about when he sang, "She Thinks My Tractors Sexy.") If only the poor could get themselves some debt, then the world might be a better place.

---

16 Ibid. page 240

Conclusion

We have seen that profit is not a dirty word, nor is it synonymous with greed. The pursuit of profit is not the only goal of life. Greed (an unhealthy concern with profits) is a sign of an unbalanced life. Not pursuing profit can be wasteful. A worker deserves his wages, so we should not begrudge people money they have rightly earned. We have also seen that profit is a necessary expense for any business. Money provides the resources and opportunities needed for companies to pursue their mission. Companies that are mission-focused tend to outperform profit-focused corporations. Business cannot raise its prices simply because it would like to make more money. It is supply, demand, and competition that really set prices.

Despite concerns to the contrary, making money largely does not result in someone else losing money. There is not a fixed amount of wealth in the world. Making money can and often does lead to an increase in the overall amount of wealth in the world. Global poverty has been cut in half in the last thirty years, and most of this is due to business, not governments or charities.

We have seen that capitalism is not based on evil, but self-interest that requires concern for our neighbor's needs. Corporations are not evil in and of themselves, but are a mixed bag of both good and evil. This is because they are made up of people who themselves are mixed bags. If we look at most corporations, they have probably done more good in helping humans flourish than harm.

Lastly, a world with debt is not a worse world. Rather, a world filled with dead capital because people cannot attain loans keeps many in poverty. The great Christian leader, Apostle Paul, is often misquoted by people as saying, "Money is the root of all evil." Rather, Paul actually said, "For the *love* of money is a root of all kinds of evil (I Tm. 6:10)." Profit or money is a tool: It can be used to great benefit or misused to great evil. The mistake is to throw away your hammer because it can smash your thumb.

Part 2

The Concepts

Chapter 6

The things you should understand before you invest

"Our acts can be no wiser than our thoughts."

— George S. Clason, The Richest Man in Babylon

There are some basic concepts we should look at to help us speak the language of investment. Understanding these terms keeps you in the conversation and avoids the deer-in-the- headlight look that says, "Say what?" There are quite a few terms here, but I will do my level best to make them as understandable as I can. So strap on your learning shoes and let's dig right in.

Under consumption

This is one of the most important things to get out of this book. We're going to go straight into an analogy to help set this idea up for you. There is a great little book called, *"How an Economy Grows and Why It Crashes"* by Andrew J. Schiff and Peter D Schiff where they tell a story that I paraphrase here:

The things you should understand before you invest

Once upon a time there are three men on an island and each man, if he works all day, is capable of catching one fish. That one fish is enough to feed him for one day. One night one of the men can't sleep. He has an idea for a "netty" thing. He is sure this net thing will enable him to catch fish more easily. His problem is that he is using all of his time to catch enough fish just to survive. How will he have the time to actually make his idea for a net a reality?

After much deliberation, he decides to pony up and take the plunge. One day the other two men are out diligently catching fish, but the first man is off working on his net. He chooses to go hungry (under-consume) and completes his net. It cost him his days' food and his tummy was not too happy with him, but his "Fish Buster 9000" (just cause they live on an island doesn't mean they can't come up with a cool name) is a success. The first day it allows him to catch two fish instead of one. To celebrate, he cooks and stuffs himself with the two fish he caught that day.

Suddenly options appear in our hero's head. He now can fish every other day if he wants to, and can finally take a day off. Or maybe he can fish half as long each day. Then he has a real capitalist epiphany: He can catch two fish today; eat one fish, and save one for tomorrow. Tomorrow comes and he builds a second net that day. He now rents the two nets out to the other two guys charging them each one half a fish a day. This guy is a genius. He never has to go fishing again. The others are happy because they get an extra half a fish out of this deal. The fish net inventor is now working on a line of coconut scented body washes and exfoliating creams. (Just because they live on an island doesn't mean they can't smell nice.) The End.

This illustrates the idea of under-consumption perfectly in a very simple way. Use as little as you can to pool your resources now so you can create a surplus later. The only resource our hero had was time. He had to starve to save the time he needed to invest in something that assured him he would never need to starve again. In other words, "You pay now to play later." This gives you the flexibility to do what you want later. Under-consumption might not just be going without to bring an idea to market. It might be saving to invest.

You are probably thinking: So wait, the point to everything I have read up until now is to live within my means? Really? People have probably been telling you that since as far back as you can remember. But what we are saying

The Roadmap to the American Dream

is to live *below* your means. If you are investing the amount you are saving from under-consuming, your means will always be increasing, which results in short order to living well above your previous means while still saving to invest even more. Your paycheck no longer becomes the only source of your income, instead it becomes one among many. As crazy as it may seem, eventually your job income may become entirely unnecessary. Think of our net inventor above. Does he need to work anymore?

Am I telling you to live debt free, and if you just paid off and cut up your credit cards the world will be hunky dory? Not even a little bit. We discuss debt later and why if used properly, debt is one of the best paths to wealth. We are saying that incurring bad debts like credit card debt for the hover board (because everybody in your family *needed* to have one in each color, with the built-in vibrating foot warmers, Bluetooth audio and spinning hub caps) is *not* a very good idea. On the other hand, credit card debt to put a kitchen in the rental property you just bought is probably good debt. The trick here is to not focus solely on decreasing your spending, but also on increasing your income so that you can increase your spending.

> **TIP:** *Saving just to save is not a great idea either. We discuss what to do with saved money later in the book. Spoiler alert: The answer is not, "Put it in the bank". Having a reserve is a good idea, but there are better places to put money. Read on to find out where.*

Saying no to yourself now can mean saying many more yeses later. We discuss the time value of money next and why investing early is so important later.

> *"Wealth, like a tree, grows from a tiny seed. The first copper you save is the seed from which your tree of wealth shall grow. The sooner you plant that seed the sooner shall the tree grow. And the more faithfully you nourish and water that tree with consistent savings, the sooner may you bask in contentment beneath its shade."*
>
> — GEORGE S. CLASON, THE RICHEST MAN IN BABYLON

Time value of money (TVM)

The idea behind **TVM** in the simplest terms is that a dollar today is worth more than a dollar tomorrow. The reason for this is that you have the use of the money today, and the interest it can earn between today and tomorrow.

An example would be if on Monday, Bill lent his friend Steve ten dollars with the promise to pay back eleven dollars Tuesday. Steve comes in on Tuesday and asks if he can pay the money back on Wednesday instead (apparently, the dog ate his wallet). Now the normal response would be to think that it doesn't really cost Bill anything to do this, and if he were a nice guy, he would cut his friend some slack. An investor realizes the issue. The problem comes from the fact that Bill wanted to lend the same ten dollars to Harvey on Tuesday with the same terms he gave Steve. To summarize, Bill had ten dollars, but based upon his investments (lending money to his friends) the actual value of his ten dollars on Wednesday would be twelve dollars (the one dollar from Steve and one dollar from Harvey added to the initial ten dollars). The delay in payment from Steve actually costs Bill one dollar or ten percent. Final thoughts: Steve is a jerk and Bill's annualized interest rate is outstanding.

Compounding interest

Compounding is when an initial investment generates interest over the course of a period of time (can be yearly, monthly, etc.), and the original investment plus the interest is then carried forward as the new amount on which interest is calculated. Simple, right? Not so much. Let's get back with Bill, Steve, and Harvey and see if they can help. If you recall, Bill lent ten dollars and asked for one dollar in interest from Steve. That works out to be a ten percent interest rate he was charging (daily, which makes Bill a loan shark, but it works for this example). We calculate the interest rate by dividing the amount of interest being charged (one dollar) by the amount being borrowed (ten dollars), which gives us a result of .1 in our calculator.

> **Note**: *For those of you that napped in high school through how all of this fun stuff works, here you go: When we use the percent symbol, it means we add two zeros to the right of our answer in the calculator (so .1 becomes*

The Roadmap to the American Dream

.100), and move the decimal point two spaces right (so .100 becomes 10.0 percent). One easy way to remember is the percent symbol itself has two zeroes in it.

This means that after Bill and his good friend Bruiser had a very persuasive conversation with Steve, his wife quickly brought the money on Tuesday. Bill now has eleven dollars to invest. If he invests that eleven dollars at the same interest rate, he makes $1.10 in interest on Wednesday. That means instead of twelve dollars, he will have $12.10. Not much huh? Why is this such a big deal? Wait until you see what happens over time. First let's see if you have it:

Try to fill in the chart below through year four:

Year	Investment-Beginning of Year	Interest Rate	Interest Amount	Investment Plus Interest-End of Year
1	$100,000	6%	$6,000	$106,000
2	$106,000	6%	$6,360	$112,360
3	$112,360	6%		
4		6%		

If you came up with $126,247.70, you did it perfectly. With this example, we made over $26,000 in just four years. So you want to see something that will really blow your mind? Take a look at this chart comparing two different investors.

One investor starts investing $2,400 a year ($200 a month) at age twenty-five until he is sixty-five-years of age at 12.5 percent interest. The second investor starts at age sixteen investing the same amount annually, at the same interest rate, until he is twenty-four, at which point he stops investing altogether. When they are both sixty-five, who do you think will have more? See the chart:

The things you should understand before you invest

Investor 1 at age 25 after graduating college starts investing $2400 at 12.5 % interest in a tax deferred account.			Investor 2 starts investing $2400 for 9 years in the same tax deferred account at age 16. No more money is added for 41 years.	
Age	Yearly Investment	Total	Yearly Investment	Total
16	$0	$0	$2,400.00	$2,700.00
17	$0	$0	$2,400.00	$5,100.00
18	$0	$0	$2,400.00	$8,137.50
19	$0	$0	$2,400.00	$11,554.69
20	$0	$0	$2,400.00	$15,399.02
21	$0	$0	$2,400.00	$19,732.90
22	$0	$0	$2,400.00	$24,589.39
23	$0	$0	$2,400.00	$30,063.06
24	$0	$0	$2,400.00	$36,220.95
25	$2,400.00	$2,700.00	$0	$40,748.57
26	$2,400.00	$5,100.00	$0	$45,842.14
27	$2,400.00	$8,137.50	$0	$51,572.41
30	$2,400.00	$19,723.90	$0	$73,430.24
35	$2,400.00	$50,942.13	$0	$132,323.68
45	$2,400.00	$208,574.03	$0	$429,697.48
55	$2,400.00	$720,455.39	$0	$1,395,365.67
65	$2,400.00	$2,382,698.49	$0	$4,531,200.27
Total Investment for Investor 1 $98,400.00			Total Investment for Investor 2 $21,600	

This is why this is such a big deal—the difference of $76,800! You can clearly see the power of compounding interest, and also how much difference having money working sooner rather than later makes. Having money to invest at sixteen is obviously worth much more than money at age twenty-five. How much more? We will figure that out a little later on.

Inflation

Inflation is when you pay fifteen dollars for the ten-dollar haircut you used to get for five dollars when you had hair.

-SAM EWING

The Roadmap to the American Dream

How much was a can of Coke from a vending when you were a kid? Is it more or less now? More, right? Did that frosty beverage change much since you were young? Is the vending machine much better? Is the can significantly different? The answer to all of these is no. Then why are you paying more? The reason is inflation. The amount of buying power your money possesses is constantly diminishing. It does so at a rate of about 3 to 3.5 percent a year.

When I was a kid a can of Coke cost 50 cents and now it is about $1.50. If my dad had said to me as I went to buy that frosty can of yumminess, "No son, don't be a dummy and waste your money on that can of soda. You do the smart thing and put your money in the bank," would he have been right? I wanted to know, so I used the TVM formula above to find out what the bank would have paid after all these years at the whopping .5 percent interest they pay. My 50 cents would now be worth—drum roll please—56 cents. That was anticlimactic wasn't it? This basically means that my dad's advice cost me around two thirds of a can of Coke. I would have been, in fact, far better off investing in the can of Coke, not drinking it, and then loading it in a vending machine today where it could be sold for $1.50.

The reason for the small return for my money in the bank is the low half percent interest rate the bank pays. If you recall, the money we have is losing value at around 3.5 percent a year. That means the net loss of buying power for my money is 3 percent a year when invested in the bank. It is like having a bucket that has a drop of water dripping into it every second, but has a hole in the bottom that allows seven drops to fall out for every drop that comes in. It won't be long till there is nothing left in the bucket. That is why earlier I mentioned that investing for investment sake is foolish. You need to invest in things, which at a minimum, keep pace with inflation (as many drops going in as coming out). Much like the price of that can of Coke, which went up in sync with inflation, you need to find assets that do at least the same. Now where can we find an asset that is like the can of Coke? Real estate.

Real estate prices are tied to the cost of living and income indexes, which are all tied to inflation. For this reason, the cost of real estate tends to go up to keep pace with the loss of buying power of money (like the can of Coke). That means that buying a house is actually a better method of saving than a bank savings account (even though the bank has "savings" in the name).

The things you should understand before you invest

What is even better than owning a home you live in, however, is a home you own and rent out to tenants. Why? Well does the value of the real estate go up with inflation? Yes, over time the prices do go up with inflation. How about the rents? Do they go up with inflation? You bet your biscuits they do. This means that while you own the house, it is appreciating (like the can of Coke), and the rents you are collecting go up as well. So you actually get a double benefit for owning an investment property. This is like getting three dollars for that can of Coke today. (There is a third benefit, which I discuss in the mortgages section.)

We are making an assumption that home prices continue to rise, but obviously, we immediately think of the housing crisis as means of disproving this. In actuality, this kind of crisis bears out this idea. Home prices during the housing bubble got way out of sync with the other indicators of inflation. In other words, the home prices were artificially inflated. Once the bubble burst and the markets re-stabilized, home prices in most markets were back to being right about where they should be, based on historical precedent. There are issues with a house though like a **lack of liquidity** (your money is tied up in the property and can't be spent) that we will talk about later, but homes do offer a hedge (protection) from inflation.

What is inflation? Inflation is a thief, and it quietly steals from the old and savers. It steals from the old as they are living on their savings, which buy less each day than they did yesterday, and it steals from savers by leaving them with less buying power when they go to spend their savings than when the money was initially put in the bank.

So what is the answer? To spend every red cent as soon as we get it? Well, if you have been paying attention, this is actually a credible idea as the money has its highest possible value as soon as it is acquired. But there are a few problems: first, we don't always know what we need in advance before we need it. For example, you mistakenly swallow your fork because you were so anxious to get at the Chinese food that you got a little too excited about the Homey garlic chicken, and then someone bumped you and the next thing you know you are on your way to the emergency room. Did you see that coming? Probably not. Things happen, and for this reason, some sort of financial safety net is needed. Typically we call this net "savings".

Second, we need to continuously earn money to survive. If we can't work we are broke. Third, there are some big ticket items like a car or home that require savings of some sort in order to be purchased and retirement and vacations are not gonna happen if we spend it all at once. How do we work around these problems? A suggestion would be limited savings, with all amounts exceeding those savings being put toward active investments.

In practice

If there is the option to have $20,000 in the bank or use $15,000 as down payment on a house to live in, I would look at the down payment as a much better long term investment. I would be earning higher appreciation (around 3.5 percent a year) on the home than I would be earning interest in the bank (.5 percent). The issue would be having only $5,000 in savings. While I would be doing a better job of saving my money by buying a home, I would be sacrificing liquidity (the ability to have the money immediately available) for this higher return. I would have to determine if that cushion would be enough for unforeseen events, especially given my affinity for Chinese food and the poor fork management skills cited above. If I determine that $5,000 is enough, I could reallocate a large portion of my savings from my below-inflation-returning bank account to the inflation neutral purchase of a home. In this way, I would be using my home as a long term savings account with a higher interest rate than the bank.

Risk part 2

Risk is probably the most widely recognized, but poorly understood concept in business. There are many types of risk and many ways to mitigate, or hedge, risk. Things like insurance and corporate structures are all tools we use to lessen our risk exposure. It can't be avoided. You run the risk of being struck by a meteorite if you step out of your house; actually, it could probably get you while you were in your house. You run risks every time you do most anything, and you weigh that risk against the potential reward. Do I pull out into traffic now or wait and be even later for the meeting? As we discussed earlier, learning to recognize risk and minimize it is a critical life skill toward achieving the American Dream.

The things you should understand before you invest

Let's look at our buddy, the inventor of the "Fish Buster 9000". What risks did he expose himself to: That the net wouldn't catch fish? That he couldn't make it with the materials he had available? That he would go hungry and never be able to make up for that one fish he would never get to go back and eat?

What helped minimize his risk? Well, he had been fishing for a while so he had a pretty good idea of what it takes to catch a fish. He also had been on the island and had in his data base of knowledge ways to use materials found on the island, which he felt confident would stand up to his application. As to the going hungry risk, there wasn't much he could do about that except maybe mug one of the other two guys for his fish and then blame it on the third guy.

> **Tip:** *The biggest mistakes people make when investing are one of two things: Either not understanding the risk of the investment fully, or thinking they understand the risk when they don't. Take the time to check out how people that lost in similar investments did so, and plan how you will adjust to avoid these mistakes. Homework is no fun, but losing money is even less fun.*

Risk for a long time was a huge stumbling block to investment. One of the early battles to mitigate risk gave us something we still use today: The corporation. A corporation is a separate legal entity in the eyes of the law. Why does that matter you may ask?

It all started hundreds of years ago in Europe where merchants would borrow investor funds to purchase goods from other parts of the world, and then ship them to other ports where the goods were wanted. It was a very risky business. Ships sank quite often, and when they did, the cargo would be lost. Before corporations, a successful merchant could be completely wiped out by a bad storm season. This is not wiped out like we think of it, where someone loses their Beamer and has to opt for a used Hyundai or cancel their membership to "The Club" (where the towels handed out in the washrooms by the steward are individually heated by a 47-step three- hour process). They may even have to start going to LA Fitness or, God forbid, the YMCA. Yes, the kids might have to go to public school and even get jobs. Barbaric, I know!

In days before corporations, if your business failed, your creditors could come after you personally. They could take all of your money, your house, your children, and even your freedom. You would be sent to debtor's prison, and your children would be sent to the workhouse until everyone died or the debt was paid back. This reality forced merchants to charge very high prices to compensate for their risk. It also hurt consumers because they had to pay these prices if they wanted the goods. Nobody won.

Enter the corporate structure, which limits the exposure of the owner to the amount of assets actually in the corporation. It is looked upon, by the law, as its own body (corpus in Latin), and therefore, only has the assets that its body possesses. This means that if your company does not own your personal home and your business fails, the creditors cannot take it away from you to pay your company's debt. It limits the risk to the business owner. In England, where corporations were first widely adopted, the country turned into the center of maritime commerce. Merchants could be more ambitious in meeting the needs of their customers because they were not being forced to risk so much. You can see, using this piece of history, that limiting risk promotes business activity and growth. We discuss various types of corporations later.

Risk is something that you must compensate others for, when they accept it. An example of this would be insurance. You pay a company to accept the risk that your house will flood. If that event never happens, they win. If your house floods, however, they have to pay to fix it (typically after denying your claim for six months). Or if you buy a house and the seller agrees to hold a mortgage. The seller will expect an interest payment in order to provide an investment return and compensate for the risk that you will not pay it back. This is the reason why people with lower credit pay higher interest rates for many loans.

Consider the story of the restaurant manager who saw the amount of money his servers were making, and realized they had fewer responsibilities but were actually making as much as he was. He then hired himself as a server and let the owner know he was quitting as the manager. The manager was not being compensated for the risk and additional responsibilities he was facing, and therefore, realized that a server's position was really the better deal for him.

What is interesting about the story is the former manager shows up a couple of weeks later and sees the owner serving tables. He had never seen the owner do anything like this, and so he asked the owner what was the deal. The owner told him that after the manager quit, he thought about it and

The things you should understand before you invest

realized the servers were making as much as he was and didn't have to worry about payroll, suppliers ripping them off, or managers quitting to become servers. He said, "They go home when their shift is done and they are smiling. I barely make it home then have to come right back, and I toss and turn all night with worry. So I sold the restaurant with the understanding that I could stay on as a server." This is an apocryphal tale, but it illustrates well that risk must be compensated for. Somebody has to pay for the antacid.

You can also accept risk and be compensated for it. Let's say you buy a house, which is a "fixer-upper". It can be purchased for $80,000. You determine it needs $20,000 in work. If a fixed-up house in that area is worth $100,000, this is a bad deal. I could go buy a similar house in good condition for $100,000 and not do anything. I am not being compensated for the all of the risk I am taking on. Things like cost overruns on the work, latent (unseen) defects, somebody getting hurt on the job and suing, the city wanting me to make the diving board for the pool ADA compliant, or any other crazy thing you can think of (believe me, they come up with some stuff) all could happen. If, however, the home would be worth $130,000 when the work is complete, I am being compensated for my risk. This is a deal I would look into.

We are always looking for ways to minimize risk. Often the person that does this best is the one that gets the deal. They get the deal because they have figured out a way to be able to pay more. They can do this because the amount of risk they assume is not as great. Let's say for the above example that another buyer was really good friends with the chief code compliance inspector for the city. His risk of needing to spend $500 to pull a permit for a new kitchen he's putting in is probably way less than another investor has to worry about, not to mention the extra things the inspector wants when they inspect, including time lost to comply. Because this investor has less risk, he can offer 85,000 or 90,000 for the same house. This is how mitigating risk works.

Is buying cases of scotch for the inspectors the only way to minimize risk on a real estate investment? No, it's not, and it is very far from ethical. A more realistic method would be to hire a really good contractor who brings their work in for a price that is consistent with their estimates.

To summarize, there are two similar investments but one is more risky, the riskier investment needs to be priced less, return more, or be eliminated from consideration. If there are two investors and the first one mitigates risk better than the other, then that investor will be able to pay more. We will touch more on risk more as we go because these factors affect every investment.

Profit is a cost of doing business

This is the idea that if something is not profitable, it won't get done. For example, look at the first mega company ever formed: U.S. Steel. This company was formed by Elbert H. Gary and J.P. Morgan, and brought together into one conglomerate most of the largest American steel companies. Think of it like merging Amazon, Google, and Facebook—kind of big. The company was hugely successful for decades, but eventually tighter margins, union workers forcing ever-higher wages, inability to afford newer equipment for modernization, and competition led to the death of U.S Steel. When it went out of business, the returns annually to their investors were two percent. Was there a major event that ended the giant's life? No, it was the slow reallocation of funds by the investors to better uses. It was no longer profitable enough to keep the investors from placing their funds somewhere else that produced better.

People and especially politicians miss this point. If there is not enough profit to compensate a business owner for the time, aggravation, and risk associated with their business, that company will go out of business. Another way of looking at it is this: The business owner will invest their time in more profitable uses.

We make this determination all of the time, and each of us actually has the requisite skills. Think of it this way. If a casual acquaintance tells you their car is broken down, they really need you to drive them someplace four hours away, and they will give you thirty dollars, what would you say? Most people would think that this kind of deal won't even pay for my gas, and it will take me four hours there and four hours back. I lose a whole day.

Now if the same person offered you one million dollars to do the same thing, you would probably offer to give them a piggyback ride the whole way if they wanted. The amount of profit changed, and so did your willingness to find a way to get this task done.

Highest and best use

There are two ways where this term can be applied. (Actually, there are a bunch more, like highest and best use of time—binge watch *Game of Thrones* or finishing this book); highest and best use of fuel (not drag racing the idiot that is revving his car alongside you at the stop light); and so on. But highest and best use is most commonly applied to real estate. It is used to describe the most profitable use of land or building possible. This is important because this allows for the highest possible price to be paid for a property.

Let's say you see a corner lot available for sale by your local supermarket. You think it would be a good site for a rare bookstore because you are nerdy like that. You determine that the profit you require to go through the aggravation of opening and running the business is a minimum of 10 percent per year, because you read this book. You do your projections of sales $250,000 a year, initial set up costs of $500,000 for inventory plus construction, and your operating costs will be $180,000 and determine that in order to make 10 percent on your investment, the most you can spend for the land is $200,000.

> **Note**: *Some of you may ask how we got to this number. We did so by looking at our income projection of $250,000 and subtracting our operating costs of $180,000 a year. This leaves us with $70,000 in yearly profit. We want to make 10 percent on our investment so we have to work backwards. We have our profit number, we just need to figure out what number it is 10 percent of. We do this by dividing $70,000 by 10 percent or .10 on our calculator. This tells us that the most we can spend in order to have our desired return is $700,000. We now subtract the amount of money we initially had, taking $500,000 to build and stock the store from the $700,000. This leaves us with $200,000, which is all we can spend for the land and still maintain our minimum return.*

The Roadmap to the American Dream

What you don't know is that Bobby "Sudsy" McSudsy-Bright (his mom kept her last name) is looking at the site and determines that it would be great for his new car wash location. He works his numbers and realizes it will cost him one million to build a state-of-the-art car wash. His projected sales are $800,000 with operating costs of $200,000. He also wants a 10 percent minimum rate of return. Using the same formula above, he figures out he can afford to pay five million for the same piece of land.

Answer: He has $600,000 of profit, which is 10 percent of $6,000,000. If we subtract his building costs, we can see that the bookstore guy is not going to be the one making the best offer for this piece of land.

In summary, we can see that the investor who came up with the best use can afford to pay more for the same property. What happened to the property above? Sudsy felt really good about his offer up until Starbucks came along and blew his car wash dreams away with an offer of twelve million dollars. The better use wins. As I write this, I can feel the caffeine junkie's approval at this outcome. One more site somewhere in the world for their coffee fix—you know who you are.

On to the second type of highest and best use: This is the highest and best use of an investor's individual resources. If you have worked as a ranch hand you probably have knowledge that would help you in investing in a related field. If you had camped for six months at Yellowstone with nothing but a tarp and some fishing line, all without breaking a sweat, you probably are better than someone like me (a big sissy that whines if his hotel isn't at least three stars) at running a survivalist camp for adults. Each of us has specialized knowledge and experience that allows us to have a leg up in an investment of this type. Could someone like me run the same camp? Probably, but it would be tougher, and it would not be the best use of my existing knowledge and skills.

This all means that if you are going to invest in real estate, you should do so in areas where you have some knowledge. If you plan on opening a business, do so in a field where you have some type of experience. Even when buying securities like stock and bonds, it is usually best to at least initially, stick with companies you know and understand. Any knowledge you have

The things you should understand before you invest

is making highest and best use of your skills. There are no style points for investing with half of your ability tied behind your back.

Another thing to take into account is your personality and risk tolerance level. Not everyone is the same. It may make sense to take a lower rate of return in an investment you are comfortable with or understand better, than in one that returns better but keeps you up at night. If you can take tons of pressure and risk, and really love and understand the stock market, then day trading may be the best way for you to go. If you prefer a longer, steadier method and like tangible assets, then real estate is a great method for long term wealth creation. If you hate the idea of having to deal with tenants and leaky pipes, or even management companies, but would instead like to never have to work for someone else again, then opening a business might be a way to go.

> **Tip:** *One major caveat with opening a business is that in order for it to be considered a true asset, you must be able to get yourself eventually out of the operation. An investment generates passive income. This means you do not actively have to work for this income. We have a name for income streams that require you to constantly work at them they are called "jobs". This book is about developing passive income. We use our jobs to make the initial investment capital, but the goal is to remove the necessity for having a job at all. We want you working because you want to, and not because you have to.*

The take-away from this section is: Analysis. You need to analyze your current knowledge and temperament to determine the highest and best use for your skills. What type of investor are you? You also need to analyze the investments you make for the highest and best potential uses they might have. Should I rent the house I just bought, or am I better selling it for a profit and buying two smaller ones and renting both out? If I keep the house, then perhaps I get a mortgage and use the money to buy the second house anyway. Constantly be looking for a better way to do things. Building your skills in this way directs you to the best opportunities.

Chapter 7

Debt

Debt is one person's liability, but another person's asset.

-Paul Krugman

Is debt inherently bad?

Nope. It is sort of like asking if a chainsaw inherently bad? No, it is a tool that can be used in good and bad ways. If you use it to cut down the fallen tree branch blocking your driveway, the chainsaw is good because it is being used well. If you happened to find yourself trapped in a 1980s' horror film after having had sex, while doing drugs and are near a place called Camp Crystal Lake, a chainsaw may be a bad thing (#Jason).

I hear people say that they are planning on living a debt free life. On the surface, this sounds wise. Unfortunately, living debt free often also means living wealth free. It is like telling a kid never to touch the stove. We tell them not touch it because they can get hurt. This is good when they don't know how to use it, but unless you want to damn them to a life of Ramen noodles and microwavable mac 'n' cheese, they need to learn to use the stove properly at some point. Living *bad* debt free is a good thing. *Good* debt, however, allows you to make better use of what you have. Here's an example that explains the power of good debt.

Debt

We have two farmers. Farmer one listened to a bunch of information on the glories of a debt free living. He follows these suggestions. He has a small mortgage on his home. He refuses to take on any more debt. He has two hundred acres of land that he works with his family. Sadly, they are only able to work about fifty acres of this land a year because that is all they can cultivate with the old fashioned tools they can afford. These fifty acres provide enough for them to feed their family, sell some at market for other necessities, and put about $2,000 a year toward savings (as long as they don't eat out, go on vacation, or have cable). No NFL TV package for farmer one :-(.

Farmer two also has two hundred acres, but he immediately attains a mortgage on this property and buys new modern equipment like tractors, harvesters, etc. to work the land. He is able, with the help of this equipment and his family, to work the entire two hundred acres. The revenue from the one hundred and fifty acres of additional land allows the farmer to not only pay for the mortgage on the land, but also save much more than the other farmer. This is done while taking his wife out to a weekly date night, an annual vacation to the local Renaissance fair, and having Showtime because they too are into *Game of Thrones* and the NFL package (#GoDolphins).

Farmer two is not done, however. He is using his savings for a down payment on the land next door, which will give him four hundred more acres to work. He will have to hire help, but he figures in three years he will make enough to afford to give his wife the vacation she has always wanted to a Star Trek Convention. The end.

Don't let farmer two's taste in vacation locals and sports' teams put you off. He is using debt to acquire productive assets. He currently has to work the land himself, but eventually if he acquires enough, he will have enough profit leftover to hire a manager in order to remove him from the operation. That will transition his farm from a job to an investment.

Now the naysayers say ah, but what happens to him if there is any kind of financial setback? What if the price of whatever he is growing falls dramatically? Farmer number two could lose everything. This is potentially true, but farmer one, in this circumstance, would probably starve as well; or if not starve, he would not be able to buy the goods his family needs from the market as he only has fifty acres of a less valuable crop.

The reality is that farmer two has the greater ability to save because he is earning far more. He is taking on more risk and expenses to do so, but the reward is more leftover to put toward saving and thus minimizing that risk. Caveat: I am not a farmer and if these acreages or number of people to work them are ridiculous, I apologize. My disclaimer *: The analogy is correct but the number of workers and size of land have been changed to protect the ignorant.*

Good debt allows you to keep your property or goods, but gives you a portion of their value as if you had sold them. The key to good debt is that you use this money for the purchase of additional income-generating assets that more than pay for the cost of the debt. There are ways to take on *good* debt in a *bad* way. Debt is often referred to as "leverage". Being over-leveraged can lead to large losses when things go badly. Too much of a good thing can be a very bad thing. There are ways to minimize this risk though. One of the ways to do this is by maintaining "equity".

Equity

Equity is the difference between what is owed on a property, and what the property is worth. Loans are typically made on a ratio called "loan to value" or LTV (based on the current appraised value of the property). This indicates how much of a loan you get versus how much equity you have leftover in the property according to its value. For example, if we were buying a home appraised for $100,000 and the bank was going to give us a loan based on an 80/20LTV (loan to value), they would lend us $80,000 and we would put up $20,000, which would be both our down payment and our equity. The reason we call this equity is because if we had to sell the home, we know it is worth $100,000, and so we could pay the bank back their $80,000 loan and still have our $20,000. When the home appreciates (grows in value), our equity increases. For example, if the home we bought for $100,000 can be sold for $110,000 a year after we bought it, our loan is $80,000, but our equity is now $30,000. So if we sold the house, the bank would get $80,000 and we would

Debt

get $30,000. This is also true as we pay down (or retire) our mortgage on the property. The portion of the home we own goes up. This means if something happened that required us to have cash, we could sell our home and generate the cash (from the equity) we would need to address the emergency.

Let's use farmer two to further explain the idea of maintaining equity. Farmer two took a loan on his land, which is worth $500,000. His two hundred acres generates an additional $8,000 a month in profit before he pays any loans. He uses $4,000 to support his family and that leaves him with 4,000 to pay his loan. The terms of that loan determines how risky this is. If the farmer borrowed 100 percent of the value of his land ($500,000) he has exposed himself to some very big risks. He will have a very large payment ($2,864 a month based on 5 percent interest rate), no ability to sell to get money if an emergency occurs (he has already borrowed 100 percent of the value, which means his equity is $0), and the risk that the value of the property may go down in the short term and the bank forces him to make up the difference. (Believe it or not, if the value fell by 10 percent or $50,000, farmer two could get a call from his bank asking him to write a check for $50,000 so that the loan is not upside down anymore.) Let's also say he borrows to buy his equipment and has a $1,500 a month payment for that. He also puts a down payment on the land next door and has another payment of $2,864 a month. He is now in a position where he is dependent on that just-purchased land succeeding in order to be able to pay his bills. If it works, he will theoretically generate an additional $8,000 from the land he is buying. However, if there is any hiccup in his income, he has no safety net.

This sounds about as risky as sleeping on the bottom of a child's bunk bed with an NFL offensive lineman above you who suffers from night terrors. Pancakes are not the only thing likely to be flat in the morning. These are some big risks, right? What could farmer two do to lower his risks? He could choose to take a smaller loan. Let's say the farmer only borrowed 75 percent ($375,000) of value of his land. Based on the same terms as the 100 percent loan above, his payment would only be $2,013 a month, that's a savings $851 a month from the $2,864 he was paying above. This would leave him with that much less money to buy equipment. However, to make the money he

The Roadmap to the American Dream

does have go further. He could choose to buy used equipment. In so doing, he could bring his equipment payment down from the above example of $1500 to $1,000 a month. So to summarize, his monthly savings over the 100 percent loan we looked at above: He is saving $500 on his equipment payment plus $851 on his mortgage payment, which gives him a monthly total monthly savings of over $1,300. That is $15,600 a year. If he had to sell his land, even with a market downturn of 10 percent, he would still have equity of 15 percent ($75,000).

To be fair, when analyzing which farmer has the greater risks we need to take into account the greater earning potential of farmer two. Farmer two makes more from his land than farmer one. This means that he has greater discretionary income ($2,000 for farmer one and $15,600 for farmer two). This is income that is not needed in order to pay any fixed bills, that is, money that can be used to go to the movies, go bungee jumping, buy eggs and toilet paper, welcome new neighbors to the block, or save and invest. If farmer two wants to be conservative, he can set aside his discretionary income to form a reserve. This reserve could be for three months' worth of expenses, or even up to a year depending upon his "risk profile" (how much risk he can handle before he needs to invest in stock for the company that makes his antacid of choice).

Remember, funds held in reserve are in a safe and liquid locations. This means they typically do not generate enough return to keep pace with inflation. They are there in the event that something we don't want to happen—happens. What does this look like for farmer one? Farmer one at peak capacity is only capable of generating $2,000 a year in reserves (as opposed to farmer two's $15,600). That is the extent of the first farmer's discretionary income. That means he needs to save all he makes, and if anything unforeseen happens his reserves are wiped out. Farmer two has a much better capacity to survive and recover from an emergency than farmer one because of his greater earning/saving power. But doesn't farmer two have more risk? Actually, not really based upon the above. The wise use of debt can actually reduce your risk. This is what *good* debt actual does. Bad debt: we look at this more when we discuss rates of return. Right now, let's look at how much this money we borrow is going to cost us.

Interest rates and what they mean

An interest rate is not an arbitrary number, which "The Man" makes you pay because he is a rich jerk who wants to screw you over. It is an amount of profit necessary to justify giving you the use of the money instead of using it to do something else (like invest in cans of Coke). An interest rate is determined based upon the risk you pose as a borrower and the likelihood of you paying the loan back. We are going to go on a quick tangent here to discuss the two main types of loans that exist. The interest you are charged is very different for them. The two types of loans are "collateralized and non-collateralized loans".

I know what you may be thinking: What the hell does that mean? Glad you asked, because we are going on a double tangent here. To understand these two loan types, we need to first understand what collateral is. Collateral is something you pledge to give to the lender if a debt is not paid. When we take a mortgage on a house, we pledge the house as collateral. It is saying to the bank, "If I do not pay this loan, you can take this home away from me to recover the loss of the money you allowed me to borrow."

Collateralized loans

A collateralized loan is a loan where something, typically the item being bought, is pledged to the lender as compensation if payments are not made. Loans are usually made for less than the value of the pledged asset. The lender might give you eight or ninety percent of the money you need in order to buy something, which leaves you with a small amount of cash needed to make the purchase. We call this money the "down payment". Car loans work like this as do home mortgages. Loans with collateral typically have much lower interest rates than their non-collateralized cousins. This is because the lender has less risk of losing their entire investment as the asset is worth more than the money that was lent. That way if they have to repossess or foreclose on the collateral, they can sell it and recover their money. Even a pawn shop is a type of collateralized loan. It is one where the lender is holding the collateral as opposed to the borrower.

Non-collateralized loans

Non-collateralized loans typically have only intangible things pledged against them (your reputation, credit score, etc.) The most common type of this loan would be a credit card. Credit cards have to charge a much higher rate of interest as they bear a much higher risk of not being repaid. The only leverage they have is to destroy your credit and hopefully annoy you into paying by calling you over and over again. If you don't pay, they sell your debt to a collection company for a small percentage of the actual debt. Say you owe $20,000. They might sell the debt to them for $1,000 and the collection company then proceeds to make your life miserable.

> **Note:** *To answer the question some of the wacky folks like me are out there asking: When you borrow money from Bruno (my apologies to anyone named Bruno) and agree to pay twenty-five percent interest a week, this is a quasi-collateralized loan. Your physical wellbeing is the collateral, but Bruno's ability to sell you for repayment of the debt largely depends upon his connections to human traffic rings.*

Back to interest rates: The amount you pay in interest is a cost for the use of money. If you are lending money to someone, then you are not using that money to do something else. This means that you need to be paid for this lost opportunity. This is referred to as "opportunity cost". This is a fancy way of saying an interest rate, and in many ways, a better way to think of it. When you pay an interest rate, you are paying someone for choosing your investment over the many others that exist out there.

One way to significantly lower your costs to borrow funds is to make yourself a better risk. This can be done through a key factor known as "credit score".

Credit score

Credit score is very important in one's ability to achieve the American Dream. Can it be done without a good credit score? Sure, but it is a much tougher row to hoe. Credit score is a number based upon items that historically show

Debt

a borrower's likelihood of paying a loan back. Late payments, too many hard credit checks, too little credit history, credit card debt that exceeds one third of the total amount of credit available on the credit card. (That is: If you have a $6,000 limit on your card, and you have more than $2,000 on the card as a balance, it hurts your credit.) Remember, lenders want to be repaid. The more risk shown by your credit history, the more you have to pay for the use of their money.

Maintaining great credit is a key to having more money and investing successfully using debt. If we can pay less interest when we buy a car, we get to keep that savings. We would otherwise have to spend more to pay the lender for risking their money with us. With better credit, we have more money to spend or even better invest. If we find an investment and we can earn 10 percent on it, but borrowing money cost us 12 percent, we are losing 2 percent on every dollar we borrow. If we have better credit and can get a loan at six percent, we are earning 3 percent on every dollar we borrow. This means if we borrowed $100,000 and earned 1percent, we would have 10,000. We would pay our lender 6 percent or $6,000 and have 4 percent or $4,000 left for ourselves that we earned on someone else's money. So simply by being a better risk, we were able to make money where someone who is a poorer risk could not.

Making yourself the best possible credit risk gives you discounts throughout life that leaves more money on the table for you. This allows you the capital (money) to take advantage of opportunities that otherwise would not be available for you.

> **Tip:** *If you have bad credit, there are people that help to fix bad credit. Whatever issues you have in your past can be fixed with discipline and hard work. Get a professional to look at your situation and develop a strategy to set your credit score right.*

Chapter 8

Common types of debt and how they work

*When your outgo exceeds your income
your upkeep is your downfall.*

-AUTHOR UNKNOWN

Credit cards

Credit cards are the bane of so many people's existence. Credit card debt is really rough because of the high interest rates charged by credit card companies. They do this because as we stated above, credit card debt is non-collateralized debt, and therefore, credit card companies have to charge more to make up for customer defaults. Is there any good use for credit cards at all? Well, actually the idea of being able to buy things and have a delay before paying for them can be a very nice tool at your disposal. If we were say buying hamburger buns for our food truck and then selling hamburgers for a profit, we would theoretically be paying for these buns with money we made from selling them and never be paying out of our pocket. In other words, if we had $10 to our name and we use our credit card to buy the buns for the hamburgers, we never actually touch that $10. The profit from the sale of our hamburgers pays for it (provided our profits are not used to buy a liter of tequila and a bag of limes as a personal bonus to celebrate our great sales).

Common types of debt and how they work

Note: *The basis of credit cards is actually not greed, as so many people assume; it is a transaction based on trust. Credit card companies are advancing you the money in good faith and trusting you to pay the bill for what you spent.*

Tip: *Credit cards are a critical part of building up a good credit score. For this reason, burning your credit cards to stop an overspending problem is probably not the best choice. I refer to it as the "nuclear option" and should only be employed if your will power is so low that your resistance to the siren call of the plastic is impossible for you to ignore. Instead we should focus on paying down bad debts.*

*Once cleared of bad debts, your credit cards should be used with discipline, and function as tools to build credit. This is done by paying with the card for things that you would normally buy with cash, always setting aside the cash to pay the full balance each billing cycle. Some cards even provide cash back bonuses that will give you a portion of all money spent back each month. These bonuses are often only one or two percent but it is a net positive, over cash, when paying for **necessary** expenses.*

The only time carrying a balance on a credit card should be considered is for acquisition of income generating assets. (Obviously if someone needs to go to the hospital to get a machete removed from their skull due to a freak piñata accident, you can use the card, but realize this is a last resort that hinders your ability to generate wealth.) What are "income generating assets" you may ask? Is the jet ski you just saw at the local watersport store? It depends. If you plan to use it to try and knock your friends off while doing sixty miles per hour to watch them skip across the water, no, sadly, it is not an asset. If, however, you are renting the jet ski out to others, and a reasonable business plan shows that based upon all expenses from operating the jet ski you will be able to use profits to pay it off in a reasonable time period, then it is worth considering. If there are less expensive forms of financing (lower interest rates, not necessarily lower payments), those should be used instead.

The Roadmap to the American Dream

TIP: *As we discussed above, the reason why we want to consider the interest rate and not so much the payment amount is that the interest rate is the actual cost you are paying to use the money. The payment could be lower but it will take forty years to pay the loan back, while the higher payment will have it paid off in five years. The total amount you pay over those forty years of payments could easily be four or five times as much as the five-year loan.*

It is sort of like renting a truck. One company wants to charge $50 and the other charges $35. Based on this info, truck two is looking pretty sexy. But in the fine print, you read that the first company charges $.10 a mile while the second charges $1. You will be driving forty miles total with the truck. Truck two is not looking so sexy anymore. It's kind of like the really hot person you were checking out all night just smiled at you but their teeth are super nasty (#buzzKill). So, your brief flirtation with truck two comes to an end as you go back to your first choice and take truck one home with you. The mileage is like the interest rate. It is the cost you pay for using the money.

Always remember to pay attention to the interest rate.

Another place where using a credit card can be wise is with real estate. Not to buy a house, but to get it ready to be rented. This is for *assets* only! The proper use of a credit card would be to put in a kitchen in a home you are getting ready to rent out. Putting in the hot tub you always wanted on the credit card does not count. As long as the income from the property supports paying this debt down in a reasonable time frame, then this is a very good way to build an asset when money is tight. It is even a better practice for a home that is being re-sold (flipped). If you have done your numbers correctly you will be like the guy with the hamburger buns, although homes take longer to sell. The odds of a home selling before a payment is needed, is highly unlikely. We need to consider how long it will take and what type of profit to expect. We will be doing more of this as we go. Okay, we have covered a risky type of debt here. Now let's look at a more stable type.

Common types of debt and how they work

Mortgages

This section is going to be a bit of an orgy of acronyms. I am not doing this to confuse you—quite the opposite, actually. I am giving you these examples because they are used often in the field, and if you understand them now you will not be confused by people that may want to take advantage of you.

Mortgages are a type of loan made on real property (real estate). They are a collateralized loan and therefore the interest rate typically is low. Some criteria are taken into account when a lender considers giving you a mortgage. The less information you can provide, the higher the interest rate. The lender also lowers the amount of money they lend you as well. (Remember from earlier, when we discussed Loan to Value (LTV) during the discussion about equity. It is the percentage of the value of the property that the lender lends to you). This is going to make up the first critical part of the loan, which is your "principal" (the amount of money you borrow). The equity (your down payment) and principal together make up the total value of the home.

The next part we need to understand is the **term.** This is the length of time the loan is made for. There are all kinds of terms, from very short to very long. The term of a loan can range from one to two years to over forty.

> **Rate** is the interest rate on the loan (which we discuss below).
> **Payment** is the amount you pay on your mortgage, normally monthly (can be biweekly or some other fixed interval of time).
> **Balloon** is the amount left to be paid, if a loan is not fully amortized (relax, I explain what it means in a minute).
> **Call** is a point at which the loan must be repaid. Normally this would be a time agreed upon between the borrower and lender before the loan is completed. It can also be an action taken by the lender for a breach by the borrower. If it is an agreed upon call it is not a bad thing. I explain this a bit more when we discuss partially amortized loans in just a second.
> **Amortization** is something we need to discuss now because it will be rearing its ugly head all over the place soon.

Fully amortizing or full AM loans

An **amortizing loan** is one that pays itself off completely as long as all payments are made. So on a typical thirty-year home mortgage that is fully amortizing when you make the last payment on the loan, you do not owe any more money and you own the home. On a **non-amortizing loan** (**non-am or interest only**), you just simply pay interest. You still owe the original amount you borrowed. You could make payments for forty years and you will still owe the same amount. The payment on an interest-only loan is lower because you are not paying back any principal.

Partially amortizing loans

This is a little bit more complicated. Typically, these are loans that are designed for people to refinance. A loan like this might be a thirty-year amortizing loan with a five-year call. That means the payment is be based upon paying the property off in thirty years, but at the end of the five-year term the loan is over and a balloon payment of the remaining loan amount is required. This is normally done by refinancing, but it could also be paid off if the borrower has the money and chooses to do so. There are financial benefits to this, which we discuss when we get to taxes and depreciation.

Hard money or hard equity loans

Mortgages that require the least documentation are called "hard money" or "hard equity" loans. They typically only lend fifty to sixty percent LTV ($50,000- to 60,000 on a $100,000 property), and they do not require any credit check or documentation of income from the borrower. Normally they only want an appraisal of the property, and charge an interest rate of twelve to fifteen percent (*ouch*!). These types of loans are possible because the lender really doesn't care if the borrower defaults. If the lender does have to foreclose, they are basically getting the property for fifty-sixty percent of its value because that is all that they lent. It pays the investor for the risk.

Common types of debt and how they work

Hard equity loans can be good if the property you are buying is a quick flip because if you hold it for only three months (based on the 12 percent interest rate), you only be pay 3 percent interest over that time (interest rate that is quoted is the total interest you pay for the year. In this case, you only held the property for a quarter of the year, therefore you only pay 3 percent). This is another example where we look at the cost of money and compare it to the potential return. This is a critical skill that is needed for the use of debt. What does debt cost versus what we make?

Conventional, Veterans Administration (VA) and Federal Housing Administrative (FHA) Loans

These mortgages are much less expensive interest rate-wise, and give you a much greater percentage of the purchase price of what you are buying than a hard money loan. The down side is they require you to provide all kinds of things such as: tax returns, pay stubs, proof of current employment, credit checks, navel lint, a DNA sample from your mother-in-law's Pekinese's left hind paw (maybe not that, but some other crazy stuff.) The lender also checks your DTI (debt to income ratio). This is a ratio of how much you make compared to your recurring bills. Car payments, child support, credit card bills all count as debts, which limits how much you can borrow. If you make $2,000 a month and have $3,000 a month in expenses, you will not be getting a loan. Lenders do this to lower their risk in lending to you. They want to make sure you can actually pay them back.

My problem lies in reconciling my gross habits with my net income.

-Errol Flynn

Once lenders calculate your bills, they calculate your total housing expenses, which are made up of four things: principal, interest, taxes, and insurance. You can remember this with the acronym PITI, think Mr. T with his line, "I pity (piti) the fool." These four things are very important for you to know as they determine how much your home will cost you to live in compared to how much you could make from an investment property.

FHA and VA typically have very similar DTIs, usually around the low the 40 percent range. Conventional loans are usually in the high 30 percent range. These change so you should check what they are with your lender. There are special programs for those with very good credit that can allow DTI into the mid 40 percent's with conventional loans right now. If the lender allows a higher DTI that means you can have more bills and still get a loan. Remember when I said that credit score is super important?

Conventional loans require a higher credit core than VA and FHA loans do, and VA and FHA loans also require less down than conventional.

I know what you are thinking, "Why the hell would anyone want a conventional loan then?" Conventional loans are cheaper. Conventional loans are made by banks and comply with a pre-set criterion (typically Fannie Mae), which allows the bank to resell the mortgage. Once the loan is made, it is then be bundled with other loans that comply to the pre-set criterion and sold as investments to Wall Street. This is a bit of an over simplification, but it is basically how it works. This system makes it possible for the banks to not run out of money, and to continue making loans. Because these loans are sold to investors, they need to have a very low rate of default. That is the reason why a higher credit score and higher down payment are required. So when do we get the cheaper part?

Glad you asked. FHA and VA loans normally have a higher interest rate than do conventional loans. Lower credit scores equals more defaults, which equal higher risk, which means more compensation to the investors for that risk (higher interest rates.) Also, FHA and VA incur greater cost from the bank or mortgage broker making them. A conventional loan costs one to 2 percent less at the time of purchase than their FHA/VA brethren.

There is another issue: Loans that are made at a greater than eighty percent LTV require mortgage insurance. Standard conventional loans are 80 percent, whereas FHA loans are normally 96.5 percent LTV. This means the borrower must pay for insurance for the lender each month in addition to their mortgage payment. The borrower receives no benefit from this insurance. They only pay out to the lender when and if they default and get foreclosed upon. VA does not have mortgage insurance because they are government guaranteed loans for veterans.

VA/FHA loans also take more time to get done, often an additional fifteen to thirty days are required to close one of these loans compared with a conventional loans. In addition, they have standards for the home you are buying. It must be in a certain minimum condition for the government to lend you money. For these reasons, sellers do not like to accept VA or FHA offers.

The last big knock against VA/FHA is they are for primary residences only. While we want to give you the knowledge to buy the home you live in (VA/FHA may be a good way to do that for you), the primary goal is to show you how to invest. Your primary residence does not generate income. It keeps pace with inflation, but not much more than that. Conventional as well as hard money loans can allow you to buy homes that need work, and can be turned into income generating assets. VH/FHA loans *cannot* be applied beyond a primary residence.

Annual percentage rate (APR)

There is no way to discuss mortgages and fees without touching on this. APR stands for the annual percentage rate. This takes the base interest rate you are charged, and adds points for mortgage brokers fees and other charges that are paid out for the privilege of borrowing money. Your interest rate is what you are paying the person that is actually lending you the money. The other fees are for the mortgage broker, for the people that deal with the loan once it is made, and any other costs that can be tacked on. APR gives you a better idea of what you will be paying compared to the base quoted interest rate alone.

> **Note:** *Watch your costs. When you invest, all extra costs come from one place—your profit. If your mortgage broker didn't charge you a $100 "air way restoration" fee (they picked their nose and charged you for it), then you would have exactly $100 more in profit on your deal. You are always the last one to get paid.*

Principal

This is the amount you are borrowing. As you make payments on an amortizing loan, the principal amount goes down. With this type of loan, you have a fixed payment (unless a variable interest rate loan is involved). In the early portion of a mortgage, the principal goes down very little because the majority of the payment represents interest. Each time you make a payment, the principal portion of what you are paying becomes greater, and the interest portion becomes less. Toward the end of the loan your payment is almost entirely principal.

An amortization schedule tells you what portion of each payment represents principal and interest respectively. By paying more than your payment amount in the early part of a loan, you can greatly decrease the length of it. If we borrow $100,000 with a fully amortized loan at 5 percent interest, our payment will be $536.82 (trust me, I did the math). We make one payment a month for thirty years (360 total) and owe zero at the end of the loan term. If, however, we pay an extra $200 a month, our loan only lasts a little less than sixteen years and nine months. Why? Once the principal is paid back, the loan ends. If you expedite the payment of the principal, the loan gets much shorter. If you make all 360 payments, you actually pay $193,255.78 over the thirty years. If you pay the extra $200 a month, you only pay $147,747.47. The difference is the interest that you are paying (a whopping $45,508.31!)

Mortgage interest

There are two main ways that interest is set on loans: Fixed and variable rate loans. A **fixed rate loan** normally has a higher initial rate than a variable rate loan, but it stays the same for the life of the loan. On a thirty-year fixed rate loan, you make 360 payments (one each month for thirty years) and the amount is always the same. These are very stable loans and are good if you want less risk.

A **variable rate loan** uses an index for its base rate, and then adds a spread, which provides the rate the lender charges. The lender gets the index from a well-known source, typically "Libor[17]," which is the rate banks

---

17   LIBOR stands for London Interbank Offered Rate. It is the average of interest rates estimated by each of the leading banks in London that it would be charged were it to borrow from other banks.

Common types of debt and how they work

charge each other to borrow money. This is a very low rate as these loans are not very risky. To that the lender adds their spread. So, if the Libor is at 1.5 percent and the lenders spread is 3.2 percent, you are charged an interest rate of 4.7 percent. The thing is, if Libor goes up, so do your payments. Typically the variable rate loan has a time period set in which it will adjust. This means your payments won't change every month, but only when the pre-set dates are reached. This could be every six months or two years. The time line varies, but if you plan on using this type of debt it is something you should pay attention to.

Just like other forms of interest, each of us pays for the benefit we get from the use of someone else's money. As we saw above, we could pay a loan back sooner to save a bunch of money and we would own our home sooner. Seems like a no brainer right? Buy wait a sec. Some of the least expensive money to use is money in a home. The interest rates are low, and if we use this money for another opportunity, it means we do not have to be a huge success to make a profit on the money we borrowed. What does that mean?

If I borrow on my credit card and they charge me 18 percent, I need to use that money on an investment that makes more than 18 percent or I am losing money. If I borrow on a home and am paying 5 percent, then this is much easier. Let's say I had a mutual fund that has been returning about 11 percent each year. If I borrowed money from my home at 5 percent to invest in this, I would be making 6 percent on the money I borrowed. I would earn 11 percent from the investment and have to pay 5 percent to my lender for the privilege of using their money. This leaves me with a profit of 6 percent I made on someone else's money. On the other hand, if I did this with a credit card at 18 percent, I would be losing 7 percent a month.

Well, that is the bad stuff—now for the good stuff. Mortgages are the best way to start to buy real estate, or start a business. It is hard to save enough to buy a property for cash or fund your startup. With a loan, you can put down a smaller amount and be able to purchase a property. Or you can get seed capital to bring your business idea to market. The use of these relatively inexpensive funds to get your money out and working is a great way to start down the pathway to prosperity.

Tip: *People that start a business overwhelmingly get their startup capital from borrowing against their homes. It is a good thing that we have the ability to do this, but obviously a setback means we need to be looking for a quiet street corner and a high quality card board box to live in (preferable wax coated and double ply so you can be the envy of the other box dwellers). We highly recommend investing (in case you somehow missed it, this is what this book is about), but we especially want you to do it safely and wisely. Sometimes the only place there is money to invest is in one's home, and for this reason we recommend caution.*

If you are going to use money taken from where you live, you need to be very certain of the deal. That being said, we are going back to the same thought we've discussed before: You need to look at the deal and determine the projected return; then compare that return to what the use of the money you borrow is going to cost you.

The last two items that made up housing expense are **taxes** and **insurance.** **Taxes** refer to the real estate tax that you pay for the property, but not your personal taxes, sales tax, or any other crazy tax they come up with (sorry, you still have to pay all the other taxes). We just don't have to count them toward whether you get a loan or not. **Insurance** refers to your homeowner's insurance. Your lender makes you buys this. They need to make sure that if something happens to their collateral, you have insurance to repair or replace it so that their investment is protected.

Student loans

These are the real anchor around the neck of this generation. Many people have asked me how to handle their college debt. Should I pay it back as fast as I can, or pay the minimum? The answer is—it depends. (I know, I should be a politician with answers like that.) But the reason why it depends is that more information is needed for a correct answer. We would need to know the interest rate of your college loan. We would also need to know what investment opportunities you have. Let's say, for instance, your student loans are at

Common types of debt and how they work

6.5 percent and you have an investment opportunity that allows you to invest incrementally but returns 11.5 percent. That means that for every dollar of the loan you do not pay back sooner than you must, you earn 5 percent. If you pay the money back sooner, you save 6.5 percent in interest but you lose the 11.5 percent you could have earned. By paying the money back sooner, you are losing 5 percent that you could have earned in profit on someone else's money. So in this case, paying the loan back right away isn't the right answer.

There are a few reasons why the above is very important. We discussed earlier why investing early is important because it gives your money more time to grow. If you squander your late twenties into your thirties paying back student loans as fast as you can instead of investing, you lose your prime investing years. There is another other big reason: this is an opportunity that you only get once. A college loan is usually a large uncollateralized debt at a fairly low interest rate. It is very difficult to go out and get someone to give you a $100,000 loan with no collateral at 7 percent interest just because you ask for it. A college loan once paid back is gone. You do not have access to this kind of borrowed money again. You already got the benefit. You got the education. The longer you use the money to pay it back to make money the better the deal for you is.

This is *not* saying to default on your loans. Instead, we are proposing that you invest any extra amount (over the minimum payment) you would pay on your loans for investments that perform better than the interest rate of your college loan.

The final piece to the "why it depends" is the antacid factor (risk profile). If having debt makes it impossible for you to sleep at night, or if you viscerally feel the burden of owing every waking moment, then this strategy may not be the best for you. You typically will not be making a ton of money fresh out of college and so managing your resources well is critical. First, try to redirect how you think about investing and debt so that you are not as focused on the risk but more so on the opportunity. Investment can be scary, but so is any field before you know what you are doing. Luckily, when you are fresh out of college you are very familiar with the technique for fixing that problem: You research and educate yourself.

The Roadmap to the American Dream

"In investing, what is comfortable is rarely profitable."

- Robert Arnott

Auto loans and leases

This is an area that really divides people. Some people do not care what they drive. If the gas mileage on a pogo stick was better than a Prius and it had, heat and air conditioning, there are people that would be all over it. Others would rather be keel hauled on an aircraft carrier with a serious barnacle problem than be caught dead in a Prius. So in summary: Some people are real car people and others just don't care. (By way of full disclosure, I am one of those car folks. If I rent a car and get stuck with a ride I deem as crappy, I'm somewhere between bummed and pissed. I've built race cars, and driven way too fast way too often. This is a part of me. It has cost me a lot of money I could otherwise have allocated to investment. Do I regret these decisions? I have to be honest, some yes and some no. But I get a lot of joy from having a car that I like.)

The above is one of those areas where you have to know yourself, and be honest. If you are going to be miserable driving a beater around today so you can have a great car you can really afford a few years from now, you have two options: One, grow up, suck it up, and get the beater, or two, work harder to be able to afford the thing that gives you joy while still investing. I've opted for option two a lot. Currently I am doing a hybrid of option one and two: I drive a car that I'm indifferent about—lots of options and gadgets—but every time I introduce mister gas pedal to Señor floor board, I die a little inside (the little hamsters that pass for an engine just don't like to run, it seems). I also still work hard and try to invest every dime I can. This took some growing up for me. I still look at the new Corvette longingly and whisper the words, "You will once again be mine." I hate growing up. Those of you that think I'm nuts at this point are not car people and will never get this. The rest of you know where I am coming from.

Okay, back to the actual subject at hand and why any of this introduction matters. If you are okay driving a used car into the ground, then buying a car is probably your best bet. If you are the type of person that works harder to be able to have a new car every three to four years and don't drive too far, a lease may be your best answer. Here's why: When you buy a new car, it immediately depreciates (loses value) of about one third of what you just paid. In other words, you paid $30,000 and drove the car home. The next day you decide to go back and trade it in. You are amazed (or rather, dismayed) when they offer you around $20,00 when you just paid $30,000.

New versus used cars

People that buy a used car do not typically experience that kind of "fall off of a cliff" depreciation. The risk they run is that the car they just bought was owned by someone that took their Smart car off-roading on weekends and tried to get the brakes hot enough to cook on when they went camping—every weekend. You can mitigate this by getting a warranty from where you buy your used car, or possibly knowing the folks you are buying from and how they kept the car. Folks that are cool with buying these types of cars understand that: Cars are not assets. They are a means of conveyance. Now if you are the type of person that doesn't know anything about cars, doesn't want any hassles with breakdowns, are okay with anything on wheels as long as it is new, and doesn't mind the depreciation so much; then a new car is what you should do. But how do you buy it?

Paying cash versus financing

We can buy a car for cash if we have it, and our friend "Debt Free Dan" will be somewhere smiling, or we can finance it. (We get to leases a little later.) If we pay cash, we only have the expense of gas and routine maintenance while the car is under warranty. This gives us the lowest monthly cost for using the vehicle. Once the warranty is over, we are responsible for any repairs the car needs, which gives us a variable monthly expense that is tough to budget for. We do have equity when it is time to sell. This means that when we want to get a new car, we can sell the old one. If we financed the purchase, we would need to wait to have it paid off, or at least not owe more than the car was worth in order to have any equity. The money you get from selling the car is really just a refund of the money you have spent when you bought it.

If we pay cash for the car, we experience the ultimate in payment reduction, but also the ultimate in opportunity reduction. We have spent a pile of cash and have a car, but no ability to make money with the money we just spent. In other words, if we buy a car with financing or with cash, there is no difference in how we use the car. We can still drive when we want, park where we want, etc. The only difference is how we pay for it. Therefore, if we pay cash, we get the peace of mind of having no payments. If we finance, we get all the usage rights we have as owners, but also the use of the money we would otherwise have had to spend to pay for the car. Once again, this is a good thing if the money that is not spent upfront to buy the car is invested, and then only removed from the investment to make the payments on the car as they become due.

If we finance the car, we have the option to put more or less money down. (Ugghhh! I just want a car with a stinking back-up camera—why does this have to be so complex? Hang in there. We are going to power through this, and I have faith in you.) A monthly car payment means that you have this payment on top of gas and routine maintenance. Your car is under warranty for the first few years you own it, and so you have fairly fixed costs during this time. When the warranty ends, you will probably still be making car payments plus you are responsible for things that break on the vehicle.

> *Car sickness is the feeling you get when the monthly payment is due.*
>
> -*Author Unknown*

As investors who are using any extra money we have to make money for us, we need to consider what opportunities we may be missing because we are spending this money. If we have the option to earn 10 percent on an investment, and the rate being charged to borrow money for the car is 5 percent, we would be best served by putting the minimum down on the car and investing the rest. Our car payment would be higher by doing this, but the income we earn from our investment returns is double of what the difference in the payment would be. To say it another way and applying arbitrary numbers to the scenario above: It costs us an extra $25 a month to finance the car at the minimum payment, and our extra earnings from our investment will be $50 a month. We can use half of that money to pay the difference in the car payment and use the other half to reinvest and earn even more. Think back to the TVM table from chapter six and consider what that $25 will be worth in twenty or thirty years.

Sometimes a dealership offers you different interest rates for the car you are thinking about buying based on how much you put down. The more you put down, the lower the rate. Based upon what we discussed about lenders' risk earlier, this should make sense. The option to put more down for a lower rate can be very tempting. It might even be a good decision based upon the discount. Once again, you need to compare what potential earnings loss you have by putting funds into a non-asset. Said more simply: How much possible investment gains are you losing by putting money into a car that is never going to return what you put into it. Remember, money has two uses: Buy things or be put to work making money. Dollars you use to buy things are gone and can't be used to help you reach your financial goals.

Leasing

Leasing can be a good option, as you are paying for the use of the vehicle and not for the purchase of it. The pluses of a lease are: Payments are usually lower, you have a new car every few years, your car is always under warranty, and you never experience depreciation. The downsides are: Mileage restrictions, you have no equity in the car so when your lease is up you need a new down payment for your next lease, and you need a higher level of insurance on the car (to protect the leasing company). One major benefit with a lease is that you have a very dependable car expense. Repairs never enter into the equation because the car you lease is, almost always, under warranty. Leases are good for companies too as they can count the payments as an expense on their books. We discuss expenses more when we talk about taxes and deductions later. You can see how leases have their good and bad side. Let's elaborate and look a little deeper at some of them.

Your payments are lower because you are only paying for the use of the car and are not buying it. For this reason you are really only paying for the depreciation on the car and some profit to the owner, which is the leasing company.

You are in a new car sort of by force. If you don't get a new car, you have no car at all. When a lease is up, you have to turn the car back in or exercise the option that they give you of buying it. You know you were doing donuts in the parking lot of the local mall after hours each weekend, not to mention the drag races so in most instances, you are not going to want to buy the car.

Because you are in a new car all of the time and have a mileage limitation, the entire time you are using the car you are protected by the warranty. The major issue for many folks with leasing winds up being the mileage limit. They need to limit your mileage, as the leasing company will be selling your car as a used car when they get it back. The more miles on the car, the less it is worth. If you want to lease, but the mileage they are offering is not enough, the leasing company can increase the miles. This, however, also increases the payments.

A portion of the savings that you have in your payments, with a lease, needs to be saved. The reason for this is that when your lease ends, you do not have any value in the vehicle (as you would with a purchase) to use for a down payment on your next lease. Usually you need at least $1,000 or more for a new down payment. But because you do not own the vehicle you are driving, the leasing company requires you to carry insurance with much higher limits than the normally allowable minimums. This is done to protect the leasing company, but it drives your monthly vehicle costs up.

As you can see, leasing has some good and some bad consequences. It also has some hidden costs that must be considered when deciding how best to get a vehicle.

Lines of credit

A line of credit is a type of collateralized loan usually given by banks. Typically, the bank offers this to you when you need it least, which is really their favorite time to lend money. They want to make sure you have plenty of

Common types of debt and how they work

assets, income, and money in the bank. So, if you find yourself saying, "I have all of those things" don't be surprised to get a call from your banker asking if you would like a line of credit. These types of loans are normally made against receivables. That means if you or your company is owed money from customers, the bank lends you money and you pledge the amounts you are scheduled to receive in order to repay that loan. If you fail to make the payments, the bank steps in and takes the money your customers were supposed to pay you.

One of the key benefits of a line of credit is that you only pay interest on the portion of the money you use and only while the money is out. This means if you have a $100,000 line of credit but only take out $10,000, you only pay interest on the $10,000. If the interest on the line of credit is 5 percent and you borrow the $10,000 for six months, you pay $250 interest or 2.5 percent on the amount you borrowed. (Remember, interest rates are calculated on an annual basis. For this reason, you are only paying half of the 5 percent interest rate because the money was only borrowed for half of the year.)

Let's go to the playground for an example: Tommy and Billy, a couple of fourth graders, owe Guido, a fourteen-year-old sixth grader, half of their lunch money every day because they have found Guido's "punch or lunch" initiative very compelling. Little Leon sees a business opportunity. He realizes that Guido's income gives him $2 a day. But some days Guido needs more capital than others, as he is a huge fan of pizza day and not so much when it's chipped beef day. Leon agrees to allow Guido a line of credit up to $5. He agrees to pay 10 cents interest a week on every dollar he borrows for any part of the week.

Guido finds himself "jonesing" for a honey bun around two o'clock on Monday, but he's already spent all of his cash. He meets up with Leon and borrows a dollar. Later that week on Pizza day, Guido asks Leon for another $2. He has $3 out for the week and owes Leon 30 cents of interest. By the end of the following week, Guido has paid Leon back $2.30. He still owes interest on the $1 he has not paid back yet. Guido has learned how a line of credit works. He also realizes at this point that the free market is hard. He introduces Leon to his new "no money left behind" program where he takes all of Leon's money and leaves none behind. Guido obviously has a future in politics. The end.

A common type of line of credit is a **Home Equity Line of Credit** (HELOC). This is exactly the same as the above-mentioned lines of credit except that instead of the collateral being your accounts receivables it is instead your home that provides the security for the loan. This can be a very good tool to help with providing cash if an emergency occurs without having a cost when the funds are not in use. So, if Joshua and Kathryn had a home equity line of credit on their penthouse condo in New York of $300,000 and they did not use it you would pay $0 to the lender. If Joshua suffered a freak tap dancing injury, and had to miss 6 weeks of work, this couple could use their HELOC to help them pay their bills.

Lines of credit function very similarly to credit cards. Their interest rates are lower because your collateral (you property or receivables: customers that haven't paid yet) are securing the repayment of the loan. These can be very helpful if you have good income, but need large amounts of cash intermittently. If we were buying real estate and had a nice portfolio of rental properties, we should be in a good place for a line of credit. We could use the income from our rental properties and even the properties themselves to secure the line of credit. This means we could use the line of credit to both buy properties, but even more importantly, pay for the renovations. Homes are easy to get a mortgage on, but renovation costs are very difficult to finance. You can sometimes pay for them with a credit card, but as discussed earlier, the interest rates on credit cards are very high. The line of credit works well here because when we sell the property we renovated, we can pay the entire loan back. The line of credit gives us a much cheaper source of funds, which like a credit card, we only pay for while we are using the money. The savings on the interest is pure profit to you, and profit is a wonderful thing.

Buying on margin

This is a type of loan that is unique to securities. It is a loan that is secured by the total portfolio you own. It allows you, much like a home mortgage, to put down only a percentage of the money needed to buy the security, and borrow the rest of the cash needed to complete the purchase. The interest rates being charged vary between brokers. Typically, the rates are on the high side, around 8 percent. For this reason, you want to be very certain of an investment's success before you use this type of loan. These loans are for the savvy investor only.

If your investments are losing value, the broker can do what is called a **margin call.** This is where you are forced to sell some of your portfolio to pay down your loan. The issue with this is that you are forced to actually realize the loss when this happens. That is different from a bar of gold that you might own. Let's say you bought it for $600 an ounce and the price fell to $300 an ounce. This really hurts your feelings and you probably need several additional drinks each night to help console yourself over this down turn, but you haven't actually realized the loss yet. However, if you were to sell the gold, you would. If you held onto your gold and the price went up to $700 an ounce, you would not have to realize a loss at all. In fact, you would have a nice little profit, which is good. Then you could pay for your alcohol rehab after all the drinking you did while gold was at $300 an ounce.

This type of loan allows you to leverage limited funds to buy larger amounts of securities. This is its main benefit. If we did our research and felt that due to some new technology, Tesla's stock was going to go up 10 to 15 percent in the next six months, then we have found an opportunity. You call your stockbroker and buy their stock on margin. Your broker allows you to put down 10 percent and they lend you the rest. Because of this you will be able to buy ten times the number of shares you could without the loan. If the stock goes up you will also receive ten times the amount of gains (minus the interest you pay on the margin funds). If the stock goes up as you anticipate, you reap huge gains, but if it goes down, you could experience huge losses as well.

Margin is like so many things we have discussed here—a great and powerful tool. It's like watching someone that is really good on a fork lift; it gives one a sense of respect for what the operator and machine can do; but seeing an eight-year-old on that same fork lift may give you a sense of unbridled terror (#RUN!!!). Knowing when and how to use a powerful tool is what separates those that should and shouldn't consider buying on margin.

Summary

> *The only reason a great many American families don't own an elephant is that they have never been offered an elephant for a dollar down and easy weekly payments.*
>
> -MAD MAGAZINE

We have looked at several types of debt and hopefully removed some of the mystery there may have been for you. Debt has the ability to make or lose you a lot of money. In fact, it has been said that "if you want to make a lot of money in real estate, borrow a lot of money, and if you want to lose a lot of money in real estate, borrow a lot of money." That sums up the use of debt well. The difference between the winners and losers are not necessarily what they do, but how they do it. Do you remember farmer two's decision of whether to borrow 100 percent on his farm or 75 percent? Both options had him borrowing, but the lower loan amount actually reduced his risk from not borrowing at all.

Debt can allow you to not only own and use things, but also use the money to buy the thing in the first place. It is like baking your cake and eating it too, and everybody loves cake—especially with ice cream.

Buying assets is the key to making debt work for you. If you find yourself reading everything "Debt Free Dan" ever wrote, and listening to him every day on the radio where he tells everybody that avoiding risk and getting debt free is the only way to live, you are only getting and reinforcing one position. Try instead to learn more about an investment type you think you would enjoy. Dan is making the assumption that you do not have the intelligence or discipline to use debt to buy income-generating assets. That position makes him emphasize the risks without discussing the rewards. It is very possible to be too focused on the upside of investing and be foolhardy, but the opposite position (being super risk averse) is foolish too.

Being debt free is great advice for the uninformed and those that just don't know how to invest. Learning how to be well informed with money and get it working for you cures both of those issues. Try to find a balance between the two. Remember: Time is on your side when you are young, but you're getting older every day.

> *"How many millionaires do you know who have become wealthy by investing in savings accounts? I rest my case."*
>
> - ROBERT G. ALLEN

Chapter 9

A little detail on methods to avoid risk

It isn't what you know that gets you into trouble it's what you know that isn't so.

-Bob Cadillac

Because risk is such a big part of our everyday life, there exists many ways to help us deal with it. We will look at some of them here. One obvious way to deal with risk is to pay someone else to take the risk for us. "I'll give you five bucks to see if there are any landmines in that field." We call companies that get paid to handle risk " insurance companies". Something as simple as having access to cash (liquidity) is an important means of protection as well. Owning a five million-dollar commercial lot and dying of thirst because you don't have cash to buy a bottle of water is an example of great assets and no liquidity to protect us.

Another tool we use is a corporate structure. We discussed some of the reasons for corporations earlier, but in this chapter we are going to look at some of the different types and the differences between them. Finally, we discuss understanding supply and demand. The ability to recognize the type of market you are in and adjust your strategy accordingly can be one of the best risk mitigating (minimizing) tools in your arsenal.

A little detail on methods to avoid risk

Insurance

Insurance companies and the policies they issue are one of the tools used to minimize this risk. This is done by taking on many risks to lower the statistical odds of a catastrophic loss. In plain English: If your house burns down; then this is a catastrophic loss to you. The odds of this happening are very low. Unfortunately, if your house actually does burn down, the low odds don't matter much. The insurance company handles these catastrophic risks by not just insuring your house, but by insuring hundreds or thousands of other homes. The odds are probably good that one or more of these homes will eventually burn down. Luckily for the insurance company, the insurance payments made by the other policyholders not only cover the cost of paying the **claim** (the amount they must pay the person whose house burned down), but also, leave a healthy profit for the insurance company. The large buildings owned by insurance companies are paid for by following this simple business model.

Insurance folks make their money insuring all sorts of different things, from people's health, lives, businesses, and homes, to Jennifer Lopez's butt. Yes, there is a twenty-seven million dollar insurance policy on J-Lo's buns (#@$$). Companies can issue policies like this based upon the statistical risk that, in this case, J-Lo will not get into a car accident backside first. Obviously, the risk of some tooshie-mangling mishap is fairly low, and despite the high value of the policy (twenty-seven million), the payments are probably fairly low. Plus, there would probably be a very uncomfortable process of trying to collect. How would that phone call go? "Hi Mr. Insurance Man. I ugh…sorta…kinda broke my butt." Not an easy conversation. The point of this is to illustrate that because the risk to the insurance company of a claim being filed is low, the **premium** (payment amount) can also be very low. This is different from auto policies where the risk of someone getting into an accident in their life is very high. The amount of a typical policy will be a small fraction of Ms. Lopez's "booty" policy, but the premiums paid by the driver will probably be more.

There are three basic numbers to be aware of with insurance: The policy amount, the premium and the deductible.

The **amount of the policy** is the maximum amount the policy will pay. There are different ways this number can be reached. Some policies have multiple policy amounts, for example auto policies. Auto policies have separate limits for collision, liability, personal injury, and uninsured motorist coverages. This is because there are a lot of different types of risk for how this policy covers you, and the insurer wants to clearly spell out their limits. Some policies have a limit per occurrence, and this is called an **aggregate limit**.

What the heck is an aggregate limit? An aggregate limit is a really smart sounding way of saying a combined limit. For example, if you had a two million dollar liability policy that would pay one million per occurrence; then the most the insurance company would pay any individual person is one million, but the total protection of the policy is still two million. This comes in handy if something happened where more than one person was hurt. The guy tripping on the pathway in front of your business bumps into the lever on your crane, which releases the piece of steel that drops on a bus full of retired litigation attorneys who were visiting the international lawsuit museum. You are getting sued—a lot.

Now for a real world example of why an aggregate limit matters. When the World Trade Center was attacked, there was an insurance company some place saying, "Oh crap!" This is because the building was covered for acts of terror. The company that wrote the policy, Swiss RE, had a per occurrence limit on the policy of 3.55 billion and a total limit of around 7.1 billion. The owner of the World Trade Center filed two separate claims on the company, sighting the attack as two separate events. He did this because he would only receive 3.55 billion if it was one event, but if it were two, he would be able to claim the full 7.1 billion value of the policy. Big difference, right? This was of course argued in court as the insurance company felt it was one single act of terrorism. The result, for those that are curious, is that the court found the events to be two separate acts of terrorism. There may have been a "completely unrelated" increase in the number of Swiss RE executives suffering from alcoholism.

The second major item of concern is the **premium**. This is the amount that the person buying the insurance pays for the protection the insurance

A little detail on methods to avoid risk

policy provides. These payments can be made monthly, quarterly, bi-annually, or annually depending on the policy and the insurer. Sometimes the insurer offers you a discount for paying the premium up front instead of through installments. Once again, we put our investor hats on to decide if the discount they offer is a better value to us than an alternative investment, for which we could have used the money.

Often it is better to make the monthly payments to preserve **liquidity** (cash on hand) for other unforeseen issues that could arise. Lots of things affect premiums but they all have the same impact; they make you a better or worse risk for the insurer (insurance company), and make your premium payments higher or lower, respectively. Bob smokes and is out of breath half way up a flight of stairs. Do you think he is a higher or lower risk to his insurer when buying health insurance? Do you think Bob's premiums will be higher or lower than Brody, the vegan guy who runs marathons for fun? If you guessed that our wheezing friend Bob is forking out more for his medical insurance, you would be correct.

The third thing to pay attention to is your **deductible**. This is the portion of the loss that the insurer won't pay and the insured (you) does pay. The higher your deductible, the lower your payments. So, if I own a $40,000 car and I have a $1,000 deductible, every accident over $1,000 requires the insurance company to pay. This means if I had a total loss (that is, the car is totaled), I would receive a check for $39,000 ($40,000 value-$1,000 deductible= $39,000 insurance check). On the other hand, if I had an accident that cost $1,000 to fix, the insurance company would pay nothing, and I would have to pay the full amount out of pocket.

In other words, the deductible is always the first part paid—whatever remains after that, is paid by the insurer. The co-pay at the doctor's office is a form of a deductible. It is similar to a per occurrence deductible. Every time you go, you pay until your yearly deductible is met.

You can see how high deductibles expose you to risk. The lower payments are pretty nice too. To quote an old movie line, "What's a girl to do"? Luckily there is a way to try and manage this risk. A higher deductible strategy can be used to great effect. We basically play the insurance companies game by assuming we won't get sued for someone tripping on our property the same week we get into a car accident, our house burns down, we get hurt and miss work (#quack), and we contract a hybrid strain of chicken pox and leprosy.

If you are paying a higher premium to lower your deductible, you are really just giving money to the insurer, which they will give right back to you if there is a claim. That is the real issue. If there was a way to protect ourselves from the risk of not being able to afford one of those big deductibles when we make a claim, then that would be fantasti-magical (yep, made it up). The thing that makes it possible for us to do this is having the cash reserves on hand to handle one of these deductibles if they come due. We call this liquidity, which we discuss soon.

Let's look at a couple of basic types of insurance here and see how they work.

Life insurance exists because everybody dies, and dying is expensive. There are two types of life insurance, **whole life** and **term**. Whole life is a good news bad news policy. The good news: This is the one policy where there is a 100 percent chance of collecting on it. The bad news: You will be dead so, you won't be the one collecting on it. The person listed as your "beneficiary" will be the one cashing in on your "investment". With a whole life policy, you make a fixed payment for the rest of your life until you die. At that point, the policy pays out the full amount for which you were insured. The payment amount is calculated based upon your age, health, and risk indicators. So, if you are mainlining heroin, you pay more than our buddy Brody from earlier, who is a vegan marathon runner, that never lets anything but hemp touch his skin, and lives in the organic isle at Whole Foods. Basically, this type of policy is the best deal if you are in great shape when you get the policy and then die young; not for you obviously, although I know some people that would be grinning from ear to ear in their casket knowing they stuck it to the insurance company.

Is whole life a good deal? Typically, not as an investment. It is, however, a good tool for estate planning. It is a poor investment because the rate of return your heirs receive for what you paid in, on average, is very low. Also, consider TVM (Time Value of Money). A dollar is worth more today than it is in the

A little detail on methods to avoid risk

future. You are using more valuable "today money" to make payments to get a less valuable "future money" lump sum in the future.

Now, you can use whole life insurance's powers for good. If you have a lot of assets that would be hard or impossible to liquidate, a life insurance policy could provide the cash your heirs would need to pay the taxes on your estate. Let's say Frank and Joy have built a really great business together making environmentally-friendly, paper-free, interactive text books for mathematics, biology, and music. They own several patents, machinery, a factory, and a lot of inventory, which are all valuable but hard to sell quickly without having to discount severely. This makes up the bulk of their wealth. Frank and Joy also have some cash, but the vast majority of their estate is in their business.

Unfortunately, if Frank and Joy were to die in a freak violin bow string-snapping incident, their children would have a very large tax bill to pay. The government is going to assess the value of Frank and Joy's estate, and their children will need to pay a hefty tax bill on whatever assets they inherit. The amount of this tax has changed a lot over the years, so just be aware of the "death tax" (as it is called). Obviously, if the kids want to keep the business going, they will need to sell assets to pay this tax. But the assets they must sell are probably needed to maintain the business. Talk about a Catch-22. Enter the whole life policy that Frank and Joy took out (because they are cool like that). This provides the kids with an influx of cash to pay this tax, allows them to preserve the business and grow what their parents built for them.

On to **term life,** the "lease" of the life insurance world. This is a policy you buy for a specific period of time (called a term), and pay for it only during that period of time. If you die after the term, you get nothing. If you die during the term, the policy pays the full amount. This is like a lease because you are basically renting a policy. You pay and when the rental is up you turn it back in.

Term life would be a good type of policy for our friends Frank and Joy if they planned on selling their business in the next five to ten years, and hanging on to all of the cash they make from the sale. A ten-year term policy would protect them if they were to die while they still own their business, and then it would expire after the business was sold. They would not need the policy anymore because they would have cash, which could then be used by their heirs to pay any tax consequences created by their death. This means Frank and Joy are not paying premiums when they no longer need the protection the policy offers them.

The major benefit of a term policy is that the premiums are typically much lower. This is because the insurance company often does not have to pay these out as often the term expires (and not the policy holder), compared to whole life policies, which always pay out. It is a gamble for the insurance company, and a way of protecting loved ones for the person buying a term policy.

Liability insurance is something you need as soon as you start to have assets. Why? Because as soon as something goes wrong, the attorneys always look for people with assets to sue. If you have nothing, normally, you won't get sued, but you also have nothing (which is bad). If having nothing just won't cut it, then you need to learn to cover *your assets*. We do this with a liability policy.

Where there is a will there is a lawsuit.

-Addison Mizner

Liability insurance is the type of policy we would want to have when those retired litigators, from earlier in the chapter, had the piece of steel fall on their bus. It is typically the catch-all policy for anything that anybody can get a jury to decide might, in some small way, be your fault. A liability policy, therefore, is an extra policy that covers some of the other things for which you may already be insured, but it does so in a way that protects you if things go really, really badly.

For example, the insurance you had on your crane might have covered the piece of steel falling on the bus, but only up $200,000 in total liability. Your liability policy would probably cover you up to several million dollars for the same bus load of blood suckers (I mean, "honored and valued officers of the court"). Typically, this type of policy is referred to as an umbrella policy. It

A little detail on methods to avoid risk

is called that because it covers you over and above your other insurance. The type of business you are in and the other policies you have, determine the cost of this policy. Because we live in a country where anyone can sue anyone for pretty much anything, you need to be aware that people *will* sue and often do. The risks are high because one judgment against you could be devastating. Protecting yourself from a lawsuit is just a cost of doing business.

> *Lawsuit: A machine which you go into as*
> *a pig and come out of as a sausage.*
>
> -Ambrose Bierce

Homeowners insurance is designed to protect your home in the event of damage. This policy typically covers a lot of other things as well. If the neighbor's kid falls off of your trampoline, normally your homeowner's policy will cover it if the neighbors sue you or just ask you to pay the medical bills. If your dog bites someone, it is your homeowner's policy once again that should protect you. These policies cover most things that happen on your property.

You do need to be aware of any exclusions that exist. This is something to ask the fellow selling you the policy. Normally, if you have a mortgage on your property the bank forces you to have a policy and provides minimum standards for what that policy needs to cover. The bank does this to protect their collateral. Remember, if you don't pay, they will take the house back, so they want to make sure it is in the best possible condition.

Things that can affect the price you pay for a homeowner's policy include how and where the house you are insuring was built. If you built your home in a flood zone and happened to build it lower than any other homes in the area (and you think sunken living rooms are just awesome) two things could happen: One, after the first big rain you will probably have a very nice indoor pool where that living room once was, and two, your insurance premiums for the flood portion of your homeowner's policy are really going to hurt your feelings. It would be like building a house on stilts on the side of a mountain in a place known to have earthquakes (people actually do this). Again, you are going to have a really big insurance payment.

There are ways to pay less, however. If you wanted to build in a place where there are hurricanes, such as Florida, but you do a really good job of building the home to make it hurricane resistant, then you would actually get price breaks on your policy. A good insurer would give you discounts for using better roof attachments, hurricane windows and doors, etc. This is a way to lower your payments to the insurer. Insurance is a pain until you need it, and then it is a pain in the butt until the insurance company agrees to pay the claim, but when they do, you are very grateful to have it.

Health insurance has changed a lot over the last few years, and probably will continue to do so. As the price of medicine and malpractice insurance continues to rise, so will the cost of health insurance. Being too cheap when it comes to a plan may leave you unprotected when you go to pick up your prescription and they want to charge you $800 for five pills. Or it may not let you go to the doctor you prefer.

Learning the difference between policies is very important when buying health insurance. Two policies can both be called health insurance, just like a Yugo and a Ferrari are both cars (in the Yugo's case, barely), but that does not make them equal. The differences with health insurance can be just as stark. Watch out for things such as, can you choose your own doctor, use your own pharmacy, the cost of your co pays, the prescriptions they do and do not cover, just to name a few. If you do not have the funds to do a full-blown health insurance policy, there are policies called "major medical". This means you are on your own to pay unless something major happens. If you cut your foot off trying to do a wheelie on your new riding lawn mower, you will be covered to get it sewed back on. If you do not end up going into the hospital, however, you are pretty much on your own. Major medical, is a risk, and to that extent it is a business decision. Do you spend less, take on the risk of needing medical help and then pay out of pocket if needed, or do you pay each month to be protected from such risk.

We have discussed auto insurance earlier. Suffice it to say, the state usually requires that you have auto insurance and they dictate the minimums you

A little detail on methods to avoid risk

need to carry. Carrying more can be good, especially if you have a nicer car or assets to protect. There is a liability portion to auto insurance and so the higher that limit, the more protection you have.

One type of insurance that auto dealers often offer you when you buy a car is **Gap Insurance.** This is a policy that protects you in case you are in an accident and you owe more on the car than it is worth. The insurance company is only going to pay the folks that gave you your auto loan the current value of the car, *not* the amount you owe them. So if you bought a car for $30,000, and you get in an accident a week later and total the car, you still owe $30,000 on the car even though the value of the car is probably closer to $20,000 now. This means you would need to write a check for around $10,000 to pay off your car loan. No fun. Gap insurance, however, pays the difference, so you would owe nothing instead.

There are a lot more types of insurance we could go into but I will end this with a very important one.

Long term care is the policy that pays for you to live in "Happy Oaks", the nice old age home where the old folks have clubs, sing songs, and have a grand ol'time as opposed to the state run "Skanky Acres" for the old, crotchety and decrepit, where their motto is "we have more residents than teeth in our facility." A long term care policy is one that you pay for with your own money, but when you reach the point where you need care, the insurer pays a dollar amount each day for it. These policies differ in how long and how much they pay for per day. Some pay for life and others only pay for a certain number of years. Obviously, you are reading this book so you can invest well and live out the remainder of your years on your private island attended to by the world's best doctors, but in case you don't quite get there (and keeping in mind the increasing cost of care), it might be wise to consider protecting yourself in this manner.

My grandfather has this type of coverage. He has been collecting on it since his eighties, and he is now ninety-years-old. Long term care insurance wound up being a real life saver for him as he would not have had the money to live in a place anywhere nearly as nice as the beautiful place where he currently lives. It also was a huge help when my father needed a lot of medical care near the end of his life. He was able to come home and have nurses and medical treatments there so that he could live out the end of his life the way he wanted to. He could do this because he had a really good policy that paid a very high amount per day. The earlier you buy this type of policy the cheaper it is, much like life insurance.

Being prepared for death, old age, accidents etc. are all parts of living a successful life. Things go wrong, and having a game plan and resources to meet those challenges is often the difference between living life the way you want to versus the way you are forced to. Skanky Acres is not where most of us want to wind up. We can avoid this by using tools like insurance to help us.

One of the benefits of being successful financially is that it gives you the ability to afford to protect yourself and your family. Making money is great, but once you make it, we want to do our best to ensure that people, taxes, and circumstances don't have an easy time taking it away. You may say, "This sounds like a lot of premium payments there, Mr. Book-Writer-Man. How do you expect us to pay all of this and still have anything left to invest?" Well, we don't buy all of this insurance upfront. We use another tool to keep those payments small, which protects us early on so we can afford more of these types of protection (insurance) later on. That tool is liquidity.

Liquidity

Liquidity is simply having cash reserves. It is a type of self-insurance. You keep some of the money your investments throw off in places that can readily be turned into cash. Or it could be a line of credit that you don't use except if there is an emergency. (No, a sale at Bass Pro Shops does not qualify as an emergency.) If you have invested over-aggressively and have a situation where you need to pay an attorney for an eviction but don't have the cash, you have a serious issue. You have an asset that will not be working at all because you didn't leave enough in the bank for contingencies.

I'm not going to lie here, I have been cash poor and asset rich many times and it is no fun. Usually it works out, but there is definitely pain and suffering in the interim. It is basically like playing Monopoly and owning all the

A little detail on methods to avoid risk

best properties, but while you are waiting for someone to land on one of your hotel-adorned spots, you draw a card and get sent to Mediterranean Avenue and find you can't pay the $2 rent. After you curse the gods of bad luck with your fist in the air, you begin the process of selling assets at bargain basement prices to raise the lousy few bucks you need to pay the blood-sucking landlord—grandma.

You need reserves, both personal and business. Personal reserves allow you to be prepared for unforeseen issues, and changes in employment status. You should always have a minimum of three months but preferably 6 months of personal reserves. Your business reserves, on the other hand, should increase with the size of your portfolio, but not necessarily in direct proportion to each other. This means when you are small, you probably want to have a bare minimum of three months reserves. More is better but may be unrealistic, depending on your circumstances. As your portfolio increases the risk actually goes down. If you own one rental property and it is vacant, you have a 100 percent vacancy factor. All expenses for this house now must come directly from your reserves until you can get it performing (rented) again. If you own two homes and one is vacant, you are only 50 percent vacant and the income from the rented property should provide enough to limit how much you need to take from reserves while waiting to rent the other unit.

This is similar to what the insurance companies do. When you have one hundred properties, each vacancy represents only 1 percent and your need for reserves goes down. Your reserves still need to be much more, in actual dollars, than they were when you only had one property, but they represent a much smaller portion of your portfolio and income. We will discuss this more later. Here is the tie-in with the insurance that we discussed above. By having strong reserves, we can increase our income and decrease our expenses by paying lower insurance amounts. For those who have managed to stay awake to this point in this chapter, you may recall we do this by getting insurance with higher deductibles.

When we keep low deductibles, we are basically betting that everything we are insured for will happen to us (or at least, we don't know what will happen to us, and we don't want to guess wrong so we pay a lot more for all of our insurance policies). By having higher deductibles, we are only paying for bad things that actually *do* happen to us. By maintaining good cash reserves and lowering your insurance payments, you can have more money to invest and still be well protected from risk. Obviously, having the discipline to maintain the reserves is critical to implementation of this strategy.

The other benefit to having access to cash is being able to deal with the unexpected. This could mean anything from cost overruns on a project, to a really great opportunity that arises. The unexpected does not need to be something bad. Having cash on hand gives you options. This should always be balanced against the loss of earnings you experience from keeping funds in places where they are easily converted to cash. Having to rob Peter to pay Paul often happens early on in an investor's career. This occurs because of the very limited funds folks are usually working with at that point.

Let's say that Cody and Jessica are buying their first rental property. It is a great deal ($80,000) and even with the work the house needs ($13,000), it will generate a 16 percent rate of return when it is rented. The couple saved for the last several years to have a small nest egg and now plan to use all of it with a mortgage to buy this property. They calculated the repair cost and will have a small margin for error ($2,000) with their available funds. As they are completing the renovation, it is determined that the house has a termite issue and the roof the contractor said they would be able to save now needs to be replaced. This couple does not have the funds to do this work ($7,000) and there is no option to finance the roof.

A sleazy investor named "Con Man" Keith hears of their troubles and offers them $85,000 to buy the house even though they told him they have now spent $93,000 on the house ($80,000 plus $13,000 in renovation costs). Cody and Jessica are now left with the option of either being forced to sell the house and take a loss, or find some other way out. If they could complete the work, the house would still generate a great rate of return, but now they are really stuck. Their issue is a lack of liquidity. They are trying to make something happen and do not have much margin for error.

The pressure you are under when you *have* to make the deal work can be intense and lead to poor choices. Maintaining some liquid funds (even if it is

A little detail on methods to avoid risk

credit cards) can bail you out when things go sideways. For this couple, they are stuck in "hat in hand" mode, and going to parents or friends to raise the needed funds might be their only play. What if they'd had a line of credit on the home they lived in before they made this deal and had decided to only use this money for emergencies? (Remember, they would not pay interest on a credit line unless they use it.) If this had been the case, they could have used their line of credit to pay for the work on the new house, and then used the cash flow from the rental to pay back the line of credit. Once the investment property was completed, they could probably have refinanced it, taken out more money to pay back their line of credit and reestablished their safety net.

Investments are often full of unexpected events and cost. Having an emergency source of cash can rescue you from a loss and ensure that your deals remain profitable. This leaves you free to assume a Captain Morgan pose with your friends when describing your successfully completed deal, while saying in your best stage voice, "I *meant* to do that".

Corporate structures

As we discussed earlier, corporate structures are a way to insulate our personal assets from a business setback. They basically function like a "fall guy" if something goes wrong. To be fair, it would be more like using one of your children as a fall guy, as most people that own a business put their heart and soul into their company. To understand why this is necessary, we need to look at the life of the business. We need to think about what forming a business looks like, and why a business owner should use a corporate structure as a way of limiting their liability.

When you start a business, typically there is little money but a passion for what you are trying to do. Anyone that watches *Shark Tank* knows what we are talking about. No matter how bad the idea might be, the people that get beat up on the show always say some version of the same thing: "This is the next big thing, and the sharks missed out." They do this because they have a single-minded passion that people that are successful usually possess. They need this passion because opening and running a new business is hard. If your new business needs a ditch dug, guess who the head ditch digger on staff usually is—if you guessed yourself, you are on the money.

This means that early on you not only do the thing you are passionate about with your business, but also all the stuff you might hate, that is, marketing, prospecting for customers, prospecting for manufacturers, accounting, just to name a few. We could throw in trade shows, attorney's visits, chasing customers that owe you money, and dodging people to whom you owe money, all without going into anything that might be too specific for the business you are into. Because there is a lot of effort, worry, work and risk associated with owning a business, and because these are all a critical part of the growth of an economy, this kind of "fall guy" allowance is made.

There are a limited number of people willing to do the work of starting a business. If these people were completely wiped out financially and personally when their business died, they would be much more limited in their ability to start a new one. If you read the foreword to this book, you may recall that my grandpa started nine other companies that failed before starting one that is still in business today. The company that survived employed several hundred workers. It provided great pay, steady work, pensions, and profit sharing plans. My grandpa and later my dad and I are very proud of the company that we built, and made sure it was a place where our workers are happy to work.

If Gramps had been personally wiped out by his earlier failures, thrown in debtor's prison, etc. his workers, his family, and the economy as a whole would have been deprived of the economic benefit of his successful company. In a similar way, it does not seem right that a merchant shipper should be personally wiped out after decades of successful business just because some ships sank due to some weather. That would be a lot more risk, wouldn't it? Similarly, if my Grandfather or the merchant shipper knew that their personal resources could be wiped out and they and their family sent to debtor's prison (until they died or their debts were paid off), then they would want to be paid more for that very serious risk.

A little detail on methods to avoid risk

Tip: *Remember the earlier section on risk? We talked about risk needing compensation. This is an example of that principle.*

Well, if risk needs to be compensated for, then who is the one paying for it? The answer —the customers! They pay for this risk in the form of higher prices. This means the customers have less money to spend on other things. Thus, they are limited in their choices. It would kind of be like being forced to choose between two parts of the delicious preassembled confectionary delight known as the double stuffed Oreo instead of eating the entire cookie. Because the cost of both would exceed the cookie budget, you would have to decide between chocolate crunchiness and white creamy sweetness. As a confirmed fat kid myself, I apologize for presenting such a horrifying and irreconcilable quandary—I need to take a second as I'm still a little shaken up thinking of an Oreo free world—no one should be put through this type of torture even in an example.

Note: *Actually the Oreo is one great example of synergy, as neither the cookie nor the filling are nearly half as good as the whole cookie when it comes together. So, when looking for a business partner, look for someone that provides a true synergy for both of you. In this way, you each have an incentive to continue to work together. If you both help each other to get more out of yourselves, you both have a good reason to maintain the business relationship. The business, and by extension, the customers benefit from your synergy.*

We can see that by allowing business owners to protect their private assets from failure of the company, a business is able to limit their risks and the consumers benefit in the form of lower prices. This kind of protection from liability is similar to what someone working for the company experiences.

If a car company gets sued, no one knocks on the door of the fellow on the assembly line asking him to pay for part of it. The worker has no liability for his company's' debts. He is limited in his risk only to the loss of his job. With a corporate structure, the business owner has the same protection.

The Roadmap to the American Dream

The owner's risk, however, is the loss of the company and all of the assets that the owner probably poured blood, sweat, and tears into creating. The owner's responsibility in a financial setback is going to be much more than the assembly line worker (unless that worker is the guy that dropped that piece of steel on that bus full of litigation attorneys). The loss the owner takes (losing the company) compared to the loss the employee takes (losing their job) is much more as well. When looked at this way, the system that gives us corporate structures to protect owners seems to be one that allows for more likelihood of success, not just for the business owner but also for their customers and people in general.

The critical thing to understand about corporate structures is that they are their own entity. If you do not use them as such, your personal assets could be at risk. There is what is called the "corporate veil," which separates the owner and their assets from the company and its holdings. If you are commingling assets and not keeping good books, an attorney could come in and pierce that corporate veil. They could claim that you are not running your business as a separate corpus ("body" in Latin, because everything is cooler in Latin).

It is important to treat your company as its own person. If you put money into your company, it needs to be considered either a loan or an equity investment. So no, you should not take $700 from your bookie to pay your employees in cash. You need to put the money first into the company, record it properly, and then pay your people. There are other ways this corporate veil can be pierced. These all stem from treating the business like it is you.

It is not you—and to demonstrate the point, we'll call the company Steve (unless, of course, your name is Steve, in which case it is Shauna). If you loan money to Steve, you make records. If it is an investment in Steve's company, you get documentation. If it is a loan, you sign a promissory note. If you have some of Steve's guys come help you build a deck on your house during work hours, you pay Steve and let Steve pay the employees. You don't borrow Steve's tools. If Steve has provided a car for you, you use it to do work for Steve. The idea is to treat your company like a separate entity so that if there is a setback the courts will do the same. When in doubt just think "what would Steve do?".

A little detail on methods to avoid risk

Now for some specific types of common corporate structures and what they are used for:

The C-corp

This is the corporation type that most people think of when they think of a corporation. This is your large corporation: Wal-Mart, Best Buy, GM, etc. In reality, the benefits to a C-corp are fairly negligible; however, since any corporation with more than one hundred shareholders is required to be a C-corp, it is the corporation of choice for big business. There is no greater corporate veil than with a C-corp.

That being said, the negatives far outweigh the positives for any small to medium sized business. The biggest one (and really the only one that we should be concerned about) is taxation. Because there is no flow-through income with a C-corp to the shareholders' individual tax returns, the corporation must pay a separate corporate tax on its earnings. This means the money the company makes is taxed for its income at a rate that is usually lower than the individual tax rate, but at times, has been higher. In order for the owners to get money back out of the company, a distribution to the shareholders must be made. All distributions to the shareholders are then considered dividends and paid at the dividend tax rate, leaving us with a double taxation situation. This we do not like. Also, when it comes to flexibility, C-corps are the most limiting. If you intend on having a huge company and "taking it public" (selling stock on the stock exchange), your company will probably need to be in the form of a C-corp. That does not mean you need to start your company as a C-corp.

Lets look at a structure that is a little more user-friendly:

The S-corp

This is the most commonly used corporate structure in the U.S., however, it is quickly losing ground to the LLC, which we discuss shortly. First and foremost, you are limited to one hundred shareholder with an S-corp, though for most people, this is not an issue. Usually when you get over one hundred shareholders, you've already outgrown this type of structure anyway. The S-corp does, however, do away with the issue of double taxation, as the profits of the company pass directly through to the shareholders' individual tax returns.

One issue to be wary of is the reduction in the amount of protection that this type of corporation can provide for you. Since all income is pass-through, it is very easy to commingle personal funds with corporate funds if you are not careful. This allows a savvy attorney to pursue you personally, as they can make the case that the business is not its own entity and therefore does not deserve the protection of the corporate veil. This is why you must run your business like a business. Like we said before, treat your stuff like your stuff and the businesses as its stuff. Let's note that this is exactly the same as when dealing with an LLC, so we will not go over it in the next section. One of the main reasons S-sorp are losing popularity to LLC's is that they do not allow for unequal distributions of profits.

This is something where I've had personal experience. Later on in my dad's life, he had a business he owned with his sister. She was much older than he was and had no interest in running the company. The company ran a small catering operation at a school and was not really profitable, but my Dad wanted to do continue it for the kids in the school so they had access to good fresh food. He also wanted to teach his kids to work, and this was a good place to do it. (#MyFirstJob) The business lost money and my Dad had to put money into the company to keep it going. He didn't want to ask his sister to contribute because she had no interest in the business.

Now here's where the problem occurs. When my father wanted to claim the losses on his tax returns for the money he paid into the company, he could only claim half because the S-corp requires the losses to be split based on ownership. So even though my father put in all of the money, he could only claim a loss for half of it, despite the fact that he lost all of it. The technical term for this is "adding insult to injury."

Note: *First, time for a disclaimer. We are not teaching you to be attorneys. There are many differences between corporate structures and you*

A little detail on methods to avoid risk

should consult an attorney if you want more than the cursory overview, which we are providing. Don't drink and drive. Just say no to drugs. Don't run with scissors.

The LLC or Limited Liability Corporation

Now that we have finished with all of our disclaimers, the primary reason people choose an LLC over an S-corp is flexibility—more specifically, flexibility with distributions. This is a major fix from the S-corp. What does unequal distribution mean exactly?

Here is an example: There is an S-corp with two shareholders, each with 50 percent ownership. If one owner needs $10,000, they each must take a distribution of $10,000, removing $20,000 from the business. This is problematic because sometimes the business cannot afford to do without the money needed to equalize the distributions. Also, corporate losses are split based upon share distribution. This can also cause issues when contributions are made unequally. The story of my father and aunt illustrates this point. If this structure had been available to them, there would have been no issues with my father receiving the losses for the money he actually lost.

Now let's look at an LLC. Owner A puts up 100 percent of the equity for owner B's idea. In order to protect his investment, owner A requires that he owns greater than a 50 percent stake in the company. The partners agree to a share distribution of 75 percent to owner A and 25 percent to owner B. Because this is an LLC, they can do this and still share all profits 50/50, or any other agreed upon amount without running afoul of the law. This is not possible with an S-corp.

Sole proprietorships and partnerships

Both are the above are not corporations. They do not provide a corporate veil and therefore should be used with extreme caution, and with the advice of legal counsel. Sole proprietorship is the default business type. It is what you chose when you chose no corporate structure. A sole proprietorship lacks liability protection. This is its main drawback.

Supply and demand

The final tool to discuss is the idea of supply and demand. You should always understand your business and what drives it. If your business is investing, then knowing the impact of market forces is critical. Let's look at some markets and how they affect things.

As we discussed earlier, even the number of people working is affected by the supply of available workers and demand for those workers. If the demand is higher, the workers can ask for more money. If the supply is too high, wages fall and unemployment is higher. If we are looking at a real estate market, we need to look at things like how many new houses are being built (this affects supply), and the rate of unemployment is (this affects demand). If there are more houses, available prices come down, and if people don't have jobs they can't buy. There is another set of factors— median income and mortgage rates. If median income goes up, people can pay more for houses, and if interest rates go up, the cost to borrow money is more, so people cannot afford as expensive of a house.

> *"What most of these doomsday scenarios have gotten wrong is the fundamental idea of economics: people respond to incentives. If the price of a good goes up, people demand less of it, the companies that make it figure out how to make more of it, and everyone tries to figure out how to produce substitutes for it."*
>
> — STEVEN D. LEVITT

You are thinking, "Why the hell is this in the risk chapter?" First, I felt like putting it here, and the second, this kind of understanding can help you make more good decisions. It translates into fewer bad decisions, and therefore less risk. Here's how it works. If I am thinking of changing jobs and I know the

A little detail on methods to avoid risk

labor market has an overabundance of supply (high unemployment), I will be more cautious. If the new job doesn't work out, I will have a harder time finding a new one. If, however the job market is strong (low unemployment), I can take the risk with more certainty.

Let's look at the real estate market indicators we discussed. If there are new homes being built at a high rate, I need to know if they are competitive with the properties I am buying. Why? Because if I am buying homes in the $200,000 to 300,000 range, and the homes being built are in the $1-2 million range the new homes are not competitive with mine. The buyers for my homes will not be lured away by the new ones because they are not in my customer's price range. This is much like a new feature introduced on the Chevy Cruze. It may be great for Chevy Cruze owners, but it does not have any effect on the business model of Ferrari.

How about interest rates? Let's look at this as if we are buying and flipping houses. If rates are higher, two things happen: One, it costs you more money to borrow funds to buy properties, and two, it costs buyers more to pay for your house when you sell it. This means that buyers have less incentive to buy, which lowers demand, and the greater interest cost for you means you have less profit available to insulate you from a loss. Both things create greater risk. The factor that makes a deal a good deal is profit. If you don't make any money, or even worse, lose money, then it is a bad deal. Unexpected things that come up in a deal eat into your profit. So, the more profit you have, the safer you are. Borrowing money at the lowest possible interest rate is usually a very good thing. (Obviously, provided that the terms of the loan are the same.)

Now let's take a look at a different type of real estate example, and see how understanding supply and demand can be helpful. Your spouse's Grammy just passed away and left you her condo near Miami Beach. You feel that this is adequate payment for the terrible fruitcakes she has been forcing you to eat for the last way-too-many-years-to-count. You are thinking of either selling the unit or keeping it as a rental. How do you handle this? What information do you need in order to understand the supply and demand for this market? What should you do?

You call a few real estate agents in the area and do some research. Most are salivating at getting the sales commission and try to discourage you from

The Roadmap to the American Dream

renting, but you persevere. You discover that in the building where the unit is located there are twenty-five units, similar to Grammy's, for sale, and in the past six months only five have sold. Based upon this, we can determine that it will take two and one half years to sell the current inventory of available units in the building. Because you know a little about supply and demand, you know that a normal supply of units in a market is six months. This means that the market in this building is skewed very much toward the buyers. In other words, it is a buyers' market.

There are twenty-five units to choose from and there are only five buyers every six months. We have to have a very attractive (low) price, or it will take quite a while to sell this unit. We also see that there is only one unit in the building for rent and seventy that have rented in the past six months. We determine that the rent we can receive will give us a 9.8 percent rate of return on the value of the condo based on current market value. (Remember, if we sell the condo, we have the money we receive from the sale to use toward other investments. We must take that into account.) What should you do?

The market data makes it pretty easy to see where the best market opportunity is. There is a high demand for rental units right now. You will be able to charge a high rent, have a short time to find a tenant, and be able to be more selective of the type of tenant you ultimately accept. It is clear that this would be a good rental right now. Understanding the supply and demand of the market makes this clear.

To finish the above illustration, we would wait for a change in the market that made it more advantageous for us to sell. If demand for that building were to increase, we would need to compare the new market value to what we receive in rent. If we could find other investments for the money we'd earn from a sale that would give us a higher return than Grammy's condo, then it might be time to kick the condo to the curb (sell it).

This same type of analysis can be done with most things. "I hear there is a drought in Columbia. Stock up on coffee now before the price goes up." or :"Apple is coming out with a smart toilet called the iPoop (if it looks like a good idea) buy their stock. The dollar is weak against foreign currencies so expect American goods to be bought more than foreign products."

A little detail on methods to avoid risk

"Successful investing is anticipating the anticipations of others.

- JOHN MAYNARD KEYNES"

Note: *Is a weak dollar a good thing or a bad thing? It depends. We like to think of our money as strong. I mean, like ready for the World's Strongest Man (for money) competition, on ESPN 6 type of strong. A strong dollar is very good if Americans want to buy things in other countries. It is very good for traveling as things cost less for Americans when they visit places with weaker currencies.*

But the issue is that as strong dollar makes imported goods cheaper. This means that people start buying imported instead of domestic goods based on price. For American companies that export their products, a strong dollar means foreign buyers have to pay more in their money to buy our goods. This means that international buyers look to other countries suppliers that produce similar goods, which do not have such strong currencies and then buy from them.

A weak dollar improves sales of American products both at home and abroad, but makes investing or buying overseas for Americans expensive, and traveling overseas even pricier. So, Strong dollar equals cheap travel and international purchases. Weak dollar equals higher sales of American products, and a good excuse to limit yourself to domestic travel.

Figuring out how a change in supply or demand is going to affect a market is sometimes tricky, but often it is not that difficult. You want to think about how the change might affect a buyer or seller's willingness to buy or sell. It is not hard to see how supply and demand affect prices, and because prices ultimately are what determine the amount of profit we make, it is critical to understand supply and demand in order to minimize risk. We have talked about paying someone to assume your risk (with insurance), staying liquid to pay for risks, picking a corporate structure to protect from risk, and understanding the market to avoid risk. Now let's take a look at some of the more common types of investment markets that exist.

Chapter 10

The markets

"Under ordinary competitive conditions, any long and serious maladjustment between supply and demand cannot last."

— George W. Stocking

A market is any place where supply and demand for anything meet. If we owned something that was so expensive that no one could afford to buy it, there would be no market for that item. Let's say we had the cure for male pattern baldness, but the treatments were ten billion dollars each and needed to be applied three times a day for the rest of your life. You could perhaps create a market by discounting the price for your cranial miracle grow, and thus create demand. If you could get the price down to $300 a treatment, some very wealthy and vain individual would probably fork out the $27,000 a month for it.

As the price comes down, the demand for the product goes up. This is an important idea: Demand is not the number of people that want a product, but will only buy it at a cheaper price. Demand is the people willing to pay for the product at its current price. A market exists when the price of

The markets

a product is low enough to match the price some people are willing to pay for it.

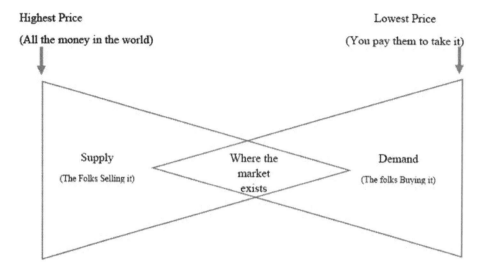

We can see that that the higher the price goes, the less demand there is for the product. We can also see when the price is lower, fewer suppliers are willing to sell at that price.

If we wanted to see what it would look like if demand were to increase and supply were to remain the same, imagine the right hand triangle sliding to the left. Also, the suppliers probably would not sell at the lowest price like they would before. Therefore, the supply side (left hand) triangle would also move to left some. If more people wanted the product, there would be more movement on the right side than the left side, leaving a larger market section to meet their needs. If the product became too expensive for some of the demand (the folks buying it), they might look for an alternative product. This would result in lower demand, which would have the opposite effect than what we have just looked at.

The price a product sells at is a collection of a ton of different factors that go into the making of that product. Some common ones are: labor, regulatory compliance, materials to make the product, insurance, competition, rents, and of course, profit.

The Roadmap to the American Dream

Is it possible to create demand from something that is considered valueless? Consider a product like particleboard. This product is used to make the majority of furniture and kitchen cabinets purchased each year. The crazy part is that particleboard is basically made from not much more than floor sweepings and resin pressed together. Somebody probably looked at all of the wood chips and shavings in a lumberyard one day, or at some other place wood is cut and thought, "These guys are paying somebody to take this crap away as junk. If I could figure out a use for this stuff, I could make it, sell the product, and still get them to pay me to take it away. I'd get paid on both ends, and could charge the lumber mill less for picking it up. *Win-win.*" There would also be a demand for this product if there were a demand for a cheaper alternative to lumber. By seeing the demand and figuring out a means of producing this wood substitute, a market for particleboard was born.

Finally, let's look at another location I learned all about on a recent cruise. In 1897, there was a massive gold rush in Alaska. This meant that thousands of people came to work in Alaska. It is interesting that nearly all the people that went there were men. Talk about your Alaskan sausage fest! The men folk were not the only ones to spot opportunity, however. Some ladies could see a simmering market bursting with opportunity. You see, from the beginning of time, fellas on their own tend to get a bit lonesome and a little female companionship is the age-old cure. These industrious women went to the nearest cities and provided "entertainment"—for the boys. What is interesting is the prices they were able to charge for their "wares". They could charge as much as a week's wages for fifteen minutes of their time. This was much higher than in other markets around the country but they could get away with it because there was a lot of demand and minimal supply. These Alaskan "ladies of the night" became very wealthy from recognizing and exploiting a market.

So where do we actually put our money? There are a ton of markets out there, and new ones being created (think particleboard) every day. We are going to discuss the most common investment markets. Remember the lessons from the examples above. These can help you identify markets that are ready for investment.

The markets

Stocks

The stock market has been around for quite a while. There are several different stock exchanges, but the largest two in the U.S. are the New York Stock Exchange, and NASDAQ. At a basic level, a stock is a partial ownership interest in a company that is backed by the assets of the company after all of their other debts are paid. Typically, common stock is what we deal with in the markets. A stock is a way to place a bet on the future success of a company by buying a partial interest in that company.

There are different methods and techniques to investing, but most can be broken down into one of two categories.

> **Speculation:** This is where you try to figure out where the market is going to go and then take advantage of that movement. Day traders and most investors actually follow some form of this model.
>
> **Value investors:** This means looking for stocks that are selling for less than the actual value of the company. These are the bargain hunters. Charlie Munger and Warren Buffet are proponents of this type of investing. Speculators are always trying to work out a system or formula that gives them a competitive advantage over the fickle short-term movements of the market. Value investors go in for a longer play in companies they understand and believe in, based on their value and management.

If I were writing this book and going to give you advice on speculation in the stock market, I would probably need to include advice on horseracing, roulette, and buying lottery tickets. There are people that are successful at all of those things I suppose, but there are a lot more that are not. I prefer to focus on disciplined approaches that have a much greater likelihood of giving positive returns. For this reason, we are going to focus on the idea and skills needed to be a value investor.

> *There is a very easy way to return from a casino with
> a small fortune: go there with a large one.*
>
> -JACK YELTON

The Roadmap to the American Dream

For starters, we have to discuss the way the market moves. It tends to move in waves of overreaction. The reason are many, but the primary one is that people are still the ones buying and selling in the market and people are emotional. Most people are upset if they buy a stock for $10, and then sell it for $12 before the stock goes up to $15. Similarly, they are happy if they buy a stock for $10, and then sell it for $8before it continues going down to $4. This means we are actually happy in some instance when we lose money, and mad when we make money—it also means that people are freaking nuts.

This is why value investing is hard. It is hard to sit there while a stock you own continues to go down, even though you know the value of the stock is higher than the share price reflects. It is also hard to sell a stock that has done well for you when the numbers tell you it is no longer underpriced in the market. What if it keeps going up? A value investor sticks to the numbers and makes his investment based on the valuation model they have established.

> *The most important quality for an investor is temperament, not intellect."*
>
> *- Warren Buffett*

The number of shares that exist of a given company are based upon the value the market feels that company is worth. This is called a company's **market capitalization**. Let say the company is worth $1,000. It might issue one thousand shares at $1 apiece. If the company becomes more valuable due to a new product or a new cheaper manufacturing process, the price of the company's stock should go up to reflect that increase in its value. Therefore, our $1,000 company just signed a new deal with a buyer and they are going to sell much more product. The company is now worth, let's say, $2,000. The shares of the stock then should be worth $2. What usually happens, however, is the market over reacts and the price of the stock goes to $2.50, and then down to $1.80, before eventually settling out at $2.

The tough part of value investing is that it requires that you understand a business very well before you invest in that business. You need to know what their business and business model are worth, and then determine if the

The markets

share price for the stock is too high or low based upon that valuation. If the price is too low, then there is a good opportunity to buy, and if it is too high and you own some shares, then it is a time to sell. So if we look at the company above and see that the shares are selling for $1 and we know there are one thousand shares. If we do our calculations and feel that the real value of the company is $1,350, we realize that this company is undervalued and may be a good buy as the shares should be worth $1.35 each.

Typically, opportunities to buy occur when the market goes down a lot. Stocks tend to go down below what their value, as a business, should be due to the emotional nature of the market. If you know that the real value of a company is $100 million, and its shares go down to the point where the total value of outstanding shares is only $80 million, there are two possible options: Either this is a really good value to buy, or there is a problem with your valuation of the company.

One last piece to cover is the number of shares that exist. We discussed how the number of shares issued is determined by the company's value when they do their **IPO (Initial Public Offering).** This is when a company first lists their stock for sale on a stock exchange. It is also referred to as **"going public"**. (It is called going public because the public now own a piece of the company.)

Let's say a company issues a bunch of shares and then proceeds to do really well. Their stock price was $50, the company doubled their business after a few years, and then tripled it a few years later. By then, the company shares should be selling for $300. That might be too expensive for some investors so some companies do a stock split. This is when a company issues new shares, and the price of the shares are reduced to reflect the market value of the company based on the new number of shares. Confusing, right? It is simpler than it seems. This is how it works: Let's say, for example, the company above decided to split three for one. If we owned 100 shares valued at $300 before the split, we would own 300 shares at $100 at the end of the split. The company has made the stock more affordable, and they have given each investor exactly the previous value they had before. We leave stocks alone at this point and move on to debt instruments called bonds.

Bonds

There are two basic ways for a company to raise capital. One is the sale of equity, which is common or preferred stock. With a stock, someone is buying a piece of the company, and if the company does well they make money. But if the company does poorly, they lose money. The other way to raise capital is debt, and this is what a bond is. A bond is a debt instrument that has to be repaid with a certain amount of interest each year. Bonds are a less risky investment than a stock because if the company does not do well, the bond holders still are paid while the stock folks actually lose money. Because bonds have less risk, they also have less upside. While the stock does really well when a company prospers, the bond holders still only earn the interest on the bond. Bonds are a steadier investment that provides a fixed rate of return for the term of the bond.

The interest rates bonds pay are based upon the riskiness of the loan. The way risk is measured for bonds is with a rating scale. Companies' bonds are analyzed by a rating agency and based upon the strength of the company, or government for that matter, a rating is given. There are market rates for the amount of interest any bond needs to pay for all of the different ratings out there. Any bond rated between AAA and BBB is considered investment grade, any bond below that is considered a junk bond. Typically when we talk about bonds we are talking about investment grade ones like U.S. Government Treasury Bills (T-Bills). These bonds are AAA rated which is the highest rating that exists. This means there is a very high likelihood that these loans will be paid back and therefore low risk. This lower risk means that the interest rate we earn on these T-Bills will also be lower. So, the interest rate on bonds that a D rated company, that is in the manual type writer business, will have to pay is going to be quite a bit higher than AAA rated, Microsoft, would pay.

From an investment standpoint, when you are looking at bonds you have to think of them as a hedging vehicle. OK, hedging: This is when you invest in something to limit the downside of another investment. Think of real estate, it is a hedge against inflation (we will cover that later). Anyway, the idea is interest rates and markets tend to fluctuate. I know—shocker. But without getting too into the weeds here, let me give you an idea of how it works.

The markets

The value of a bond that you purchased actually goes down as interest rates rise. This is an issue of rate of return and cost of money. I paid $1,000 for a bond that pays 6 percent, which is great because I am receiving $60 a year and I like receiving money. However, all of a sudden the Feds decide that inflation is too high, or maybe they just consulted their magic eight-ball (who knows), but they raise interest rates. Now the same AAA rated bonds I just bought are selling at 7.5 percent. Crap. This means I could be earning $75 a year instead of $60, which is at least three candy bars and a six-pack. That would be a far better use of my money. However, in order to get that $75 a year, I need to sell my bond because I don't have money to buy the new one. The thing is this: All the other investors out there know they can get 7.5 percent from the new bonds, so I have to sell my bonds at a discount. This is how bond pricing works. It also works the opposite way if interest rates go down.

Now, how is this a hedge? Well, when interest rates are going up, it is usually an indication of a strong economy. Not a good time to buy bonds right? Wrong. Allocating a portion of your total investment portfolio to the purchase of bonds is your protection (hedge) for when the economy cycles to bad. Let's say the economy (and inflation) was hot and interest rates went up to 8 percent. You, being the smart investor that you are, thought that even though the rates and market are rising, so you were going to continue to invest a portion of your assets in bonds in order to protect the gains you've made. Low and behold, due to high interest rates home sales drop and take the rest of the market with them (we've never seen this before, right?). The Feds respond as they often do by dropping interest rates. Wait a second— when rates go down, my bond values go up, in fact, the more they go down the better I do. So while my stocks are imitating Jules Verne and going 20,000 leagues under the sea, my bonds are doing just fine and keeping my portfolio stable.

The above is a very cursory glance at bonds. There is much more to them, and if you really want to dig deeper into these types of investments there are plenty of great sources for this information (see our reading list at the end of this book). I am providing you a general overview so you can see what types of investments appeal to you. We also hope you use it to impress your buddies.

Options

Options allow you to bet on the movement of a stock without having to own the stock. This can be helpful if you have limited capital. There are two different common types of options: **Puts and Calls**. Both types of these option types can be either bought or sold. This means there are four possible transactions that can occur. You can buy a put, sell a put, buy a call, or sell a call. Options are sold in what are called **contracts,** each one consist of one hundred shares. If the price an option is trading at is $1.85, it costs you $185 to buy one contract. We will explain how they work and some cursory ideas of how they can be used.

A put is an agreement to allow the investor to sell (put) the stock to the investor who sold the put to them at an agreed to price. This is called an option contract and these are good for a limited period of time. It might be thirty, sixty, ninety days, or more. Kind of like when you go to dinner with a finicky friend who can't decide what to order. You say something like, "Order this and if you don't like it, I will allow you to put your food to me (I'll eat it)." It is a bit more complicated than this analogy, but let's take a look now in more detail at the transaction.

Buying a Put

This takes place if you bought a put on a stock that was trading at $10, but with the right to put the stock to someone at a price of $10 for a period of the next thirty days. You would pay a premium for this ability. In this case, let's say it cost 50 cents per share. You would do this if you thought the stock was going to go down in price. If the stock went down to $9, you would have the right to buy shares of the stock at $9 and sell them to the person that sold the put to you for $10. It cost you 50 cents to buy the put, so you made 50 cents. What actually happens is a little different. There is a market for options that allows you to sell your option to someone else rather than actually buying the shares and putting the stock to someone. You can just sell your option to someone else because the value of the put has now risen 50 cents.

The markets

The amount of time left on the contract and the share price of the stock is what determines how much the option is worth. In our example, we said that you bought the put option with thirty days left on the contract. If it took ten days for the stock to fall to $9 the value of the right to put the stock to someone has increased by $1; but for the person buying the put from you, the period of time left for the stock to fall further is only twenty days. For this reason, the price of the put option after the stock has fallen $1 might not be $1 more ($1.50); it might be $1.45 due to less time. An easy way to understand this is to change the time lines. If you bought the right to sell me a share of that $10 stock for a stock that is currently trading for $10, and the right was good for the next fifty years, you would have a very good chance that at some point the stock would go down and you would make money. Your risk would be low.

You might think that an option like that would be pretty expensive. If, however, the right to put the stock to me at $10 was only good for the next ten minutes, how much would you be willing to pay for that right? Not very much, probably.

The downside to buying a put: If the stock goes up in value, eventually your option becomes valueless. You lose the total amount of money you spent to buy it.

Use: Buying a put can be used like insurance, and in this way, its use is interesting to note. If you own a stock that has been performing well and you want to lock in your profit, you can spend a few cents a share to buy a put. If you had our $10 stock that you bought a few months ago for $6, and you want to make sure you don't lose a bunch of money, you could buy the $.50 put option for the right to put the stock to someone at $10. You effectively limit your possible down side to $9.50 (the $10 price you can sell it for minus the cost of the put price of $.50).

Selling a put: When you sell a put, someone pays you money and you agree to allow them to sell your stock at a certain price for a certain period of time. It is the opposite side of the same transaction just discussed. You are now the one selling the right to put the stock to you. You would do this if you thought a stock were going to go up in value. If you sold the right to have a stock put to you at $10, a stock which is currently selling at $10 for $.50 per share, and the stock goes up to $12, you received 50 centrs per share profit (called a **premium**) and no one is going to put the stock to you at $10 because it is currently selling for $12.

The downside: If the stock goes down to $8, you are required to buy the stock for $10. You have the 50 cents premium to help offset the pain, but you still lose $1.50 per share.

Use: This is an interesting choice if you wanted to buy the stock above at $10 because your research shows it was a good deal and you could sell a $10 put and make the premium. If the stock goes down, you have the premium to offset your loss (remember you were ready to pay $10 a share to buy it). If the stock goes up a little, you have made money and can still buy the stock if you want to; if it goes up a lot, you still made your premium, and as they say, "Next…".

Buying a call

When you buy a call, you have the right to buy a stock from someone at a given price for a given period of time. So a put is a right to sell, and call is a right to buy. The reason to buy a call over just buying the stock itself is that calls are much cheaper than the actual stock. With a call, you are really only betting on the change in price of the shares of a stock. You have no actual ownership interest in the company. It is like betting on a horse race in the sense that you make money if your horse wins, but you do not own any part of the horse.

Another benefit of a call option is that your downside is limited to the smaller amount you paid for the option versus the actual share price of the company. For example: A company's shares are selling for $20; you can buy a call option that gives you the right to buy the stock at the price of $18.50 for 30 days and this option costs you $2 per share. If you had $2,000, you could buy one hundred shares of the company or you could buy one thousand shares worth of options (ten contracts). If the stock goes up $2 and you bought the shares of the company, you have experienced a 10 percent gain (you made $2 and it took $20 to earn it: $2/$20 =.10 or 10 percent). If you had purchased

The markets

the options instead for $2 per share on one thousand shares and the stock price went up $2, your options probably have almost doubled. That is a 100 percent return. Pretty freaking cool, right?

The downside: If the stock we just looked at went down in price to $2 and we had bought the call options, we would have lost 100 percent of our investment. The other problem is that options expire. Let's say that we bought our options knowing that this is a good stock, but then something bad happens in the world and the market overreacts. Unlike when you own a stock where you can patiently wait for the market to rebound and you do not realize the loss till you sell, an option expires. If you are upside down and don't want to execute it when it expires, you lose whatever you paid for the option.

Interesting use: Buying calls is a way to leverage limited capital to grow it. You can control larger amounts of stock and reap the benefit of their gains. You can also buy **"in or out of the money calls"**: There are two ways to buy options: in the money and out of the money. An in the money purchase means you will have equity when you buy. An example of an "in the money" purchase would be buying a call option for $18 for a stock that is currently selling for $20. This option will cost more than the $2 you are currently "in the money" (your option allows you to buy shares for $18 and it is currently selling for $20. You have $2 dollars built into the buy.) Obviously, that is why the option will cost more than the amount you are "in the money" otherwise it would be like them offering to sell you $5 bills for $1.

With an "out of the money" purchase, the stock has to appreciate for your option to be worth exercising. An option to call the stock for a price higher than it is currently selling for is an example of "out of the money" purchase. A stock is selling for $20 and you buy the $21 call for .25 cents per share. These options are very inexpensive because they are riskier but if the share price goes up even a little in a couple of days that call you bought may have increased significantly in value. One more interesting use of "out of the money" call is to hedge for risk. If you take a position where you do well if the stock goes down you could buy some cheap "out of the money" calls at a higher price in case the stock goes way up so that your losses in that situation will be minimized.

Selling a call (clothed and in the buff):

If you have been paying attention, you have probably figured out that this is selling the right for someone to buy stock from you at a certain price. This transaction is typically referred to as "**writing a call**". There are two ways to do this: the safe way and the risky way. Obviously, when you do most things naked it is riskier—not that that slows most of us down much. When you sell the right for someone to take your stock from you. it is usually a good idea to have the actual stock. A covered call is just that. You have the stock and someone pays you money for the right to buy your stock from you at a given price. So you own 1,000 shares of a stock trading at $30 (thought it was time to get away from all of those $20 stocks we've been using. I know, I'm a wild man for such spontaneous risky moves). You decide to sell a covered call for $30.25 and you receive 75 cents per share or $750 for the ten contracts you sold. If the stock goes up past $30.25, someone will probably be calling your stock away from you. You made $1 per share from the time you owned at $30 if you get called. You got paid 75 cents per share for the option you sold, and the person buying paid you $30.25 per share.

The downside: It sounds great, but what are the risks? The stock goes way up and you miss the gains in the share price. Or the stock goes way down and you are stuck with the losses. Obviously, if you were planning on holding the stock and it went way down, you would be stuck with the losses as well and not have the benefit of the premium you were paid for selling the call.

Covered calls are the least risky type of option. Let's talk about something much more risky: Going Naked! When you go naked on a call, it means that you sell the right for someone to buy your stock from you at a given price—with one little problem—you *do not* actually own the stock. The risk here is that the stock goes way up in price and you are stuck trying to buy the stock to cover your call. **Naked calls** are for very well informed or crazy investors. They are very risky and are used only when the likelihood of a stock going down is very high.

Uses: You can decide you want to sell your stock in the $30 company. You sell a covered call at $29 for $1.75. If the stock stays put, then you effectively sold your stock for $30.75 ($29: sale price plus $1.75 premium). If the stock goes down to $28.50, you do not get the stock called from you. You were paid $1.75 already for the call you sold, so even though the stock went down by $1.50, you are still up 25 cents. You still have the stock, which you can now sell a new covered call on.

Options are very interesting and very specialized type of investing. You need to know what the hell you are doing if you are going to start using them to invest. We have included some good resources in the reading list at the back of the book to help you if you want to go this route. I know it is kind of weird to write a book that tells you to read other books, but there is no way to tell you everything you would need in order to wisely invest using these tools and keep this book under a bazillion pages. We have covered some heavy stuff and it is going to get a little easier now. Let's talk about outsourcing.

Mutual funds

This is basically outsourced investing. You find a fund you like, and hire them. The fund managers then take your money and invest it for you. They charge fees and make more money when they make you money. If you do not want to actively watch your investments, mutual funds are a solid option. There are a lot of different mutual funds out there, and what differentiates them is what they invest in, how risky they are, and who runs them. Some mutual funds invest in one particular sphere such as technology or energy companies.

Other funds invest in an index like the S&P 500. Still others invest in currencies or foreign countries. There is pretty much a mutual fund for just about anything you want to invest in. If you think that overalls for elephants is the next fad to hit (especially if they come equipped with an extra sleeve for the trunk), there is bound to be some fund somewhere that agrees and will invest on your behalf.

Just because the investing is being outsourced, it does not mean that you do not have to do any research. It would be like letting your friends choose a husband or wife for you: You might want to make sure you really have researched your friends' taste and success in picking the right person before committing. Even if you like and trust them (and really enjoy not having to date anymore), you are still going to want to check out their pick before you walk down the aisle.

In the case of mutual funds, instead of researching individual stocks, you need to research the fund managers and their returns. You want to make sure they know the specific sphere in which they will be investing your money. To pick a fund, do some research on a field you think will do well, and then research the funds that invest there. See how the returns have been for the last several years. The Wall Street Journal has lists of mutual funds and their past performance. It's a good place to start your search. You can also go to a financial planning group, but realize, these companies are often paid bonus commissions for recommending certain funds. It is always best to do your own research in advance.

Real estate

I am about to out myself here. I am a huge fan of real estate investment and have made the vast majority of my money there. This is true because I understand the investment well and have good experience in the field. I also will give you more on real estate than the other investment types we have discussed because there is more to understanding a real estate investment than any of the above options. I don't mean to say that real estate is more complicated, but figuring out your investment returns in real estate is a little more complex.

What do I mean by that you say, as you start to cringe? It is pretty simple. If we invest money in a bank account, we are told an interest rate the bank is going to give us. If there are no fees, the interest rate is my net return for my investment. So I put $1,000 in my account and they give me an interest rate of .1 percent. At the end of the year, I have an extra $1. I made one tenth of one percent on my money. Kinda weak sauce, huh?

With the previous listed investment types like stocks, bonds, and options, you have brokerage fees that you pay on each transaction that you do. This is an expense that needs to be removed from your profits in order to figure out how much you actually made. You invest $1,000 in some mix of stocks,

The markets

bonds, and options, and at the end of the year you made $100, but you have $30 in brokerage fees to pay. Your net earnings are $70, which is 7 percent. If we didn't subtract the brokerage fee, we might have thought we had made $100 or 10 percent.

This is important when we compare investments to each other. I'm going to go out on a limb here and say that you have limited capital (money). You have the ability to invest in a limitless number of things, from the super risk averse option of putting your money into a savings account to the "I have a death wish" option of buying a kilo of cocaine and becoming a drug dealer. Or if that offends you, please read experimental parachute tester instead. What allows you to decide your investment fit is an assessment of risk compared to the return. So you can see how understanding the return is a critical component to figuring this out.

An example of using this formula would be something like, "Gee, if I put my money in at one tenth of one percent, sure it is super safe, but inflation is higher than my interest rate, which means I am actually losing money at that rate". The potential income from allocating my funds to cocaine distribution is far better, but there is a significantly shortened life expectancy. This is a major downside for a drug dealer.

With investments funds, like mutual funds and similar "funds," you have other fees that get charged such as management fees. These are costs that you must subtract from your gross return to arrive at the actual amount of dollars that go into your bank account versus how many dollars you invested originally.

What does all of that have to do with real estate? Real estate has even more things that need to be subtracted from the gross profit in order to determine the net profit. With rental property, there are two different ways we make money, which means two different things to add.

Let's look at one more factor, which makes real estate different: You do not need to sell it to generate income. Let's look at a simpler real estate investment model, and then work our way to the more math intensive model. If you are buying and flipping (renovating and reselling) properties, you only make money when you sell, much like any of the other investment types we have discussed so far. You buy Apple stock, it goes up $10 you do not make $10 unless you sell that stock. If you improve a home so that its value goes up from $120,000 to $200,000, you do not get that $200,000 until you actually find someone to pay you that amount of money for the house.

The downside: Stocks have a liquid market, which means if a stock is trading at $60 and you want to sell at $60, your sale is guaranteed. This is not so in real estate. In real estate, the homes in the area might be selling for $200,000, but you may still wait days, weeks, or even months for someone to buy your home listed at $200,000. This difference is called liquidity. **Liquidity,** as you recall, is how quickly an asset can be turned into cash. Real estate is less liquid than several other types of investments. It is more liquid than something like a rare stamp or book collection. Liquidity is something that can be planned for or dealt with in a real estate investment portfolio, something we discuss more later.

So back to our house we are flipping: We are going to have expenses with that house we flipped. Even if we did the work very quickly, there are some real estate taxes that need to be paid, insurance we should have had for the house while we renovated, the actual cost to renovate, real estate commissions to buy and sell the property, closing costs, and debt service (mortgage payment) plus any other unusual expenses. What is left over is your profit. As you can see, real estate investment requires you to keep more accurate records of your expenses in order to see how much money your money is earning.

As we discussed earlier, real estate is a hedge against inflation. Home prices go up with the cost of living. There is no such direct correlation with other securities (stocks, bonds, etc.). That is one major advantage that owning real estate gives, but wait there's more. If you own a house and rent it out, you get income without selling the property. This is very different from securities, which must normally be sold to give you actual liquid funds. You may well say, "But wait a second. I thought the downside of real estate is that it is less liquid than other investment types." The answer is yes and no. Rental real estate provides you with a passive income stream, but part of your profits are tied up so that you cannot actual realize them till the house is sold. So if you earn 8 percent a year from the rental on a property you

The markets

own, is that rental income your only income from that property? The answer is no. The property is appreciating in value, which means that you also are probably earning at least 3 percent additional income each year. This means that for the year when you earned 8 percent, you probably earned closer to 11 percent. When we get into the math in the next chapter we discuss how to figure this out.

The fact that we can earn passive income from our rental property is not the end of the awesome part. When you rent a place, does the rent stay the same or does it go up? It goes up over the years, doesn't it? In fact, rent goes up to keep pace with inflation. This means that if you are renting the property, you are actually getting a double dip on inflation because as the home price goes up so do the rents. Does that change the rate of return on your investment? You bet your biscuits it does. If you bought a house for $100,000 and rent it out this year so that you earn $10,000 net (after all bills are paid), you have earned 10 percent. But the house also appreciated 3 to 3.5 percent while you earned that 10 percent, and next year's rent will give you $10,300 in income. The house will appreciate another 3 percent to 3.5 percent while you earn that rent, and so on. Did the amount we paid for the house change? No. So our rate of return is actually improving while we own the property because the rents go up as well as the home's value. Pretty cool right? This is why I like being a landlord.

Downside/upside: Real estate is a tangible asset and differs from stocks and other securities. Sure you could go try to get copies of the actual stock certificates. In theory, they are all backed by the tangible assets of the company, but in reality, none of these are things you really need to deal with in order to be an investor. Real estate, however, has a physical location that you can go see, feel, smell, and taste (really not recommended, especially when fertilizers are in play). If you like to have visual evidence of where your money has gone, there is not much that can beat real estate.

Unfortunately, there is a major down side to tangibility, which occurs when the tangible water heater breaks at two a.m. and floods the tangible living room, causing your tangible tenant to call you and threaten to put their tangible foot in your tangible backside if the water heater is not fixed soon.

The Roadmap to the American Dream

Fear not. If that sounds like a deal killer for you, there are folks called property managers who for a small fee handle all of that nonsense for you. But we do need to subtract their management fee from our net return to see if this if this is still our best investment option.

There are also tax advantages to owning real estate, which we cover later in a section I very creatively decided to name, "the tax advantages of real estate". I know, you are in awe of my creativity.

So we have an investment type here with income properties (real estate purchased to generate income from rent) that is unique. It requires you to track more expenses, with more hands on input, yet yields an income while continuing to increase in value. It is also a slower moving market than the other investment types in that if you buy a good stock this week that is undervalued, by the end of the week it may have gone up enough so it should be sold. On the other hand, a good property almost never becomes a bad property in a week or even a year. The need to constantly reassess what you own is much less with the real estate portion of a portfolio because a neighborhood or market does not change overnight.

Buying income generating real estate is actually a very broad statement. There are many types of income properties out there from buying a small condo to large industrial buildings. Finding the asset type that you understand best is important before investing.

The beginner's place where most folks get their feet wet is renting out a house or condo. This works because most people at some time have rented a place, so they have some idea of what the process looks like—at least from the tenants' side. Residential rentals are a great business. It is where I focus most of my investing for the simple reason people have to have a place to live. As you move to larger multi-unit buildings, you start to run into bigger versions of the same problems you have with smaller properties.

For example, you need a roof on a home you are renting and it costs $5,000—ouch—that stings as opposed to your twenty-unit building needing a roof and it is going to cost $28,000 (that doesn't sting, it freaking hurts like the, "did somebody see the donkey that just kicked me and made me regret not wearing my athletic cup" kind of hurts). You also start having laundry

The markets

rooms and common areas and fun things like that, which all make ownership a bit more complex. We could then move on to office buildings and again, you are dealing with common areas, elevators, and parking fields, but we would also start dealing with tenant improvements, common area maintenance, and a more fickle customer. The new challenges that get added when we switch property types need to be understood because they can cause you a lot of grief if you are unfamiliar with the challenges they bring.

Another example, when I owned a large mini warehouse facility, it was on seven acres of land and had 128 warehouse bays from 364 square feet up to 3000 square feet we knew that we needed someone at the property full time to deal with the tenants, but the two largest issues we had were the trash and the bathroom. Nothing quite prepares you for trying to explain to a grown man that he cannot throw his boat—yes, the whole freaking boat— into the trash compactor, not even if he cuts it up. People would have thrown anything into that thing, seriously, the stories would make you laugh and then cry for us as a species. It got to the point where cameras needed to be installed to protect the trash bin because people would just come in and leave stuff by there and drive away. It seems like a silly thing to be talking about right? The trash bill for that property was several thousand dollars a month. Eventually by managing that situation, we were able to save $3,000 to 4,000 a month. That was pure profit to us, but we first had to understand and deal with a very particular type of issue that arose from the specific type of investment property we had purchased.

As you can see, different types of real estate require different types of knowledge. Most of it is not particularly hard to come by, but you do need to go into it with your eyes wide open. If you are going to be a landlord, what types of lease will you use? What are your state's laws regarding evictions? How long do they take? How will you screen your tenants? Does your screening show if they have had evictions? These are just a few questions to think about as you consider this investment type. It is a great asset type, and for the reasons listed above, it is the one that largely makes up my investment portfolio.

The Roadmap to the American Dream

Business

Starting your own business is the dream of many in the U.S. as this is a country largely made up of very entrepreneurial people. With perhaps the exception of the Native Americans, everybody here got up and left someplace else to come here. That was not an easy thing to do, but it is indicative of the type of spirit it takes to start your own business. We very much take for granted in the U.S. the idea that if I don't like what I'm doing, or if I think I can do this better thing, and if I have the gumption to make it happen, I have a good chance to succeed. This idea permeates (is everywhere in) our society. This is a great thing. It has allowed the U.S. to create so many businesses that make people's lives so much better, and I'm not only talking about the business owners but also the consumers.

The place where a business starts is with a consumer need (known or unknown by the consumer) and someone creatively trying to meet that need. Whether it be the need for a vegetarian Mongolian Italian fusion restaurant or mobile pet psychotherapy, there is no end to the creative ideas people have for meeting, what they perceive are consumer desires. If business owners understand what people want, adjust and do a bunch of other things just right, they wind up with a successful business. If not—well the business goes to a big farm to run and play with all of the other businesses. In other words, it dies. The business owner loses money, gets bummed out, hopefully learns from their mistakes and lives to try again with another idea that works better.

On the scale of hands-off versus hands-on investments, owning a business is the most time intensive type. Think a business like a newborn baby with diarrhea versus a mutual fund, which is more like your forty-year-old kids who live in a different country. For those who are curious, stocks would be like older teenagers and real estate would be kids in grade school (like still helping with homework age). I am hoping this becomes an official scale as I think it would be hilarious to describe your business as being in the diarrhea baby phase and have people seriously shake their head and say, "Yeah, been there I know what that's like."

Why is running a business so time intensive? Usually because you are responsible for doing *everything*. You usually do not have much in the way of

The markets

income so it is tough to hire staff, and if you do have the income, you have to oversee the staff and deal will any HR issues that come up. Brenda is feeling underappreciated and believes that more positive reinforcement would help her job performance. Through great self control, some Tibetan chanting techniques and four Xanax tablets, you manage to restrain your desire to positively bury your foot up her butt. Brad, however, feels that Brenda is a cry baby and has the need to tell her this, which makes Brenda request to not be on the same shift schedule as Brad—you get the idea. Employee problems become your problems. While you deal with these earth shattering issues, you are also expected to handle purchasing anything that your business needs, make sure all the stuff you buy is paid for, make sure you have been paid for all the stuff you sold, pay all of the bills, make sure the city, state, and federal governments didn't pass some new regulation that makes your business unworkable, and there was one more thing I thought? Oh yeah, grow your business.

Recognizing that business tends to fail is an important part of doing the risk return calculation we discussed when thinking about going into business. Do plenty of advance research to understand what type of staffing you need, what they need to be paid and how much product you need to sell just to break even. The break even point is not when the business can pay all of its bills. It is when the business can pay all of its bills and pay you the income you would be earning if you were working for someone else. These are important things to look at in order to get a handle on how to have a successful business. You need to have a clear business plan with timelines and goals. Know at what time you need to pull the plug if it doesn't work. Way too many people get into a business without a clear exit plan, and winding up almost destroys them.

I did much the same thing myself. I had run successful food operations for a very long time and so I decided to go into the restaurant business. I opened two Italian restaurants. Our business was growing nicely and then the economy in the area tanked. I hung on and hung on thinking this week we will turn it around. I let go of staff, worked every single day of the week, and still couldn't make it work. I had no clear exit plan and lost over a million dollars. I have opened several successful businesses since then. I learned a very expensive lesson. I have gotten into deals that have lost money, but I am much clearer about drawing a line in the sand to say when it goes past here, we walk away. You must have discipline in business, or your passion for what you have built will blind you to reality.

Evaluating a business as an investment is very complex. Usually you are just trying to get to a breakeven point, and that typically means working eighty plus hours a week. For a business to be truly evaluated as an investment, it must not only generate a return on the amount of money you have invested into the business, it also must pay to replace you. For example, if I own a mutual fund, it might take thirty minutes of my life every six months to deal with, maybe. If I own stocks, it will take more of my time, and I will need to generate more return from my stocks if they are going to compete with the mutual fund. My time is an asset and if something is going to take more of it, then it must compensate me or be considered the inferior investment. Remember we are trying to make the investments as alike as possible for the purposes of evaluating where the best place to put our money is. If I own rental real estate, it is going to take more of my time, but I am also getting a monthly cash flow, which is a positive in its favor. My business needs to compete with all of these other possible uses for my money in order to earn my investment dollars.

So after we pay all of our bills, our staff, taxes, rent, insurance, etc. and then pay someone to do our job in our business, how much money does the business make? Then compare that amount with the money invested in the company. If it is less than double-digit returns, you probably could have done better elsewhere. You then should try to figure out how to increase the returns, sell the business, or decide to take lesser returns than you could earn somewhere else that doesn't require your blood sweat and tears.

Conclusion

We have looked at some of the different places you can invest your money, but there are a lot more. You can buy futures, get involved in commodities or currencies, heck you can even buy viaticles (which are life insurance policies that

The markets

people want to turn into cash. You buy them and pay the premiums so when they die, you get paid. Creepy, right?)

Regardless of how you chose to invest your money, the ideas of this chapter remain critical: Learn how each investment type works, and figure out your net return to make sure you are making the best available use of your money. I want to make sure my money is working as hard as it can so that later I don't have to work so hard. Keeping this in mind, we are going to delve into the math in order to help you figure out how to compare unlike investment types.

Part 3

The Math

Chapter 11

The basics

By the inch, it's a cinch by the yard it's hard.

-Bob Cadillac

I know math is scary but I will go slowly and make it as simple as I can. I will take my father's advice from the quote above. We are in this together so buckle up and hold on tight. We are going to use real estate examples to show you this math, as this investment type is best suited to using real world examples. You can use modified versions of this method for calculating any returns on anything. The critical number to get to is the **net return number** and from that number, any calculation shown here will work. We went over some of this earlier in the book, but repeat it again here so you have one place to refresh yourself if you need it. We state these examples in the most linear fashion possible so that the simplest ideas are first, and then we build to the more complex ones.

Rate of return

Very simply put, this is how many dollars I earn compared with how many dollars I have to invest to make those dollars. It cost me $200,000 to earn

The basics

$2,000 a year; that is a 1 percent rate of return. We get that result by dividing the income $2,000 by the investment $200,000, which equals .01 by moving the decimal two places to the right and adding the percentage sign we have 1 percent. If we had an investment that required $3.85 million and returned $843,000 a year, what would the return be? The answer is 22 percent. Again, divide the income (843,000) by the investment (3.85 million) and get your return (.22 which = 22 percent). All investments have a rate of return. It can be positive, which means you are making money, or negative, which means you are losing money and in need of a different investment strategy.

Cap rate

Cap rate is short for the capitalization rate, which is the rate of return for an investment. This is the same thing we just calculated, but rather than using the net income above, we use this when we have only been given a gross income and need to calculate the net before we can compare it to the total investment. In other words, we have the total amount of money the investment takes in given to us, and then need to subtract the expenses to determine the annual rate of return. Let's look more at a real world example.

We buy a house for $80,000. It is a three bedroom two bathroom home, and needs $20,000 worth of work to be ready to rent. Our total cost for this investment will be $100,000. The market rent for a property like this is $1,300 per month. We must put aside some money for repairs—let's say $75 a month—and we need to pay property taxes and insurance. Our taxes are $1,600 a year and our insurance is $1,200. The typical time it takes to rent a property in the market is two weeks so because we are super thorough, we figure a vacancy expense (lost rent) of $600. We are doing that because we are going to use the maximum potential income of the property and then subtract from that figure. Our gross potential income is $1,300 a month times 12 months, which equals $15,600 per year. We now subtract our expenses from this number to give us how much money we get to keep in our bank account at the end of the year.

$15,600 Gross potential income
- $ 900 Reserve for repairs ($75 a month times 12 months= $900)
-$1,600 Real estate taxes
-$1,200 Insurance
- $ 600 Vacancy
$11,300 Net Operating Income

This example shows that we will make $11,300 each year as profit after all expenses are paid. If our total investment cost was $100,000 ($80,000 to buy the property and $20,000 for renovation) we can calculate our **cap rate**.

* We do this by dividing how much we make ($11,300) by how much we spent to make it ($100,000).
* 11,300 divided by 100,000 equals .113, which is 11.3 percent rate of return. In real estate slang, this property would be said to be an 11.3 cap.

Now we have our net rate of return for this investment and can compare it to other things such as our bank account at its one tenth of 1 percent return. This property leaves a solid boot print in our bank accounts bottom (it kicks its butt). We could also compare it to the returns of a mutual fund or our stock portfolio—but wait a second—real estate has a few tricks up its sleeve to sweeten the deal. What would happen if we added financing (a mortgage) to this deal—and wait a second—I don't see the property appreciation figured into our income. What happens to that? Relax, young Jedi, we are getting there soon. First, a short hiatus.

> **ROI (return on investment and return of investment)** can mean two things. The more common one is return on investment, which is what we have talked about with both the rate of return and the cap rate above. It is expressed as a percentage and is a comparison of how much you make compared to how much you spent.

The basics

Return of investment is the amount of time it takes to earn back all the money you spent to purchase the investment. This calculation is done the exact opposite way from the return on investment calculation. Let's look at our property we just figured was returning money to us at 11.3 percent a year. We saw that out by dividing the profit $11,300 by the total cost of the investment $100,000, it gave us 11.3 percent. If we do it the other way and divide $100,000 by $11,300 (basically calculating how many $11,300's are in $100,000), we get 8.85. This means that in 8.85 years we will have earned $100,000 in profit from this investment.

Chapter 12

The basics when adding debt

"The speed of your success is limited only by your dedication and what you're willing to sacrifice"

— NATHAN W. MORRIS

Every trade has its tools. If you are going to be a plumber, you would probably need to know how to work a wrench, if you are going to be a carpenter you would need to know how a hammer works, and if you are going to be a lawyer, you would want to know the most economical way to screw people (you wouldn't want them to throw out their back or something—ahh, they probably sue you for that too.) That being said, if you are going to take advantage of the American economy and seek out avenues in which to invest, you are going to need some tools too. The one tool that you really need is a financial calculator. Luckily there is soooo an app for that. I use a 10bii, which is a great little tool. **Relax!** There are only a handful of keys you need to use before you go into a flashback mode, trying to use your scientific calculator for science class back in high school.

Using a financial calculator

All financial calculators have the same keys, but sometimes they have slightly different symbols that indicate their purpose. This is not a big deal because if you know the purpose of each of these keys, you can easily figure out the slightly different symbols. There are five primary keys (located across the top row just under the display on the 10bii), and one important setting used with a financial calculator for figuring compounding interest on mortgages, annuities, investments, interest rates, payment amounts, and amortization times.

Calculators are really smart and they remember tons of stuff. We just need to tell it what to remember. We are going to input values into the calculator and then touch the key we are assigning those numbers to. This tells the calculator what those numbers are and to remember them. Be aware that if you don't clear the calculator, it continues to remember the old numbers. We will use this to compare how different investments do over time.

I love the 10Bii app for the iPhone because it shows you what numbers are assigned to each key on the top row, and that is primarily where we will be working. Do not be intimidated. You cannot launch a nuclear missile with this calculator—I've tried. This next part is designed for you take out the calculator and do the samples as we go. I spent hours working on these instructions to make them easy to follow and you could learn to be comfortable with this important investment tool. It's not downloaded yet, is it??? That's okay, I'll wait—got all day—but seriously, get the freaking calculator out and use it.

Let's start with the setting we need to check before moving forward: That setting is the "number of payments per year" or basically, the time period on which the funds are compounding. This is represented on the calculator screen on the bottom of the display with "**Payments Per Year**". The key to change the setting can be seen below the **PMT** key. We will adjust that here.

Typically for a mortgage, PMT is set to 12, because you make twelve payments a year, and for an investment, it needs to be set at 1, for one payment a year. This is because a mortgage payment may be a fixed amount, but the portion of the payment dedicated to interest goes down each month, and the portion that pays down principal increases. This occurs because the mortgage is compounding on a monthly basis. With an investment, however, the income

The Roadmap to the American Dream

that comes in is calculated on a yearly compounding basis. This is regardless of how the income comes in.

We just want to know how much our money earned in the year. So in summary: If we are calculating a mortgage, we set the number of payments to 12 and for an investment we set it to 1. The way to adjust this setting is fairly simple: First type in the number of payments you want. Right now let's set it to 12. So, type in 12 on the calculator, then press the orange shift key (third key up on the far left hand side), and finally press the PMT key (second key to the left on the very top row). The display should show in small print "Payments Per Year: 12".

Next let's tackle the **"N"** key. This is where we start to tell the calculator what numbers to remember. The N key is where you put in the number of payments or years (compounding periods) you need to calculate. For an investment, this is simply the number of years that investment lasted. With a mortgage, this represents how many payments will be made. So, for a thirty-year loan that pays monthly, this is 30 x 12=360. To input the number, you just type in the number of compounding periods and touch the "N" key. For the sake of this example, let's do a thirty-year loan that pays monthly, so type in 360 and then touch the "N" key.

The **"I/YR"** key stands for **interest rate per year**, and this is where we type in the interest rate we are earning or paying. We input this exactly as above: Type in the interest amount and then press the "I/YR" key. For the sake of this example, let's type in 5.75, and then touch the "I/YR" key.

The **"PV"** key stands for the **present value**, which is either funds we are spending for an investment (in which case this number will be negative) or funds we are receiving (like a mortgage to buy a property, in which case the number will be positive). We input this exactly as above: Type in the amount we are spending or receiving and then press the "PV" key. For this example, let's say $485,000. This amount is positive as we are calculating a mortgage and this is a cash flow in to us. So you type in 485,000 and touch the PV key.

The next key is the **"PMT"** key, which stands for the **payment**. Right now, we could touch that key and the calculator tells us the payment for our thirty-year loan on $485,000 at 5.75 percent. It does so because the last key (FV) was left at 0.

The basics when adding debt

If we were calculating a payment into an annuity, like our investor charts in chapter six (the guy that invested from 25 to 65, and the other guy that invested from 16 to 25), we would put in the amount of money they were investing each month or year the same way here as with all the keys above. In this example, we solve for the mortgage payment by touching the "PMT" key. It should read -$2,830.33. This is the monthly payment amount needed to fully payoff (or amortize) this loan. If for some reason this did not match the answer on your calculator, make sure the FV was set to 0. If you run into trouble, you can always hit the orange key and then the C key, which clears everything so you can start from scratch.

The last key is the **"FV"** key. This stands for **future value**. This is where we can see how much we would still owe on our thirty-year mortgage if we sold in ten years and had to pay it off early. Let's do this now with the numbers we currently have in the calculator. This is how we would solve this is. After figuring out the payment (-$2,830.33), we change the number in the "N" key to ten years' worth of payments, or 10x12=120. We \ do this by typing in 120, and then touching the "N" key. Next we touch the "FV" key. This gives us a balance of -$403,132.72, which we still owe on our mortgage after ten years.

We can continue to play with this. What if we paid extra each month on our mortgage instead of -$2,803.33? What if we paid -$3,000?

* Make sure to make the payment amounts negative as it is money going out.
* Then leave all of the numbers the same and type in 3000, and touch the "PMT" key.
* We next touch the "FV" key and we see that we only owe $375,701.09.

What if we decided to keep the property, but continued to make the $3,000 payment? How long would it take us to pay off the loan in full?

* All we would need to do is leave all of the numbers in the calculator and change the "FV" key to $0.
* Then we touch the "N" key to find out that we will only need to make 311.72 payment instead of 360.

- This means we will shave 48.28 months off the life of the mortgage or just over 4 years.

Pretty cool, right?

Now that you feel like you can calculate the square root of a black hole as it swallows a sun preparing to super nova in the midst of an ever expanding galaxy while running down the street in the rain, all while juggling and joining Mensa, let's put down our new-found calculator friend for just a second. We get the chance to use our calculators really soon, I promise.

Cash on cash return

This is what we get when we add a mortgage to the cap rate calculation from the previous chapter. Let's look at the home from the previous chapter. We purchased it for $80,000 and had $20,000 in renovation expenses. For the sake of this example, let's assume we can finance the purchase and rehab together. We are looking at a mortgage on a $100,000 home. This is an investment property, so the bank is only going to lend us 70 percent of the purchase price. This means they will lend us $70,000 (multiply 100,000 by .7= $70,000). They are going to charge us 5 percent interest on a thirty-year fully amortizing loan. Time to break out those calculators—told you we'd need them soon.

We need to fill in our financial keys. For those of you that are brave try it on your own and skip ahead as (spoiler alert) the answer is coming up.

- First we should clear our calculator from the last calculation. We do this by pushing the orange shift key and then touching the "C" key, which will clear everything.
- For this property, we have a standard thirty-year loan, which means we will be making twelve payments a year for a total of 360 payments. We need to put 360 into the N key of the calculator.
- We are paying 5 percent interest, so we need to put 5 in I/YR key.
- For the PV key, we need to put in the loan amount (not the purchase price) so 70,000.

The basics when adding debt

* We leave the FV key alone at 0 because we will owe nothing when this loan is done as it is fully amortizing.

We now push the PMT key to get our mortgage payment of $375.78. That will be our mortgage payment for this loan.

Let's look at the expenses and income for this property:

$15,600 Gross potential income
- $ 900 Reserve for repairs ($75 a month times 12 months= $900)
-$1,600 Real estate taxes
-$1,200 Insurance
- $ 600 Vacancy
$11,300.00 Net Operating Income
Cap Rate 11.3 percent (Based on $100,000 of owners money)

We now have a mortgage payment, which needs to be subtracted from the income. We need to multiply our monthly payment by 12 to get how much it will cost for the year because our income calculation is based on our yearly income not monthly. Our yearly payment is calculated (375.78 x 12=) $4,509.30, which we need to subtract. It will look like this.

$15,600 Gross potential income
- $ 900 Reserve for repairs ($75 a month times 12 months= $900)
-$1,600 Real estate taxes
-$1,200 Insurance
- $ 600 Vacancy
$11,300.00 Net Operating Income
- $4,509.30 Debt service (mortgage payment)
$6,790.70 Cash on cash return

I know what you are probably thinking—mortgages are terrible. We are earning a lot less money. But are we? Here is the cool part. We previously spent $100,000 of our money to earn $11,300 a year. We are now only spending

$30,000 to earn $6,790.70. Here is why this math matters. Our rate of return with a mortgage is—drum roll please—**23 percent.** We get this by dividing the income $6,790.70 by the $30,000 we spent to buy the property.

Cap rate with debt service 23 percent (based on $30,000 of owner's money)

This allows us to take that same $100,000 we would have spent on one property, and instead, buy three properties. If we did, we would be earning 23 percent on all of our money as opposed to 11.3 percent. Pretty sweet, right? It gets even better. Owning more than one property actually lessens our vacancy risk. If we have one home and it is vacant, we have a 100 percent vacancy factor (percentage of units vacant), but if we have three units and one is vacant, we have a 33 percent vacancy factor. That means we are still collecting 67 percent of our rent. When we have a property, the bills do not stop coming in when it is vacant. You still have to pay the mortgage, taxes, and insurance. Having income from other properties lessens your risk to have negative cash flow (paying out more than you are taking in) because the occupied properties are still producing income for you.

There are risks with financing properties because you have additional obligations with each additional property. If you own two properties that are both financed and also both vacant, you now have a lot of bills and no income to pay them. The way to protect against that risk is to have more properties. This is true because there is a reasonable chance that if you own two properties, there will be some time that both properties are vacant. It is highly unlikely that if you own one hundred properties, there will be a point where they are all vacant.

The wise way to handle the risk of vacancy is, as we discussed earlier, through a reserve that should represent a smaller and smaller percentage of your portfolio as it grows. That means if you own one property, you might want three month's reserve (which includes the mortgage payments in addition to all other property expenses) for your entire portfolio; in other words, enough money in the bank that if the property earns no money you can pay for all of its bills. When you buy a second property, your risk of 100 percent vacancy goes down. You could probably get away with having two months of

The basics when adding debt

reserves for your whole portfolio (enough money to pay all the bills of both properties for two months). If you add two more properties, you might feel comfortable with only a single month's reserve for your property.

As the portfolio grows, you will be able to have less than one month's reserves for your portfolio because the risk of complete vacancy goes down. It is all a matter of measuring risk, and how much you feel comfortable with. You want to have reserves, but at the same time, you want to be putting that money to work for you buying more properties. You also want to be taking advantage of as much positive leverage as your risk tolerance and common sense allows. In the end, it needs to be considered a risk/reward calculation that is really more of an ulcer/profit or valium/return calculation.

Chapter 13

Advanced investment ideas and the math to use them

"Know what you own, and know why you own it."

- Peter Lynch

There are some critical ideas we need to understand so we can start really thinking about money the best possible way. In this chapter, we are going to look at these ideas by looking at examples and learning how to do the math to figure this stuff out.

TVM Calculation

Let's use your financial calculator to show us how much money we are making in a particular investment over time. This is done similarly to what we did in the previous chapter for a mortgage. We have money invested, it earns money, and we reinvest that money as soon as we get it. How much do we have after a certain amount of time? We can figure that out fairly easily.

Advanced investment ideas and the math to use them

We did something similar to this earlier in the book the hard way by figuring out the interest we earned in year one and adding it to the investment that we started with at the beginning of the year. We then used that amount as the starting amount for year two; and then we figured out the interest we would earn in year two and added that to the investment of the start of year three. Wash, rinse, repeat. To help refresh your memory, here is the chart:

Year	Investment-Beginning of Year	Interest Rate	Interest Amount	Investment Plus Interest-End of Year
1	$100,000	6%	$6,000	$106,000
2	$106,000	6%	$6,360	$112,360
3	$112,360	6%		
4		6%		

After being the heartless jerk that made you do it this way back in chapter six, I now will tell you the cool part. Your calculator can do this for you. Let's do this calculation to solve for year four without having to do the rest of the work.

Open your friend Mr. Calculator (mine prefers to be addressed formally). The first thing we need to do is adjust the setting we discussed on our calculator. Our investment here is earning interest annually so there are no monthly payments.

* We do this by typing in the number 1 then pressing the second (orange key), and then touching the PMT key, which has highlighted P/YR (short for payment per year). That key is located on the top row the fourth key over from left to right. Notice that the payments per year in the display has changed to 1.

The Roadmap to the American Dream

Now we use our financial keys at the top of the calculator to see what we earn.

* First we should clear all our previous numbers out of the calculator by doing a "clear all" using the orange key and the "C" key. Now we can begin.
* We have invested $100,000 so we need to put this in as a negative number as it is money we spent. We do this by typing in 100,000 and then touching the +/- key on the left just above the blue key.
* We then touch the PV key on the top row.
* Our interest rate is 6 percent so we put in 6 and touch the I/YR key, also in the top row.

Now we need to fill in the number of payments. For investment return we need to use how much we earn on a yearly basis on our money. Our calculators are set to figure a yearly rate of return of 6 percent. So, we need to tell the calculator how many years that will go on for.

* In this case, we want to know what we earned in 4 years so will type in 4 and hit the N key.
* We will not be making any payments, so we leave the PMT key at 0, and then touch the FV key to get the answer.

The answer is $126,247.70. That saved a couple of minutes, but the awesome part is: What if we wanted to see what we have in 20 years? Without clearing anything on the calculator, type in 20, touch the N key, and then the FV key. You will have $320,713.55. That saved a bunch of time, didn't it?

Let's use an **annuity** as an example. With an annuity, you make monthly payments for a given period of time. Those payments earn compounding interest, and then when the annuity matures (the prearranged time when you no longer need to make payments), you have a large sum of money that gets paid back to you in many different ways depending on the terms of annuity. With some types, you receive monthly payments for the rest of your life, or even

Advanced investment ideas and the math to use them

your spouse's life. Sometimes an annuity is paid out as a lump sum. I know that doesn't sound particularly helpful yet, but let's look at it quickly and then I will show you why you want to understand this.

Let's change our calculator setting back to 12 payments per year, as we will be making monthly payments into our annuity.

* Type 12, then orange key, then PMT key.

Do a clear all on the calculator and then we are ready to go.

* Let's say we have an annuity where we pay in $300 a month for thirty years at 8.5 percent interest. We will be making 360 payments (twelve payments per year times thirty years). So we put 360 in, and touch the N key.
* Our interest rate is 8.5, so we put that in and touch the I/YR key.
* We are not putting an initial starting amount into our annuity, only payments starting in month one, so we leave the PV key at 0. We then put in our payment (money going out) as -300 and touch the PMT key.
* Now we can see how much we have by pressing the FV (Future Value) key, which gives us the result of $495,211.71.

So, we invested a total of $108,000 and it grew into almost half a million dollars.

What if that is not enough for you? What if you really wanted one million when you retired. We can easily figure out how much we need to put in the annuity today in order to reach that amount.

* Type in 1,000,000 and touch the FV key (this is how much you want the Future Value to be).
* Now just touch the PV key and it tells you that if you invest $39,770.60 today and make $300 a month payments, you will have a million-dollar-annuity to enjoy thirty years from now.

As you can see, we can use this tool to figure out the investment rate we need to earn on our money in order to meet our future financial goals. If you were thinking of investing (really hope you are *at least* thinking about it, because it's kind of the point of this book), you can say, "Okay, I have this much money now, and I want to have this much more money when I retire" (hopefully at age 35). "So how much do I need to earn on my money to get there?"

For those of you without much to invest now, you need to do your best to under-consume so that you can have a nest egg to start with. Once you do, these investments can throw off money that you can reinvest, which continues to grow the amount that you are earning returns on. Now we are going to go a step farther. There is a problem with this calculation we just used. It calculates return as long as the return stays the same. What if we own rental properties and the rents go up each year? How do we calculate that? Unfortunately, our wonderful calculator has no ability to calculate how much we are earning in appreciation for our property. Seems like we are going to have to learn more math—*crap*!

IRR

To be able to evaluate a real estate investment, we can't just figure out how much money it earns in rent. That would be like figuring out the car payment for the new car we are buying but forgetting about little things like gas, repairs, tires, etc. To see the whole picture, we need to look at purchase price, current rents, and rent increases, and then project a future sale price to see how much we will actually earn on our investment in total. How do we do that you may ask? Like this: We are going to meet the CFj key on our calculators now. If you have downloaded it on your phone, that's great because this is by the far the easier way to do this compared to using the actual calculator. We will be calculating a rate of return for a property we buy, rent out, hold for five years, and then sell. It will experience 3.5% rent increases and 3.5% appreciation each year.

- * Do a clear all and then set your calculator on 1 payment per year, if it is not already set that way.
- * Now touch the CFj key in the third row down in the middle column. We are going to need to put in the first box the amount of money

Advanced investment ideas and the math to use them

  spent to buy the property. It is money going out so it is a negative number. Let's say we spent $150,000 so we will put in -150,000.
* Next we need to put in our year one net rent. For this example, we are going to say $14,400 in year one. (Now if we just quickly do a Cap rate calculation, comparing the amount we spent $150,000 to the year one net income $14,400, we are at a 9.6 percent rate of return because we would need to earn $15,000 to be at a full 10 percent. Okay, but not great.) Let's keep going though and see if things improve.
* We need to put that 14,400 in the second amount box as year one's income, and put in 1 for the # times as we only earned that amount one time for the year. I am going to add around 3.5 percent a year and round up to come up with the second and following years' rental amounts.
* For year two we earn a net rent of $15,000. We need to push the + button right at the very top left of the calculator to add a new set of boxes to fill in. This is where we can add the rent of 15,000 and again put 1 in for the # times.
* We do the same thing for year three's rent by putting in a rent of $15,400, pushing the plus sign at the top, and putting in 1 time.
* Year 4 is going to be at $15,900, so put that in.

Now we have to do a bit more work because for this example, we are going to project selling the property in year five. We are going to have to figure out how much we can expect to sell our property for.

* We do this by pushing the done button on the calculator (Relax! all of the numbers we still be here when we get back). Our rent is going to be $16,500 but that is not all we are going to make. We are also going to be getting back all of the money we invested plus all of the appreciation the property had. So, let's figure out what our property is worth.
* We use our financial keys at the top of the calculator, leaving the one payment per year setting and putting in -150,000 for the PV.

* We figure the property appreciated at 3.5 percent a year (which is pretty standard for real estate), so we can put that amount in as our interest rate (I/YR).
* Finally, the property has been growing at 3.5 percent for the past five years so we will put 5 in as our N setting. (Make sure the payment is set to 0 as we have no payment).

We can now solve for the future value of $178,152.95.

* We round the number up to $178,500, and add it to the rent money we receive for year five: $178,500+ $16,500 for a total of $194,650.
* We can now switch back to the CFj key and put $194,650 in for year five once again as 1 time.
* If we push the IRR/YR (right below the year 5 info you just put in) you get an answer of 13.10 percent. The calculation we have done here is called an Internal Rate of Return.

Here is a visual representation of what it should look like.

Year	Amount	#Times
0	-150,000	Purchase Price
1	14,400	1
2	15,000	1
3	15,400	1
4	15,900	1
5	16,500 + 178,500 = 194,650	1

IRR: 13.10 percent

Don't clear your calculators just yet. Getting 13.10 percent is a lot better than the 9.6 percent rate of return that our cap rate calculation told us we would earn. 13.10 percent means that the total of all incomes will provide the equivalent of having our $150,000 invested in an account that earns 13.10 percent compounding interest each year for five years.

Now, some may take issue that these numbers are projected and the market might be lower when we attempt to sell. This is true. The market is cyclical (goes through cycles), but the historical average of these cycles is what we are using. This means that if in year five the market is poor, there is nothing to keep us from holding the property until the market recovers. Our rents still come in and the investments continue to appreciate until the market recovers.

> *Note:* *The obvious exception to real estate always going up long term is the crash in the housing market in 2008. This crash was due to the excessive run up in home prices that preceded the crash. How do you know if a market is "run up"? There are certain places where home prices are tied to other indicators. One key place is with median income. Median home prices are usually around 2.5 to 3 times median income. This means that the median house costs somewhere between 2.5 to 3 year's salary for the median income earner. Some markets are more or less but that is a good general guide.*
>
> *Another way to look at it is this. If you can look back fifty years and see growth around 3 to 3.5 percent per year, and then you see several years of 10 to 15 percent growth, you know that you are looking at a bubble and should be figuring out how to take a short position (a position that benefits from the market going down) on real estate.*

Back to our sale in year five: By calculating all incomes, we can now compare owning this property with our projection for buying stock in ABS Company), or a portfolio of bonds, or being a lender and doing a mortgage for someone else, or perhaps starting our own business. We have our investments on equal footing for comparison.

NPV

We decide to make an offer for an investment (it can be any investment type) based upon a 13 percent rate of return. Our investment criteria says that we would be happy with as low as a 10.5 percent rate of return. How much can we pay for this investment and still receive a total return of 10.5 percent?

Enter our last major financial concept. By taking the information we had in our financial calculators from the previous IRR calculation, and inputting our desired interest rate in the calculator, we can find out how much more or less we can pay to get the desired return. This is called the **net present value (NPV)** of the investment. This is like saying: If I have an investment return, I need to have, in this case, 10.5 percent; and based upon the yearly returns that we project and the future sale price we expect to receive, the most we can pay is the NPV in order to achieve our return goal.

We have talked a lot about the time value of money and how compounding works. This is the opposite of that process. We are applying what is called a **discount rate** to the investment. Let's say you are buying a piece of art and an expert tells you it will be worth one million dollars in twenty years (and let's assume they are telling the truth). Should you pay one million for it today? No? Is that a bad deal? Yes! At what price does it cease being a bad deal, and start being a good deal?

The NPV tells us how a change in our purchase price affects our final rate of return. So, if I promise to pay you back $100 in ten years, you can apply a discount rate to that $100 and determine that based upon the interest you want to charge me (let's say 9.5 percent), you can only lend me about $40 today (a discount rate of 9.5 percent to me is also an interest rate to you of 9.5 percent).

Let's apply this to the calculation to our property where we had the 13.10 percent internal rate of return. If our goal was a 15 percent rate of return, let's see what we could pay in year zero (when we buy the property) to achieve that.

* We leave all the numbers in the calculator just as they were before and touch the NPV key (right next to the IRR key in the CFj screen). It asks us for our target rate of return, and we type in 15 percent. It then tells us we can pay -$10,144.03 for the property.

That was hard to do huh?

This means that if we subtract that NPV amount ($10,144.03) from what we initially spent to buy the property ($150,000) it will return 15 percent. So

Advanced investment ideas and the math to use them

if we pay a little less than $140,000 we would hit our target return. What if our return we are looking for is a little less ambitious? Maybe we would be okay with a 10.5 percent rate of return, so we touch NPV put our 10.5 percent rate of return. Bingo, we can afford to pay $15,547.54 more for the property and still earn that return.

Now a trick for those that like to be extra special lazy (like me). If you remove the purchase price from the first line of the IRR calculator and solve for NPV, it tells you the actual purchase price you can pay instead of the difference.

* Just remove the very first amount next to "initial cash flow", then touch the NPV key and insert the rate of return you want and the calculator will tell you exactly what to pay to get that amount. This little trick saves you from having to add or subtract. Woohoo lazy method!!!

Hopefully all of this math and fancy calculator footwork helps you to think of investments as money you spend in order to earn future cash flows. It could be either a lump sum when you sell in the future (like a stock), or intermittent payments (like an annuity), or a combination of both (like investment real estate). Now let's put some of this math to a practical use.

Chapter 14

Where this math matters in your life

"It's not how much money you make, but how much money you keep, how hard it works for you, and how many generations you keep it for."

- ROBERT KIYOSAKI

Have you ever wondered whether it is better to buy or rent? If you listen to your real estate agent friend, it is *always* a great time to buy—but is it? We can apply the tools we have learned to see if and when this is true.

Buying a home versus renting one

Instead of being the person that is struggling with this decision (as you have had to with so many in these chapters), let's say your friends ask you for advice. You say, "Why I just read a book about all of this and I have a new super cool calculator, very little idea how to use it, and quite possibly even stayed at a Holiday Inn Express last night" (old television commercial reference). "So, sure I can help."

Where this math matters in your life

Your friends are looking to rent a three-bedroom two-bath home in a nice neighborhood with an asking price of $2,550 per month. During your discussions, they have said this home is the one they want to live in for the next five years, and then upgrade. They are wondering if buying the home next door is a better decision. With a rental, they would have a fixed expense and not be responsible for major repairs.

There are some factors to consider, which at their real estate agent should make them aware of, but as an investor with a black belt in Financial Calculator Tai Kwon Do, you come up with a few questions and considerations for them to think about.

1. Rent is not tax deductible.
2. What is the current and expected inflation rate?
3. What is the current rate of appreciation for homes and how is the rental market? Appreciating, stagnant, downward trending?
4. Rent goes up most times, fixed rate mortgage payments do not.
5. Homes will appreciate over time.
6. Five years is a short timeline, and a mortgage payment does not pay off much principal in those early years.
7. What if the owner of the rental chooses to not renew their lease? Moving is time consuming and expensive.

So, you tell me if they should buy or rent:

* The purchase price for the identical house next door would be $325,000
* If they buy they would be financing FHA with an interest rate of 5.3 percent
* The term is thirty years.
* The lender will give them a loan of 96.5 percent loan to value.

We could figure out their monthly payment (but I already did). It is $1,741.57 plus $265 for mortgage insurance (insurance required on loans greater than 80 percent LTV). The annual taxes are $7,000, and hazard insurance is $4,200, which makes their monthly escrow $933.33. This brings their total monthly payment to $2,939.90.

* The home is twelve-years-old so to responsibly analyze this we must add a monthly reserve for replacement of major appliances and home systems of $200 a month (an estimate).
* Their down payment is $11,375 (3.5 percent of purchase price) with $16,250 (5 percent of purchase price) for closing costs, so their total out of pocket or cash to close would be $27,625.

They, therefore, can expect to sell the property in five years for $405,000, based upon expected 4.5 percent property appreciation. (What can I say—it's in a hot market.)

Current rentals in the area for a 3/2 SFR (three bedroom, two bath, single family residence) in similar condition is $2,550 a month, and always requires first and last month's rent plus security. They also have to pay a one-time pet deposit of $150 for their Teacup Yorkie, Thor. Also, they would be required to pay an application fee of $150. So, the total move in cost would be $8,850. The rental market is appreciating at an average of 4.5 percent annually (also a hot market), which means in five years we can project the rent to be approximately $3,177 a month.

So let's tap into our inner nerd and bust out a spreadsheet. We add all the cash flow out (expenses) for both transactions as well as the cash flow in (income) from the sale of the house, and at the end of year five see which is the better deal.

Where this math matters in your life

Costs	Costs	Rent	Costs
Down Payment/Closing Costs	$27,625.00	Move in w/o 1st Month	$6,300.00
Mortgage Payment	$37,678.80	Rent yr 1	$30,600.00
Mortgage Payment	$37,678.80	Rent yr 2	$31,977.00
Mortgage Payment	$37,678.80	Rent yr 3	$33,415.97
Mortgage Payment	$37,678.80	Rent yr 4	$34,919.68
Mortgage Payment	$37,678.80	Rent yr 5	$36,491.07
Sale Price	$405,000.00	Total living expense	$173,703.72
Mortgage Payoff after 5yrs	$289,201.00		
Closing Costs	$32,400.00		
Total living expense for 5yrs	$132,616.00		
Living cost to rent	$173,703.72		
Living cost to buy	$132,616.00		
Benefit of Purchase	**$41,087.72**		

So, the purchase of the house is over $41,000 better than the rental. In other words, the customer spends $41,000 less by buying the property than he would by renting it. Or does he?

There are other factors that affect this decision. While this seems all well and good on paper, it appears like a lot of money gets put out to buy the property and we are paying more each month. A lot of people get the gut feeling that this is not as sweet a deal as folks in real estate sell it to be. You know what?—they are right. This model only works if your friends do not have an alternative use for their money. If your friends are investors, the fact is, the higher the costs per month they are paying takes money out of their pocket they could be using to *make* money. The loss of this potential income is a real financial cost to them.

The purchase looks like a good deal only after we sell the property. Isn't there some way to factor in the difference it makes for when we have to spend the money? The good news is, yes. There is a way to show empirically the best deal. This concept is our old buddy, the time value of money or TVM. Time to get your calculators out again, as I promised.

The first thing you need to determine is the rate of return from your friend's investments. For our example, let's say they are earning 6 percent on their money. We apply that to the difference between the two investments and add those differences to the entire five-year investment to get the actual numbers for analysis.

*For the sake of this chart and simplicity, we consider all monies spent at any time in each year as spent at the beginning of the year.

	Purchase cost	Rental cost	Difference	Investors Safe Rate	Years of Lost Income	Loss of Investment Income
Year 1	$65,303.80	$36,900.00	$28,403.80	x 6%	5	$9,606.89
Year 2	$37,678.80	$31,977.00	$5,701.80	x 6%	4	$1,496.59
Year 3	$37,678.80	$33,415.97	$4,262.83	x 6%	3	$814.27
Year 4	$37,678.80	$34,919.68	$2,759.13	x 6%	2	$341.03
Year 5	$37,678.80	$36,491.07	$1,187.73	x 6%	1	$71.26
					Total	$12,330.04

Let's add this new data to our previous example. This $12,000 plus dollars is additional income if your friend was to rent. For that reason, we add it to the rental side as "cash in".

Buy	Costs	Rent	Costs
Down Payment/Closing Costs	$27,625.00	Move in w/o 1st Month	$6,300.00
Mortgage Payment	$37,678.80	Rent yr 1	$30,600.00
Mortgage Payment	$37,678.80	Rent yr 2	$31,977.00
Mortgage Payment	$37,678.80	Rent yr 3	$33,415.97
Mortgage Payment	$37,678.80	Rent yr 4	$34,919.68
Mortgage Payment	$37,678.80	Rent yr 5	$36,491.07
Sale Price	$405,000.00	Income from investment @ 6%	$12,330.04
Mortgage Payoff after 5yrs	$289,201.00	Total living expense	$161,373.68
Closing Costs	$32,400.00		
Total living expense for 5yrs	$132,616.00		
Living cost to rent	$161,373.68		
Living cost to buy	$132,616.00		
Benefit of Purchase	$28,757.68		

Where this math matters in your life

That had a major impact on the benefit of buying versus renting. It is still better to buy in this example, but not to the extent it was before this calculation. What if your friends read this book and are therefore better investors? What if they earn 12 percent instead of only 6 percent? How much do you think that affect the answer? Let's turn up the lights in our mom's basement, push aside our copy of Dungeons and Dragons while being sure to not knock over our Star Trek commemorative coffee mug, and once again redirect our nerdiness to—you guessed it—a spreadsheet.

	Purchase cost	Rental cost	Difference	Investors Safe Rate	Years of Lost Income	Loss of Investment Income
Year 1	$65,303.80	$36,900.00	$28,403.80	x 12 %	5	$21,653.40
Year 2	$37,678.80	$31,977.00	$5,701.80	x 12 %	4	$3,270.09
Year 3	$37,678.80	$33,415.97	$4,262.83	x 12 %	3	$1,726.14
Year 4	$37,678.80	$34,919.68	$2,759.13	x 12 %	2	$701.92
Year 5	$37,678.80	$36,491.07	$1,187.73	x 12 %	1	$142.53
					Total	$27,494.08

We are doing this exercise so we can start thinking like an investor and to realize the power investing has on the decisions we make.

Buy	Costs	Rent	Costs
Down Payment/Closing Costs	$27,625.00	Move in w/o 1st Month	$6,300.00
Mortgage Payment	$37,678.80	Rent yr 1	$30,600.00
Mortgage Payment	$37,678.80	Rent yr 2	$31,977.00
Mortgage Payment	$37,678.80	Rent yr 3	$33,415.97
Mortgage Payment	$37,678.80	Rent yr 4	$34,919.68
Mortgage Payment	$37,678.80	Rent yr 5	$36,491.07
Sale Price	$405,000.00	Income from investment @ 12 percent	$27,494.08
Mortgage Payoff after 5yrs	$289,201.00	Total living expense	$146,209.64
Closing Costs	$32,400.00		
Total living expense for 5yrs	$132,616.00		
Living cost to rent	$146,209.64		
Living cost to buy	$132,616.00		
Benefit of Purchase	$13,593.64		

That was quite a bit closer, but still there is an advantage to buying over renting. This should show you that the financial benefit of buying a home is quantifiable. So now if you are presented with a financial question, you do not have to just make something up. If someone was to tell you they are not buying because they are earning a lot on their investments and they want to use their down payment money towards those investments, you no longer need to say, "Oh, okay." Instead, you can ask them, "How much are your investments returning to you?" and then run the actual numbers to help them make the best financial decision.

I am trying to sell you on the idea that this book will make you more interesting at parties as well as a better investor—is it working? And if it doesn't make you more interesting, I blame your friends for just being lame.

Analyzing two investments

You are thinking of investing $120,000. One investment choice is a stock that pays an annual dividend of 3 percent. In addition, it has gone up an average of 7 percent per year for the past fifteen years. The other option you are considering is a duplex, which can be purchased for 100,000 but needs $20,000 in repairs. When the work is done, it will be worth $140,000. The market rents are currently $800 per unit. The taxes are $1,200 per year, and insurance is an additional $1,000. Tenants pay for their own utilities. Repairs are $150 a month and you are figuring a $50 a month for vacancy and incidentals. Rents as well as real estate values are anticipated to increase at 3 percent per year. Your net rent? The answer is $14,600 per year. You are planning on holding both of these for five years and then selling.

Now, what's best? It is IRR time.

Stock			Duplex		
Year	Amount	#Times	Year	Amount	#Times
0	-120,000	Purchase	0	-120000	Purchase
1	3,600	1	1	14,600	1
2	3,600	1	2	15,038	1
3	3,600	1	3	15,489	1
4	3,600	1	4	15,954	1
5	171,906.21	1	5	155,545	1
IRR: 9.64 %			IRR: 15.17 %		

Where this math matters in your life

We have a clear winner. Despite the fact that the property we own is only appreciating at a rate of 3 percent versus the 7 percent gains in the stock price, the higher cash flow generated from rents makes the duplex the better use of funds.

Chapter 15

Taxes

I'm proud to be paying taxes in the United States. The only thing is, I could be just as proud for half the money.

— Arthur Godfrey

Taxes. They're evil! On to the next chapter—fine, we can do some more details I guess. Taxes are an expense. They are the last thing removed before profit. It is like having a silent partner who splits profits with you, that is, if that partner is a mobster you are paying for protection. Finding ways to minimize taxes is something every investor needs to do because let's be honest, paying more taxes doesn't really help anyone that much, especially not the person paying them. So, we are going to focus on things that get our Uncle Sam's grubby mitts a little further out of our pockets.

First let's clarify some terms. There are two terms used to describe something that lowers your tax bill: tax credit, and a tax deduction. Tax credits are the best, which is probably why they are so rare. A tax credit is an amount that is subtracted from the total amount of tax that you owe. Let's show a simple example of a credit at work.

Let's say you earn $100,000. You have $28,000 in total tax liability (what you owe) and no deductions, but you do have a $3,000 tax credit.

Income	**$100,00**
Total Taxable Income	**$100,00**
Effective Tax Rate	28 %
Tax Liability (Sad Times)	**$28,000**
Tax Credit	$3,000
Check to IRS (Not Quite as Sad Times)	**$25,000**

A tax deduction on the other hand is an amount removed from your income before taxes are calculated. In other words, with a deduction you only receive your effective tax rate's portion of the deduction off of your tax bill. Let's use the same example above, but switch from a **credit,** to a **deduction.** It looks something like this:

Income	**$100,00**
Tax Deduction	**$3,000**
Total Taxable Income	$97,000
Effective Tax Rate	**28 %**
Tax Liability (Even More Sad Times)	**$27,160**
Check to IRS (Just as Sad Times)	**$27,160**

So, as you can see that the tax credit makes a much bigger difference on the ever-painful check to our buddies at the IRS. Let's look at some of the tax advantages specific to owning real estate.

> *Why does a slight tax increase cost you two hundred dollars and a substantial tax cut save you thirty cents?*
>
> — PEG BRACKEN

Tax advantages of real estate

One of the incentives the tax code allows for is making the interest portion of your home mortgage "tax deductible". (They do this to encourage home purchases.) This functions in the same way that a business can deduct their expenses. To make it clearer, let's look at what happens to your taxes when you rent.

Let's say you earn $100,000, you have no deductions, and an effective tax rate of 28 percent. Your median yearly rent is $33,480.74, and your real cost for the rental must factor when you have to pay rent, which is after you have paid the taxes on your income. This is what it looks like for our buy versus rent customers from last chapter.

Income	$100,00.00
Total Taxable Income	$100,00.00
Effective Tax Rate	28 %
Check to IRS (Sad Times)	$28,000.00
Money Left After Uncle Sam's Cut (Actual income)	$72,000.00
Median Rent for 5 Years	$33,480.74
Money Left Over to Live on Yearly	$38,519.26
Number of Years Renting	5
Total Money Left Over to Live on After 5 Years	$192,596.28

With a purchase, we are able to deduct the interest that we pay each month on our mortgage. We are not be able to deduct the principal we borrowed, but that interest deduction will be very helpful in the early part of the mortgage. The reason for this is that the majority of the payments at the beginning of a mortgage are almost entirely interest. As you move further along, the payments stay the same, but the portion of the payment going toward the principal diminution (to diminish) is greater and the interest is less. So back to our five-year buy versus rent customers.

The Government that robs Peter to pay Paul can always depend upon the support of Paul.

-GEORGE BERNARD SHAW

Taxes

Once again, they earn $100,000, they only have a mortgage interest deduction and their effective tax rate is 28 percent.

Income	$100,00.00
Median Interest Portion of Mortgage Payment	$16,014.17
Total Taxable Income	$83,985.83
Effective Tax Rate	28 %
Check to IRS (Still Sad Times)	$23,516.03
Money Left After Uncle Sam's Cut (Actual Income)	$76,483.97
Mortgage Payment	$37,678.80
Money Left Over to Live on	$38,805.17
Number of Years Renting	5
Total Money Left Over to Live on After 5 Years	$194,025.84

So, that is not a whole lot, is it? Actually, it is. The higher mortgage payment was already calculated into the calculation we did that took into account the home purchase performing at a net positive of $41,087.72. Now to accurately account for the tax benefit, we need to add the difference in the tax bills—aka our check to Uncle Sam.

Check to IRS Rental	$28,000.00
Check to IRS Purchase	$23,516.03
Benefit to Purchase in Taxes	$4,483.97
Number of Years of Investment	5
Benefit to Purchase Over 5 Years	$22,419.85

This benefit needs to be added to the positive side of the buy option as we have done below.

Buy	Costs	Rent	Costs
Down Payment/Closing Costs	$27,625.00	Move in w/o 1st Month	$6,300.00
Mortgage Payment	$37,678.80	Rent yr 1	$30,600.00
Mortgage Payment	$37,678.80	Rent yr 2	$31,977.00
Mortgage Payment	$37,678.80	Rent yr 3	$33,415.97
Mortgage Payment	$37,678.80	Rent yr 4	$34,919.68
Mortgage Payment	$37,678.80	Rent yr 5	$36,491.07
Sale Price	$405,000.00	Total living expense	$173,703.72
Mortgage Payoff after 5yrs	$289,201.00		
Closing Costs	$32,400.00		
Total living expense for 5yrs	$132,616.00		
Tax Benefit/Interest Deduction	$22,419.85		
Living cost to rent	$173,703.72		
Living cost to buy	$110,196.15		
Benefit of Purchase	**$63,507.57**		

There may be many benefits to home ownership, but as you can see, the financial ones can be very compelling. Investors also get some special tax advantages, none more so than those that invest in real estate.

Tax brackets

But before we do that, let's clear up a little confusion on **tax brackets**. Tax bracket confusion is heard all the time. People say, "Oh if I make more money, it will only push me into a higher tax bracket." They say this like they do not want the extra money! What needs to be understood is this: Only the amount exceeding the threshold of the tax bracket you are currently in is taxed at the higher level.

Taxes

What is the difference between a taxidermist and a tax collector? The taxidermist takes only your skin.

—— MARK TWAIN

Here is a brief example (not using real tax brackets but hypothetical ones.) If you were getting taxed at 25 percent on your first $75,000, this equals $18,750 in taxes. Anything over that $75,000 pushes you to the 28 percent tax bracket. Let's say you had the unadulterated gall to earn $95,000, what would happen? You would pay 25 percent on the first 75,000 or $18,750, and pay 28 percent on the 20,000 over that you earned, or $5,600. The total tax bill would be $24,350 —*ouch!* It is still worth it to earn more money, but you have to realize that you do not get to keep all of that nice raise you received; you only get a piece because Uncle Sam wants his taste too, and he will make you an offer you can't refuse to get it. (Hint, it involves an orange jump suit.) In other words, any raise for you is a raise for the government too.

Let's look at this in an easier format. Note: For the sake of this example, we say that the lowest tax bracket is 25 percent and all income below $75,000 is taxed at that rate.

Income	$75,000.00
Tax rate	25 %
Total taxes	$18,750.00
Total Income @ 75k After Taxes	$56,250.00
Higher Income	$95,000.00
Tax rates on the first $75,000.00	25 % x $75,000.00 = $18,750.00
Tax rates on the next $20,000.00	28 % x $20,000.00 = $5,600.00
Total taxes	$24,350.00
Total Income @ 95k After Taxes	$70,650.00

This is actually how the graduated tax system we have works in this country. There are more levels, but basically, as you make more than a certain amount, you move into a higher tax bracket. There is a schedule that tells you what the maximum tax is for each level. As you move up in levels, you add this to whatever tax you owe on the portion of your income that is in the highest tax bracket in which your income places you.

By way of clarification, let's look at the example above. The maximum you could earn in the 25 percent bracket was $75,000. This means the maximum tax you would have to pay if you earn more than that would be $18,750 plus whatever you would owe on your income over $75,000. So, all you would really need to do is calculate the amount you owe on the income over that threshold (the 20,000 at 28 percent that we calculated at $5,600), and then add the $18,750. This gives you your total **tax liability**.

All of this is done to clarify in your mind that going into a higher tax bracket does not mean you earn less money. It only means you get to keep less of what you earn as your income increases. This is important because it makes you realize that you need to know what tax bracket you are in. If you earn a lot, you may be paying north of 35 percent. So every additional dollar you earn actually only translates into 65 cents of money to you.

Profit, remember, is a cost of doing business. It is the incentive that drives people to take risk. Anything we can do to improve the incentive tips the balance in our favor. The reality is that there are many types of investments out there and investors are always looking for the lowest risk to highest reward ratio. Luckily for those in real estate, there are special incentives particular to real estate we can use to tip this balance scale in our favor.

Depreciation

The main difference between the depreciation that happens for most things compared to real estate is that depreciation is complete nonsense for real estate. With one brief exception (the burst of the real estate bubble), the prices of real estate, which is properly maintained, do not go down. This is especially true over a longer time period because there are occasional short term pricing corrections in any market. In reality, however, the depreciation of real estate is actually a tax benefit given by the government to incentivize the purchase of real estate. It does not reflect an actual devaluation of the property. So, how does it work?

For starters, there is an exception (isn't there always?). You are allowed to depreciate improvements but not land. What does this mean? It means that

Taxes

when you purchase a property, a portion of the purchase price is allocated to land value and a portion is allocated to the improvement(s). The portion that is allocated to land cannot be depreciated at all. They know that dirt does not lose value over time and so they do not let you depreciate your dirt—sorry to all of you "wanna-be" land barons out there.

So, what about the non-land portion? What exactly constitutes an improvement? Improvements are pretty much anything you add to the land. The obvious first thing we think of would be a building, but a swimming pool, fence, driveway, etc. can all be considered improvements. The percentage of purchase price allocated to land versus improvements is going to depend upon the specific property type being purchased. Often your accountant will have an industry standard for the specific type of property you are buying. For some types of investment property, a normal allocation might be 80 percent to improvements and 20 percent to land, for another type it might be 70/30. The key thing here is to make sure you are able to back these numbers up to the IRS if they come a-knocking.

So, if we were to buy a property for $1,000,000 purchase price (**total cost basis**), and use an 80/20 improvement to land ratio, we can depreciate $800,000 of that purchase price. (This is known as your **cost basis for depreciation**.) So, do we get to write off all $800,000 that year? No, not even close. You would be depreciating this property for a long, long time. How long? It depends. (Don't you hate that?)

If the property is residential, it can be depreciated over twenty seven and one half years, and if it is non-residential, it can be depreciated over thirty-nine years. I guess they figure the residential buildings get their butts kicked by the tenants and therefore go down in value quicker (just a theory). So, what does that mean? Well if our property above is residential, we get to deduct $1/27.5^{th}$ of $800,000 ($29,090.91) each year from our income. If the property is non-residential, then we get to deduct $1/39^{th}$ of $800,000 ($20,512.82) from our income each year. Taking depreciation is not an option: You must take it every year until there is no basis left in the improvements.

This tax benefit is not a gift. The government is going to want the money back. That makes it only a tax deferment, but something is better than nothing. Plus, you get the use of the money while it is deferred (think TVM).

So, how does the government get the money back, you may ask? They get it back when you sell. They charge you a special tax rate on the difference between your **book value** (the current value of the property on your books after removing the depreciation each year) and the original purchase price. That special tax is called **cost recovery tax**, and at the time of writing this book, it is at 25 percent. Any profit that you make over the initial purchase price is taxed at a different rate, called the **capital gains rate**. If the property is held for more than a year, then you pay the long term capital gains rate, which at the time of writing this book is at 15 percent. Short term capital gains rates are much higher, as high as 39 percent plus. This is something to keep in mind if you think "flipping" may be your calling.

Let's look at our deal from above. We bought a residential property for $1,000,000 and are using an 80/20 allocation for depreciation. We hold the property for ten years, and depreciate it by $29,090.91, for a total depreciation of $290,909.10. We then sell the property for $1.4 million (figuring on a 3.42 percent increase in the market value each year). So, what does that look like? For this one we use a chart.

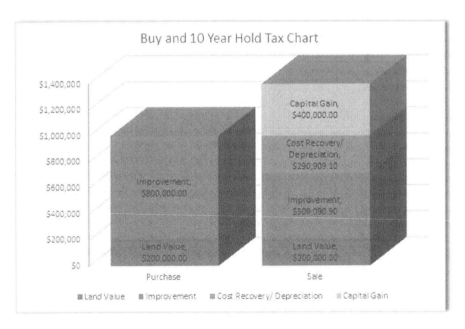

Taxes

Let's calculate the tax benefit. First we need to see what the benefit of the depreciation was on a yearly basis. Let's say that the investor's nominal tax rate is 35 percent, and if the property generates $80,000 in NOI, what is our yearly tax savings? If we did not have depreciation, the investor would have to pay $28,000 in taxes based upon the property income ($80,000 at 35 percent). But if we subtract our yearly depreciation amount from our income ($80,000-$29,090.91), we get only $50,909.09 that we have to pay taxes on. This equals only $17,531.85 in taxes we have to pay ($50,909.09 at 35 percent), and leaves us with a NOI of $62,468.15. This is a yearly savings of $10,468.15. For the ten-year hold period of the property, this equals $104,681.50. Not bad right? That is more than 10 percent of the original purchase price.

We now know what we saved on a yearly basis, so let's take a look at how the government gets paid back. We have depreciated over ten years a total of $290,909.10. When we sell the property, we are going to have to pay a tax of 25 percent on that amount, which is equal to $72,727.28. That is still less than the $104,681.50 savings we had. In fact, it is $31,954.22 better.

Gonna go all infomercial on you now:

But wait there's more! Can you guess what it is? Think TVM. We had the use of that $104,681.50, or at least $10,468.15 each year. What if we invested that money? This sounds like a job for a compounding man. (We just have to get him out of his meth lab for a minute.) For the sake of this example, we say that these funds could be invested at 10 percent. The actual value of those yearly savings invested at 10 percent is $166,835.35. This means that if we had invested the tax savings, we would have $166,835.35 and only have to pay back $72,727.28, which leaves a net gain of $94,108.07. Gosh, ain't real estate grand? That is a huge benefit, which translates to an additional 9 percent return on the initial investment.

Let's continue though and look at the rest of the tax consequence for this property. We bought the property for $1,000,000 and are selling it for $1,400,000. We have to pay cost recovery of $72,727.28 on the portion of the property basis we depreciated, but we also need to calculate the taxes on our gain over the initial basis of the property. The gain in capital that we have will be taxed at the—you guessed it—capital gains rate. We have a $400,000 capital gain, and since the tax rate is 15 percent, we have to pay an additional

The Roadmap to the American Dream

$60,000 in taxes. This means our total tax liability for the sale is $132,727.28. The actual profit after taxes is $267,272.72. If we add back in our net gain from before, however, we have a gain of $361,380.79. That's a lot better.

Lastly let's run an IRR with and without taxes so you can see the effect that taxes play on investments and their returns. For the sake of simplicity, let's say that the rents and expenses stay the same and the NOI is fixed at $80,000 per year.

Purchase Price	-$1,000,000
NOI Yearly before tax for 10yrs.	$80,000 per year
Sale Price before tax	$1,400,000.00
IRR w/o Tax	10.46 %t

Now let's do the same thing with our after tax numbers.

Purchase Price	-$1,000,000
NOI Yearly before tax	$80,000 per year
Taxes on NOI	-$17,531.85
NOI Yearly after tax	$62,468.15 per year after tax
Sale Price before tax	$1,400,000.00
Cost Recovery Tax $209,909.10 @ 25 percent	-$72,727.28
Capital Gains Tax $400,000.00 @ 15 percent	-$60,000.00
Total Taxes on Sale	-$132,727.28
Sale Price after tax	$1,262,272.72
IRR with Tax	8.05 %

And you thought you were making 10.5 percent returns? This is what an after tax calculation of a real estate investment looks like, and what it does is—it makes you sad. Even though taxes took a big chunk, this is still actually going to look better than another type of investment because of the deferred taxes from depreciation. We could do the same property with the benefit of financing, and look at how leverage and the mortgage interest deduction might affect these numbers (spoiler alert, they would be better), but we have done enough numbers for today.

Chapter 16

Basic things to know when buying real estate

*It takes considerable knowledge just to realize
the extent of your own ignorance*

- Thomas Sowell

Picking an agent

If you are not a real estate agent, you probably want to find one or a few, depending on how much you plan on buying. As an agent myself, I can tell you that the standard to get your license in most states involves fogging up a mirror and showing proof that you have had a pulse sometime within the past 6 months (and I think there is a waiver for this last item). So basically, agents run the gamut. You have some good, smart, talented ones who will save you money, and you have a lot who are probably at their best holding the door open for you and not much more than that. To pick an agent, you want to know they are, at the least, full time agents (not doing it as a hobby) and they are familiar with the market. You are an investor, so finding an agent who knows what you should be looking for is always a good idea.

To check an agent out, you should let them know what type of minimum return you are looking for, and a price range you want to buy in. If you are planning on buying to hold the property and rent it, then the agent should know that. When they show you properties to buy, they should also be telling you what rents to expect.

Based upon the rent numbers, figure out what your net rent is going to be, and then run the simple formula for cap rate to see if the agent is showing you properties that match your investment goals. If not, don't be afraid to ask them why. If they tell you your goals are unrealistic in the market, then there are two possibilities: One, they are lazy and don't want to look for properties for you. Solution: Find a new agent. Or two, the agent is correct. Solution: Your investment return goal needs to be adjusted, or you need to allocate your capital to a different type of investment (buy something else). An agent who tells you the truth and knows what they are talking about is a surprisingly rare commodity.

Remember, they only get paid when you buy, so they are always going to encourage you to purchase. This is a good thing to think about regarding all the people you choose to work with: Where are their interests? Are they aligned with yours? The answer often is no, but that's okay. You just need to be aware of this, and adjust yourself accordingly.

My attorney's goal, for example, is to point out and advise me to avoid all risks. If he could, he would wrap me and my company in bubble wrap and then throw us in a shipping container full of mattresses. My goal, however is to make money. Taking on risk is part of making that happen. I have made a lot of money going against my attorney's advice on some deals. I have also lost money on deals where I didn't listen. In summary, I listen to what my real estate agent says, and I listen to what my attorney says, weigh their advice, and then make my decision.

Picking an area

You have to figure out the type of property and the area you are going to be comfortable with. Here is the sort of lousy part: The worse the area, the better the rate of return typically. This is because the home prices are less in uglier neighborhoods. Yes, the rents are lower too, but not proportionally so.

In other words, your money earns a lower rate of return in a better neighborhood. I invest in single-family homes and condos in poorer areas because I like a high rate of return. I also like to spend a little more money to make my homes very nice so they rent quickly to good tenants.

A lot of people I know would not invest in those areas. They prefer condos because they don't have to worry about outside maintenance, they like nicer areas because they think there will be better appreciation (we discuss this more in a bit), and they think that tenants in nicer buildings will be better rent payers (not as much as you might think). In other words, they want a less "hands on" type of investment. They are willing to pay for it with a lower rate of return, or someplace they can drive their friends by to say, "Yeah, I own three units in that building."

It is true: You are probably not going to get your air conditioning unit stolen in a penthouse unit on the beach. At the same time, you will have to tie up significantly more capital for that ocean front condo. You are going to need to decide what sorts of places you are comfortable visiting to check on. Maybe you want to choose to use a property manager so the day-to-day issues are off your plate. Take the time to think through the type of portfolio you want to build, and then have the agent we hired in the previous section start sending you properties in those areas.

Rising markets versus declining markets

It is great to have a plan, but then life happens. You may want to own a portfolio of single-family homes, but the market for them is very tight. That means there are very few for sale and the ones that are for sale are priced too high to get a good return. The solution is to adjust. You look for good market opportunities wherever they are. If they are not quite in your ideal market but the price is good, it is still probably a good deal. The important thing to be aware of is the market. In my current market, if you were to look at mid to high price condos, you would think you were in a real estate crash. There are thousands of units available with very long times on market. For this reason, prices are starting to fall there. But if you look at single family home especially those in the mid to low price range, you would think it was a real estate boom. People routinely offering more than asking price and still being outbid. This is great if you own single- family homes and want to sell, but not so great if you are looking to buy.

So how do you handle changing markets? You do the research to see what type of market and sub market you are dealing with. The market for me currently in my area is stable overall, but the sub markets of mid to high price condos and low to mid-price homes are very different. That is why it is important to drill down into the numbers. If I was buying a unit in a large condo building I would want to see not just what sold in the area, but also, specifically, what the sub market of that building looks like. Maybe there is something special about the building that makes it better or more likely worse than its neighbors. You handle varying markets by "analyzing value".

More than you ever wanted to know about analyzing value

The best way to tell what something is worth is to find something similar that someone has recently paid for, and then compare it to the unit you are thinking of buying. You also need to check the current competition on market. Most folks who start investing in real estate begin with residential units, such as single family homes, condos, or town homes. You can determine a good opportunity by looking at the local MLS (multiple listing service) or even some online resources to see the available homes for sale and most recent six months closed sales.

You want to look at the sale price of the closed sales (not the asking price) as this tells you two things: What people have paid for similar properties in the same area and how much you can expect an appraiser to appraise the property for. Why does that matter? If you intend to hold the property and take advantage of leverage, your bank is going to do an appraisal to determine how much they lend to you. If you intend to flip properties, the person buying it is probably going to need to get a loan. Now guess who is going to tell his lender how much it is worth? The appraiser. The way the appraiser determines value is by looking at three available and three closed sales in the area. We try to determine value the same way so that we have good evidence to back up our value.

Basic things to know when buying real estate

It is important to understand that appraisers use similar properties, and then make adjustments to them based on whether or not they are better or worse than the property they are appraising (called the "subject property" or just "subject"). This method of determining value is called the "sales approach" to value. The properties they use for comparison are called "comparables" or "comps". If your property has three bedrooms and one of the comps has four, they try to determine the average difference in price people pay for a fourth bedroom and then subtract that from the sale price of the comparable to make it more like the subject property. It is a little confusing, but basically, if the comp is better—subtract, and if the comp is inferior— add (I use the acronyms CBS and CIA to remember these). Also important to note, the appraiser never makes adjustments to the subject, only to the comps in order to make them as similar to the subject as possible.

Speculation versus value

> *"The individual investor should act consistently as an investor and not as a speculator."*
>
> - BEN GRAHAM

Every investor who ever lost money in real estate has said, "I think this property is going to be worth double in 5 years." Some people make money by buying in areas they think will improve, but let's be very clear, this is called gambling or speculation. When speculating, there are too many factors outside of your control to have certainty that your investment will pay off. Value investing in real estate, however, looks at the rental income the property can generate to determine the price.

In my market, there was huge speculation in the condo market and dozens of new condo towers went up. Thousands of units got added to a market that was super hot. Everyone was buying condos, and in a year, could sell them and make a nice profit. But there was a problem. This was a bubble, and just like a game of musical chairs, the one holding the property is the one without a chair when the music stops and loses. "Well, can't they rent these units? So, glad you asked. The average cap rate on these units due to the inflated prices is under 3 percent. Their mortgage interest rates are higher than that.

More bad news for our buddies who bought the condos: The condo fees for these buildings are very high, as is the vacancy rate. So, *if* the unit is rented, you earn less than 3 percent. If it is vacant for anytime at all, you are losing a lot of money. If they can't sell them, they rent them, right? But there's an issue when everybody gets the same bright idea at the same time. Vacancies are so high because of the large number of folks who can't sell their units. You have a ton of units available to rent, and if landlords actually want their units to be rented, they are pressured to lower their prices.

Why did this happened? The decision to buy was a speculation play and not a value one. There is always a market to sell a good cash flow, which is why value investing is safer. This is not the case with speculation. If the market does not go up, you are in deep doo-doo. Value properties still appreciate. Maybe they are not quite as sexy or cool as the "spec" plays, but you know what is cool and sexy? Making money! You can make money doing speculation, but it is a play for folks who really know what they are doing. Even folks like developers who do it for a living still go broke all the time. You know what is the exact opposite of cool and sexy? Losing money!

Your team

Ok, so we found a property that we think is selling for less than market. We now need to check for defects or repairs. If you do not have the skill to do this, you should get a home inspector, or buy a good bottle of scotch for the general contractor who moved in down the street and ask him to look. The important thing is to try to get a handle on your total cost to purchase and get the asset performing. Early on it can be tough to find good contractors, therefore, you need to try to find a very solid deal to make up for the real risk that you might make mistakes. If you make a mistake and only make 8 percent instead of the

14 percent you were hoping for, I've got news for you: You made money, got experience, and learned some things to avoid—that's a win in my book.

Don't get discouraged by mistakes, learn from them. People take on huge losses to go to college without a guarantee they will be paid back. Yet, they do so singing the soundtrack of "Happy, Happy, Joy, Joy"(sadly a Ren and Stimpy reference—I'm not proud that I know that). I see people actually getting upset that they invested and are making money, but less than they thought they would. My conclusion once again is that people are freaking nuts.

Assembling a good team of contractors and handymen are going to be critical to a real estate investor. Properties have repairs and things break. Finding folks to fix them quickly and inexpensively keeps your tenants and your checkbook happy (happy checkbooks make for happy investors). One of the best ways to get good people is by "theft". Somebody mentions they have a good "guy" for something, so ask for their name, number, email, whatever you can get. Good contractors are worth their weight in gold (unless they are really skinny or fat, and we would need to see what the price of gold is too, I suppose. Let's just go with they are really important).

How much to pay

Once we know what we are buying the house for and have assessed the initial repairs, we can add these together to get our initial acquisition cost. We now use rental comps of what is available on the market and what has rented on the market in order to determine our potential gross rent. From there we need to figure out taxes and insurance, and subtract those from our annual rent. What is left is our net rent, which we then compare to our total acquisition cost to get our rate of return. It is a great idea to use a real estate agent to get the comps and for guidance on how to figure out taxes and insurance amounts.

A good agent can be a huge asset. If you have the time to do it, getting your own real estate license is not a bad idea either, but certainly not mandatory. Even if you get your license and never use it, you will learn more about the rules specific to your area that apply to your investments.

When comps don't exist

Often with larger commercial properties, there are not comparable sales to compare a potential purchase with. For this reason, we use the "income approach," which is to figure out the normal market rate of return for the property type you are considering, and then base your offer on that. In other words, if you are considering buying an older office building, let's say class C, (as this is how the industry differentiates between levels of building finishes) and the typical class C buildings in your market is selling at a price that gives the buyer a 9 percent rate of return (cap rate), then your final purchase price should be no higher than an amount that leaves you a 9 percent profit.

This is done by taking the NOI and dividing it by the cap rate. If we assume a 9 cap for the office building and it has an annual net income of $95,000, we would divide the $95,000 by .09 to get a market value of $1,055,555.56. So as long as you do not pay more than that amount, you earn at least 9 percent. For every dollar less you pay, you increase your rate of return.

One major caveat with commercial real estate is that each specific type is unique. It is not often that you see an investor with multiple different property types in their portfolio. If they have more than one, it is usually residential and something else. This is because the knowledge it takes to run a shopping center, for example, is very specific and different from running a self-storage property. There are often items that only experience can really help you through, for instance, where there are unique types of leases, certain preferable types of tenant mixes, parking issues, etc.

Normally an investor finds one type of real estate investment they like and sticks with it. They look for opportunities only in that one property type. Obviously, this means they miss deals in different property types, but it focuses their skills and allows them to be very good at making the properties they do buy efficient money-makers.

Chapter 17

Buying Securities

The four most dangerous words in investing: 'this time it's different.'

- Sir John Templeton

Wow, ok—how do I provide advice on buying securities? That's stocks, bonds, futures, and a bunch of other stuff you are probably not ready to mess with. Not something like Blackwater, as I'm sure some of you were thinking. Okay, that was obscure. Blackwater is a security company so buying them would not be considered securities unless they were publicly traded, but again I digress.

Now, you really can't take a crash course and jump into the stock market and be the next Warren Buffet. It just doesn't work like that. You may have a brother's wife's cousin who had a hot stock pick he picked up in the men's room and made a boatload of cash. That's not investing, it's gambling, and just like in Vegas, if you keep playing and you don't know what you are doing the house always wins. Therefore, what we are going to talk about are strategies to invest, not how to pick stocks or racehorses or using chaos theory to pick the winning lotto numbers (I know I just made a physics major smile).

Step 1: Portfolio diversification

What the hell is this? In simple terms—crap happens. You can do all the research in the world and pick a great company or companies, and still something unforeseen can crash your sector of the market or the entire market, and you get crushed. Just because Apple stock has performed exceptionally well and you really love Apple, one day Tim Cook may take over as CEO—oh wait—that already happened. I kid. We really don't know where Mr. Cook is going to take Apple over his tenure as CEO, but that doesn't change the point.

Diversification is more than just having many different stocks in your portfolio. It is also about buying assets in sectors that are unaffected by each other's movements, or better yet, which have an inverse relationship. This means that when one goes down, the other goes up. Think about being invested in a tow truck company during a recession. People are losing money (not cool), stocks are going down (even more not cool), but as people lose their vehicles to repossession, your towing company is going gangbusters (a little morbid, but hey, kind of cool). Now, you may be thinking what's the benefit of that? It's a zero sum game isn't it? The answer is no, not if you rebalance on a regular basis. Okay, time for some basic math—eeew

My simple portfolio
Small Cap stocks (little companies): $10,000
big return, higher risk

AAA Rated Bonds (we discussed these as a hedge earlier): $8,000
lowest risk to return ratio in our portfolio

Blue Chip Stocks (the big boys, your *Apple* stock is here): $15,000
Medium Risk, medium return

Bill's *Tow Trucks* (inverse bet on the market): $6,000
AKA hedge

Assume these returns: 15 percent, 4 percent, 9 percent, -2 percent

Buying Securities

At this point some of you might be saying, "Crap, drop the tow truck company and invest in small caps. I see green." This is wrong, unless you're gambling again, and as I said, we're not in Las Vegas. This is because we don't know what's going to happen next year.

Okay, so the math goes like this for year one: Beginning Balance: $39,000

Small cap: 10,000 x 1.15 = $11,500
Bonds: 8,000 x 1.04 = $8,320
Large Cap: 15,000 x 1.09 = $16,350
Hedge: 6,000 x .98 = $5,880

Total Portfolio Value: $42,050: wooohoo that's a 7.82 percent return, not bad. Could have been 15 percent but again, we're not in Vegas.

Ouch, year two returns are like this: -4 percent, 5 percent, -3 percent, 12 percent: Beginning Balance $42,050

Small cap: $11,500 x .96 = $11,040
Bonds: $8,320 x 1.05 = $8,736
Large Cap: $16,350 x .97 =$15,859.50
Hedge: $5,880 x 1.12 = $6,585.60

Total Portfolio Value: $42,221.10 hey our hedging worked—I was worried for a minute. However, 4.13 percent two-year return is not so great. Now let's imagine if we used rebalancing

Rebalancing: Changing your portfolio mix based on a predetermined percentage of portfolio

In other words, we want to have the same asset mix by percentage at all times, and we do this by buying and selling assets on a structured timeline (every quarter, every year). Basically, we have a plan. In this case, that plan is: Small Cap: 25.5 percent, Bonds: 20.5 percent, Large Cap: 38.5 percent, Hedge: 15.5 percent

Small cap: 10,000 x 1.15 = $11,500 or 27.35 percent
Bonds: 8,000 x 1.04 = $8,320 or 19.79 percent
Large Cap: 15,000 x 1.09 = $16,350 or 38.88 percent
Hedge: 6,000 x .98 = $5,880 or 13.98 percent
Total Portfolio Value: $42,050

Crap! Our portfolio is out of balance so let's do a little selling and buying to get back in line without ratios.

-4 percent, 5 percent, -3 percent, 12 percent:
Year two rebalanced portfolio numbers:

Small cap: $42,050 x 25.5 percent = $10,722.75 x .96 = $10,293.36
Bonds: $42,050 x 20.5 percent = $8,620.25 x 1.05 = $9,051.26
Large Cap: $42,050 x 38.5 percent = $16,189.25 x .97 = $15,703.57
Hedge: $42,050 x 15.5 percent = $6,517.75 x 1.12 = $7,299.88
Total Portfolio Value: $42,348.07

Granted, our rebalanced portfolio only scored a few hundred dollars higher return, but in a bad economy. Think of the difference if your small cap stocks had tanked 35 percent (not that we've ever seen that happen…)

There are a couple of key points here that we are trying to get across:

Don't go all in

This is something to keep in mind no matter what you are investing in, but I think it's especially important when dealing with equities. Remember, you are not an expert and even the experts make mistakes when picking their racehorses—I mean—their stocks. There is a reason why most investing is done in mutual funds. Well actually, there are quite a few reasons, including ease of access, low initial capital, and easy diversification (lifestyle funds). Primarily, however, it is because you are busy. You work and don't have time to search through the vast amounts of available data necessary to correctly pick a balanced stock portfolio where you can avoid the downside risk of investing in your one "sure thing." So as I was saying, don't go all in. Don't take too large of a portion of your hard earned cash and put it into one or two stocks because you like the new drone that GoPro just put out (ouch, recalls are no fun). Yes, you can make a ton of money if your bet pays out, but the risk is almost always too great.

Let me tell you what I do. I have a slush account, which is about 5 percent of my investing portfolio. I manage it myself even though the rest of my equity portfolio is managed professionally. This is my gambling money. This is where I buy calls on stocks that I think might go up in the near future. This is where I buy the penny stock my buddy told me was going to explode and turn me into a gazillionaire (none of them have paid out yet). This is where I put it on double zero. This is how I get my Vegas out. I get to have a little fun and I get to learn about the market without endangering the bulk of my capital.

Remember, even though all investing in general lives by the rule "no risk, no reward", it also lives primarily in the land of risk mitigation. As you get more knowledgeable in the area you want to focus your investing in, maybe then you can up that amount. But to start, play it safe. Money doesn't grow on trees.

Have a plan and stick to it

The most dangerous thing you can do while investing in equities is chasing returns. OMG, Amazon is killing it, I should buy more!! How many people were completely killed like that during the dot.com bubble? I know you love cats, but that doesn't mean investing 90 percent of your capital in pets.com is a good idea. Of course, it's also the hardest thing not to do, which is the reason the first thing we discussed was diversification and portfolio rebalancing.

Having a plan that allows for a diversified portfolio with consistent rebalancing greatly reduces the chance that you will suffer a dramatic loss in a volatile market. Unfortunately, it also greatly reduces your chance of striking oil with your expert stock picking technique (dartboard, blindfold, Ouija board, scotch). However, unless you are extremely well-versed in the market as well as the risks associated with your picks, it is still the best way to move forward and not get caught chasing returns.

Professional portfolio management or self-managed

I've been told that this section should have gone before diversification, but I disagreed and so here it is. Unless you understand diversification and rebalancing and why people invest in things like lifecycle funds, you can't really decide how you want to manage your money. All right, so to make this very important decision, we first must get a few things out in the open.

First, your insurance salesman is not a stock broker or an investment specialist. I've sold insurance and variable insurance products (insurance policies that buy stocks), and they are great products to be used in the correct part of your portfolio. I find this part of the finance industry slightly unnerving, however, because most insurance salesman or financial planners (as they like to be called) know very little about the markets and how to invest. Yet they still ask their clients (insurance clients) to give them their investment portfolios so they can invest it in mutual funds that pay an upfront commission. Then they set it and forget it until your next insurance review comes around, where they suggest you switch to some other mutual fund (chasing returns) and make another commission. This isn't active management and it's not worth paying for.

Second, no successful investment manager wants your $10,000. This doesn't mean that you must self-manage if all you have to invest is $10,000. It just means that if someone is willing to personally manage your investment portfolio of $10,000, they probably have no idea what they are doing. You would be better served just finding a low cost diversified mutual fund from a major company like Fidelity, and invest it yourself. I'm not trying to ruffle any feathers here, and your buddy Marv from college who wants to manage your money very well might be the next Warren Buffet. However, for everyone else who's buddy is not the next Oracle of Omaha, this advice holds water.

Finally, your mutual fund is not going to set the world on fire. By this I mean that investing in mutual funds is great; it is an excellent way to diversify risk while still making money on a fairly liquid investment. But they are not your golden ticket to riches and early retirement. The managers of most mutual funds are trying to attain solid returns with the minimal risk allotted for their specific fund profile. Their benchmark for success is to beat the market (S&P 500). So generally, you shouldn't expect returns of no greater than 7-10 percent, which is, of course, not setting the world on fire.

Now keeping those key points in mind; let's discuss how to make a decision on what to do with your money. In general, there are two different paths here, self-managed investing and using a professional portfolio manager. It's seems like a rather simplistic response but if you go down all the bunny trails it really leads to those two things. You ask the same question you ask for really every investment decision: Do I do it myself or hire someone to do it for me. Now, just to be clear, both paths still start with self-managed mutual funds. Why is this? Well, I am going on the assumption that you are just getting started and therefore do not have enough capital to gain the interest of a professional money manager who is worth using. Chances are you also probably do not have the experience or knowledge to truly self-manage just yet, so to be safe, you should have a large percentage of your assets in mutual funds anyway.

Getting started

Assuming you agree with me— that you know very little about the market and aren't cash rich—what type of mutual fund should you start with (dartboard, blindfold, Ouija board, scotch)? We've been here before. I say, start simple, you need to invest and you need to learn at the same time.

Index funds (funds that basically mirror major indexes like the S&P 500) are usually low cost, and since most fund managers don't beat the S&P 500 anyway, they are a pretty good bet. I once asked my coworker when I was working as a financial planner (insurance salesman) many years ago, what he was invested in. He told me he had money in three funds, an index fund, a bond fund, and a fund that bought mortgage backed securities. I found this incredibly interesting because

I had sat in on many meetings with him and his clients were never in index funds. They were always in small cap venture fund X and large cap dividend fund Y.

So, why would his clients not be in the same thing? It boils down to two things. The index fund paid almost zero commission, and if all he was doing was investing his client in a fund that mirrored the market, how could he justify his fee? It is telling, however, that he had his money in a fund that simply matched the market. It's a time thing, and he wasn't a stock broker or professional money manager who knew the ins and outs of the market. But he did know the same thing you now know: Be diversified (S&P index fund), use downside protection (bond fund, mortgage backed securities fund), and then rebalance on a regular basis. Remember, if you are interested in trading stocks and want to gamble a bit, use a slush fund and not your main piece of capital.

Now that your feet are wet

The point of getting started is to do just that. It's to get started investing in the market while you continue to learn, but let me repeat: *Continue to learn* about the market and where you are investing your hard-earned dollars. Doing this allows you to make the final decision regarding self-managed or professional management. That decision comes down to one key factor, the factor that decides everything—time. Yes, time is the ultimate factor here. You need to make a decision as to what type of an investor you want to be.

> **Tip:** *Let me make it perfectly clear. You cannot self-manage your investment dollars in the market if you do not have enough time to understand it. It just doesn't work. So, get started today, and then figure out while you are playing with small dollars whether or not you want to handle it yourself with large dollars, or as I would suggest handle making money yourself elsewhere while someone else helps to make it grow.*

Time spent on this research gives you a better base of knowledge for questioning a money manager before you give that money manager your accounts. Playing with your gambling account also opens your eyes as to whether you

Buying Securities

have the intestinal fortitude to sell a stock when it's going up, and not chase returns or buy a stock when its going down because you see the upside potential. If you can't do that, and trust me it's not easy, it's time to punt and get help. This is not throwing in the towel. It is realizing that your skillset is better suited to making your dollars elsewhere (maybe real estate), but still understanding that diversification also means having multiple buckets from which to make money. In your case, this particular bucket just may need a little help to be successfully carried out.

Chapter 18

Caution!

It is a good thing to learn caution from the misfortunes of others.

-PUBLILIUS SYRUS

This chapter is going to be a collection of tips based upon my experiences, pain, and suffering as an investor. While I am grateful to have been a successful investor, these are the things that have kept me from making mistakes, or cost me money and slowed my pursuit of financial prosperity. Everybody makes mistakes, but smart people learn from the mistakes of others. I am giving you—the reader—the benefit of the doubt here. Please learn from what went wrong for me so that you can avoid these pitfalls.

Go with your gut

There are a lot of ways to be taken advantage of, and lose on deals. One of the best pieces of advice I have heard is to go with your gut. Most of the time when I have been burned on a deal, it is after I had a bad feeling with someone or something but then talked myself into it. Many times, I have listened to my gut and have been offered the same deal later at a lower price, or found out

Caution!

later that the person I was dealing with was not reputable. There have been a couple of instances where I met people that I felt where full of bull plop, and wound up working with them. One fellow cost me over $200,000 in losses. Another sleaze ball sold non-performing mortgages (which is what we were buying at the time) to my group, and unfortunately, she sold the same mortgages to two other folks as well. When your gut says "no," remember there are other deals out there to be had.

Don't pay up front

When dealing with contractors, do not pay them too much up front. You need to make sure it is always in their financial interest to complete the work they agreed to do. If they have done half of the work and received 90 percent of the money, do not be surprised if they stop showing up, or if your job becomes a very low priority for them. We had a contractor who got paid about 15 percent more than where his completed work should justify. He never showed up again.(I will let you know how the lawsuit turned out in the second edition of this book.)

This contractor got paid more than he should have because we got too big for our britches. We had completed a couple of simultaneous renovation projects, and we did a little too much buying all at once (because we wanted to get our money working). We realized we did not have the contractors to work all the projects, so we started looking with new folks. We should have slowly tested them by giving each small parts of jobs, which were being done by our trusted contractors. But we didn't do this. Instead of having a year where we doubled our monthly income, the result was a year where we were only able to take it up by 20 percent. This happened because we owned properties but we could not get them to be productive in a timely manner. When properties are vacant, they still cost money.

Watch carry costs

Carry costs kill you if you are not careful. Carry costs are the expenses associated with a vacant property. If the house is empty, you still have a mortgage, taxes, insurance, and repairs. If a property stays vacant longer than you project, or work takes longer than you plan, you could find yourself in a cash crisis. Always build a safety factor into your calculation for vacancy. It is hard to hold cash off to the side for this contingency, but it is better than having to do a fire sale because you are overextended.

Never be desperate

Always try your best to leave yourself in a position where you have cash or a way to get cash fairly quickly, even if it means you have take a hard money loan on a property you own. If you become desperate, you become forced to take deep discounts on assets in order to sell them quickly enough to meet your obligations. There are bottom feeders out there who will be salivating to see how badly they can take advantage of your bad situation. Never get into their hands. It is better to grow a little slower and avoid this heartache.

Always be cautious when anyone tries to put pressure on you to do a deal quickly. The faster someone tries to get you to go, the more you should slow things down. Have an attorney look at the transaction. Do a thorough check to see if there is a rat someplace. In our case, the person who resold the same properties multiple times did so putting pressure on us to close, and a simple miscommunication with the attorney allowed her to almost get away with it. It is really interesting this was a person we had done other transactions with, without an issue. We still felt there was something fishy, but we didn't listen to our gut.

Get stuff in writing

Don't need to say much here. Any deal you do with anyone needs to be in writing. People have wonderfully short memories, and almost always in their own favor. Don't be the victim of selective amnesia. Also, get your contractor bids in writing, and have more than one copy. Keep your people on their toes. Do this with anyone you use: Stockbroker, mortgage brokers, financial advisors, accountants, etc.

Caution!

Don't chase the investment

I remember a long time ago when I was trying to buy a stock. It was really cheap, like 35 cents a share. I put an offer in at 34 cents, trying to be cute. It went to 38 cents. I changed my offer to 37 cents, still being cute. Long story short, I chased it up to $1.05 and finally got it. It topped out at $1.10, and I didn't sell because I was pissed that I missed all of the gains (and I was being a horse's posterior). It went down to 15 cents shortly thereafter. So in summary, I got my butt kicked on that investment by the donkey from the Disney movie, which was kicking the ninety-yard field goals. It hurt my feelings a wee bit. If you think you have a good buy, then buy. If you don't get it, look for the next deal.

Avoid bidding against yourself

Similar to the idea above, try to avoid bidding against yourself. When you are told by the other side that your offer is too low for a counter offer, be very careful when responding by raising your offer. You are being negotiated with, and you are giving in by increasing the price without getting anything back. When you raise your price, the seller will then take and counter that higher price. Sometimes it makes sense to do this, when the deal is good enough and your initial offer is low enough, but be cautious and recognize what is happening.

Use an attorney to craft documents

Have an attorney craft the documents you use all the time, for example, a lease you are going to use if you are renting out your properties. I would not have my regular attorney create this document because that is not necessarily what they do. I would have my eviction attorney make it because he is the one who would take it to court and have to defend it. If you are going to be a landlord, opt for a very landlord friendly lease. Most of the time, it is the landlord being screwed in a lease by tenants who don't pay. You can help counter this by having a document set up to give you the best advantages when heading to court.

Know what attorneys do

Attorneys are there to make you aware of risk and protect you from risk. Attorneys do not want you coming back to them threatening a lawsuit because they missed something. This mindset can and does kill good deals all the time.

Many attorneys are first class deal killers. You want to find one who has the confidence to not sweat the B.S. stuff. While I am a fan of asking an attorney for advice, there are times when, as a business person and investor (compensated risk taker), I have to go against their advice. Doing this is something you can start to do when you become more experienced with your investment business. You should not lose a deal because your attorney is arguing with the other side about the wording of a potential meteorite striking the asset clause of the contract. If they are doing that, they win because they are billing your backside for their time. You lose because you are paying them and probably losing the deal in the process.

I have made it clear to my counsel that I accept all meteorite risk for my assets to avoid this type of foolishness (no there is no meteorite clause, but there are equally silly things lawyers take issue with on deals).

> *Creative risk taking is essential to success in any goal where the stakes are high. Thoughtless risks are destructive, of course, but perhaps even more wasteful is thoughtless caution which prompts inaction and promotes failure to seize opportunity.*
>
> -GARY RYAN BLAIR

Beware of those bearing commissions

When using a broker to buy securities, realize they sometimes get special commissions to recommend certain products that might not be in your best interest. You need to do your research and try contacting other brokers to get their opinion of the product. Do this until you find someone you can work with and trust. The one who tells you, "Yeah, they are paying a bonus

Caution!

on XYZ stock, but it's complete garbage," is the one you want (provided their advice pans out).

Be realistic about time lines

When working with a mortgage broker never, ever, ever believe them when they tell you how long it will take to get a loan done. I use the rule of fifteen. I take however many days they tell me and add fifteen. I don't think the reason for their poor ability to deliver in a timely manner is because they are pathological liars, quite the contrary I believe they are just consummately optimistic. If they say, "Yeah, I get these loans closed in twenty days," assume that happened once four years ago and that the buyer had just won the lottery, was drafted into the NFL, and mistakenly won a Nobel Prize. Normal folks don't get that lucky. Believe me, I've tried. I have given them complete packages with every document they need the day we start. It *always* takes longer than projected. So, when you do contracts that require financing, make sure you have the time to get them closed.

Understand what it means to use a home inspector

When using a home inspector, much like a lawyer, their job is not to get sued because they missed something. Their reports are usually going to make the property seem really bad. The numbers they use for the repair amounts are usually much higher than the work actually costs. I use home inspections as a hammer in order to get the seller to knock something off the price if I can. I use the fact that they seem bad in order to approach the seller and say, "This report says the house needs $20,000 in repairs. If you give me a credit of $12,000, the buyer will move forward." Maybe we get something and maybe we don't. The report is a way to get the seller to possibly pay for some of the repairs I probably already knew needed to be done.

When you are the seller on a deal, you have leverage all the way up until you sign the contract. Once that happens, you have very little left. The buyer has potentially two more chances to renegotiate: The first is the home inspection, which we just talked about, and the second is the appraisal, which we discussed earlier. If the appraisal does not come back at the offered amount or more, the buyer can walk away. Now it is possible the buyer could pay the difference in cash, but this is highly unlikely. Usually they want the seller to lower the price. This is the same thing with the home inspection.

There are a couple of ways to handle this. One is to do the inspection before you list the property and pre-disclose it. In this way, any offers you get must have the inspection report figured into the price. The buyer could pay for another inspection, but in my experience, they rarely do. The second thing you can do is if the buyer wants a credit for repairs, you say you want to wait for the results of the appraisal so that you are not renegotiating twice. With renegotiation, the seller almost always loses.

Be aware that some securities can pay a dividend and still go down in value

I had an aunt who was happy as a clam because her investments would send her a dividend check twice a year like clockwork. But the actual value of her investment fell over time by more than 30 percent. Whatever investment avenue you pursue, you need to educate yourself enough so you are aware of the various ways you can make, or lose money.

If it seems too good to be true it probably is

If you find yourself thinking, "Wow, out of all of the investors in the world, how did I get to be soooo lucky to have this investment fall in my lap." *Run!* Bernie Madoff is just a more recent guy to make Ponzi schemes famous. There are lots of similar scams and scammers out there. If you invest and there is a nice return, try taking all of your money out. Keep it out for a while. If they are blowing up your phone with what sounds like desperation, then we've already discussed that. This is similar to "go with your gut," but instead it is "use your head".

Caution!

Finally, cover your assets

When you start to have assets and build wealth, there are parasites out there that try to take it away by any means they can. Lawsuits are just a fact of life, unfortunately. Protect yourself by having good umbrella liability coverage.

Another thing you can do is to not let any one company you form have too many assets. If someone does successfully sue, you can limit how much they can get because their suit is limited to the value of the company they are suing. As an example, if I had one company with $3 million worth of assets, I could be sued for up to $3 million, but if I had three companies each with $1 million in assets, the most I could be sued for in any of the companies would be $1million. There is a lot more to know about insurance and corporate structures, but I have tried to give you some basic ideas to start you on your way.

Part 4

Becoming an Investor

Chapter 19

• • •

Setting yourself up to invest

"Invest in yourself. Your career is the engine of your wealth."

- PAUL CLITHEROE

Let's get real. Just like you go to school to prepare for a future career, you must do some prep work in order to invest well. You invested how many years to get the skills to do the job you are doing now? Now that we have figured out that your job is probably not going to be enough on its own to get you real financial prosperity, are you ready to invest?

Over the last several years, the only group in the U.S. that have experienced real gains have been investors. This is where the sprinklers are pointing. If you want to know what skills get you paid, it is the skill to make money with money. Put those lazy greenbacks to work. To do this you need to be supplementing your knowledge base. The truth is, the vast majority of wealthy people read (much more so than the lower income earners), and if you want to have a similar bank account, it probably makes sense to engage in similar activities. Finding additional books to read to further you along as an investor is a wise allocation of time. It is far better than the stress and drama of wondering if she says, "Yes" to that dress, or what those crazy housewives are up to.

Setting yourself up to invest

My personal preference are audio books in my downtime. I find this to be a painless way to learn. It allows me to listen and learn when I otherwise would be wasting the opportunity. The first thing I do when I wake up is to put on my headphones and start listening. Brushing my teeth—I'm learning; folding laundry—I'm learning; cooking—you guessed it—I'm learning: taking a shower—well, haven't figured out how to listen in there. The point being, I am making efficient use of downtime. I could be listening to music or have the TV on, but instead, I am investing in myself.

> *"An investment in knowledge pays the best interest."*
>
> *- BENJAMIN FRANKLIN*

For those that can learn this way, I highly recommend it. If you worry that you won't catch everything that is said, don't worry about it. You are using time that would otherwise be wasted. Anything you learn is a net positive gain to you. There may be some traditionalists who try to look down their nose at those of us that listen to books instead of reading them. They can behave as they like, but anyone that mocks someone for trying to learn more and think better should probably have their motives questioned.

Be curious. Don't just take things for granted. Ask questions. If you don't know how something is done, ask someone that does know. Most people love to talk about how they do what they do. Use this reality to make them happy and expand your knowledge base. If your attorney makes a suggestion, ask him why. Learn how the laws that govern your business work. When your accountant does your taxes, ask him about the deductions and how they work. When it comes to minimizing taxes, there are many ways to skin a cat—although why you'd want a skinned cat is something you might want to think about.

There have been plenty of times when I have made suggestions to our accountants on how to minimize our tax liability, and these ideas have been better than what they were originally planning to do. This is not because they don't know their business, but because they don't know *my* business and what we can and cannot do. This life offers you daily opportunities to learn. They say you learn something new each day. If you are paying attention, you should learn several new things each day.

The world is your classroom and the curriculum is self-guided. Nobody is there to give you a bad grade if you don't put the work in. Your grade comes from the quality of life you are able to build for yourself by what you have learned from the information all around you. You know you are failing if you are not getting where you want to be. Study more because new tests are administered daily. The good news, you don't need to have all of the answers. There are new tests, so you can keep learning, and the more information you have, the better you will do with future opportunities.

Self-analysis

What kind of person are you? Are you lazy? Distracted? Compulsive? Determined? Certifiably nuts? Detail oriented? Creative? Visionary? Dreamer? Big picture person? The reality is, we are all different, In order to really be effective reaching our goals, we need to be honest with ourselves. If you are a big picture person but hate details, you need to find some way to deal with the details that do need to get done. You may need a system of reminders, which will bug you if you don't handle the details, or maybe you need a detail-oriented partner. One way or the other, you need to do an honest assessment to figure out how to improve the performance of your first employee (you). If you don't feel you know your strengths and weaknesses, ask friends and relatives. They probably have been keeping a detailed list of your shortcomings for years.

Take the information you get from your assessment of yourself and try to figure out, based upon your strengths and weaknesses, what systems you can create to set yourself up for success. If you are lazy, you need to set up a system to give you momentum to start the day. Maybe spend the last part of the evening setting out your clothes for the morning, making sure you have your lunch packed and clear out your inbox so when you get to work you are not looking at a wall of work that needs to be done. Laziness is something that you can train yourself out of, but it requires commitment and discipline.

"Hi, my name is Josh and I was a lazi-holic." I had to fight with myself for years to do what I know needed to be done. Eventually I was able to break the habit and establish one of trying to always be proactive. It took putting systems into place and setting reachable goals for myself that made me feel good when I did them, and bad when I didn't.

Kick your own butt

Sometimes using negative reinforcement is needed when dealing with yourself. This doesn't work for some people, but for others it is very helpful. This looks like saying to yourself, "I didn't get the work done I wanted to so I am not going out with my friends on Saturday." Find things you want to do and hold yourself hostage to get them. Make yourself do what you want or deny yourself the things you want. It is like being a parent to yourself except there is no psychologist sitting there telling you that you are going to damage your own psyche for holding yourself accountable for your choices.

Give yourself a cookie

Positive reinforcement works well for some people too. I call them "cookies" because let's face it, cookies are freaking awesome. They are like the fish they feed the dolphins at sea world, and those dolphins do just about anything for their "cookies". Set a goal and give yourself something you want if you achieve your goal. You want to make sure the "cookie" that you offer yourself is in keeping with your goals. If you wake up early tomorrow, you can go in late to work for the rest of the week: This is probably not a good way to go. If you save money by packing a lunch all week, you can buy a new car—also not a winner. If your goal is to get up early all week, a good "cookie" might be getting a treat on your way to work on Friday if you are successful. If your goal is saving money by packing a lunch instead of eating out each day, a good "cookie" might be taking yourself out to do something you enjoy (that obviously costs much less than what you saved). Look for things that you really enjoy, and give them to yourself only after you are able to get the work out of yourself that you need to.

Sphere of influence analysis

Choose your friends with caution; plan your future with purpose, and frame your life with faith.

-THOMAS S. MONSON

Who do you know and who do *they* know. To be successful, it usually takes more than one person and more than one skill set. See if there are people you know that might be good resources toward your future ventures. Maybe they are contractors, they have large investment portfolios, or they have money they would be willing to invest. People that you know are almost always the easiest sources for real world knowledge on how to get things done. The contractor can tell you how to pull permits or deal with a specific issue you might be having at a property.

The person with the large investment portfolio might be able to give you advice as to how they pick the securities they invest in, or maybe even a tip as to where they are buying now. The person with the cash to invest might be willing to bankroll your acquisitions to get you started more quickly. These are just a few ideas for how people you know can be a huge help going forward. It may just be that they know a person that would want the rental property you have on the market. Connect with your sphere. There are experts amongst them waiting to be called on.

The other side of your sphere of influence are the people that *think* they're experts but aren't. These folks can slow you down and screw you up. There is a simple test to determine if they are for real or if they are, as they say, "all hat and no cattle". See if they actually make money. If they don't produce, then you reduce the value of their influence in your life.

Setting yourself up to invest

*Talkers are usually more articulate than
doers, since talk is their specialty.*

-THOMAS SOWELL

There could be others in your sphere of influence that play into behaviors you would like to eliminate from your life. The guys that want you to play *Halo* till four a.m. when you have things you want to get done the next day. The "girls" who want to go out dancing when you want to focus on making your time more productive. The friends, who have seen too many frat movies in their life and end their sentences with words like "duuude". Even friends who do well but pull you into behaviors that you want to outgrow need to be looked at. They call it your sphere of influence, and while you do have influence with these folks, they also have influence on you. These folks may be great, fun, and sassy but they may also be holding you back. It may be time to clean house, or at a minimum, do a rate of return calculation on those from your sphere you want to let influence the course of your life.

*People who have time on their hands will inevitably
waste the time of people who have work to do.*

-THOMAS SOWELL

Debt analysis

How much do you owe and who do you owe it to? Are your debts for appreciating or income generating assets or are they for depreciating assets that are really "depreciating liabilities"? If you financed your furniture, that is a depreciating liability. If you bought a car with financing, that is also a depreciation liability. If you have credit card debt, which is not for an investment that gives you a positive return, this is a problem. If you have large amounts of this type of debt, you need to try to retire the highest interest parts of your debt to be able to financially afford to invest. If you owe money at 18 percent and you have an investment that is performing at 12 percent you want to get into, it is in your best interest to pay off the credit card before making that investment. The return of 12 percent does not compensate you for the cost of 18 percent to borrow the money. If you have a student loan at 8 percent and at the same time, an investment that is paying 12 percent, it would be in your best interest to *not* pay that loan back any faster than you had to. After all, you are earning 4 percent more on the money than you are paying to borrow it.

> *"I would not pre-pay. I would invest instead
> and let the investments cover it."*
>
> - DAVE RAMSEY

Figure out if your debts can be consolidated to lower your interest payments. Any savings is pure profit to your bottom line. So, finding ways to lessen your payments without hurting your credit worthiness is a very wise use of your time. The more money you can "find" is that much less you need to under consume in order to reach your goals.

Your risk profile

How much risk can you take, and what type of risk bothers you least? Is there a type of investment risk that appeals more to you? Not that risk is ever that appealing, although people do willingly jump off of perfectly good bridges, trusting their survival to what essentially is a big rubber band. Figuring out how much risk you are comfortable with, and then figuring out if this is a healthy and wise amount of risk; these are pre-investment decisions you should make. Your tolerance for risk may also change with time and experience. Some things may seem risky early on when you do not fully understand them, and then as you become more familiar with the process, it will seem less risky to you.

Be cognizant that investment and the generation of wealth is a part of life. It is not life. If you make yourself miserable and other parts of life suffer because of your pursuit of financial gain, any success will not qualify as true prosperity. It is like being a world bench press champion but neglecting any exercise for your legs to the point where you can't walk. Risk can create worry, which can make folks grumpy. Make an effort to find the level of risk that allows you to pursue your goals as ambitiously as possible without sacrificing too much from the other parts of your life. I know what you are thinking: Just find perfect balance. Well, that's no big deal at all. I never said it would be easy. I only said it was important and to be aware of it.

> *The real measure of your wealth is how much you'd be worth if you lost all your money.*
>
> -AUTHOR UNKNOWN

Under consumption

We talked about this already. Why is it here again? Whahh whahhh—because it is just that important. You need to make your money work hard for you while you are young so when you are older, you don't have to work hard for it. Under consumption is super *not* sexy, all the way up until you retire at age thirty-eight, and then it is freaking awesome. Unfortunately, it means delaying gratification, which is something we Americans are not really known for right now. But like any discipline, it takes practice.

My suggestion? Do not go to the website where you have that stuff in your shopping cart/wish list. Empty those suckers out and stop waiting for the moment of weakness when you click "confirm purchase". I don't care if it is on Prime. Set up practices that help you succeed and avoid temptation, and every day your investments will improve the quality of your life. Here is the crazy part—are you ready? Imagine being in a place where you could spend money and *not* have to feel guilty. How cool would that be? This is the path to get there.

> *"Financial peace isn't the acquisition of stuff. It's learning to live on less than you make, so you can give money back and have money to invest. You can't win until you do this."*
>
> - DAVE RAMSEY

Personal reserves

We have addressed this before, but it is important that you have the discussion with yourself regarding the amount you want in liquid reserves to protect yourself and your investments from unforeseen issues. Nobody really sees an emergency repair or medical issue coming (or it wouldn't be an emergency). For this reason, determine how much exposure you have, how much risk you are comfortable with, and then, how much you need to put aside to satisfy those two things.

Remember, that while a reserve may need to be a larger portion of your total investment, when you only have one, as you become more diversified, it can slowly become a smaller and smaller percentage of the total value of your investments. As your family grows, you need a larger reserve because people are expensive critters. In much the same way, however, you do not need to set aside as much for each new family member, but the total amount of reserves should probably increase as your family does.

Once you decide what type of personal reserves you need, figure out how much you need for the investment you are planning on buying. If you have that much money, then buy the investment. If you don't, then continued under consumption is called for. Getting to the place where your investments are helping to fund and refund your reserves is when the amount and frequency with which you can invest starts to increase rapidly. Sometimes early on you may decide to invest with less in the way of reserves than what you might prefer. That is a business decision you have to make. The debate is an old one: Risk versus reward. Welcome to the party.

Setting yourself up to invest

Over/under analyzing

Both can be a problem. The issue is, we can talk ourselves into or out of just about anything. If you don't analyze enough, you may make a mistake and lose money. If you analyze too much, you may lose the deal or convince yourself it is not a good move when it really is. I play board games and there is a phrase for the act of over analysis called "A.P.ing". This is short hand for saying someone is suffering from analysis paralysis. They think so much that they cease acting efficiently. It is very possible to think long and think wrong. Like many recommend when writing tests, "Your first answer is usually the best". That is, your gut is no dummy. It often gets things right. Determine your investment criteria, and if they are met by the investment, pull the trigger.

Now for the folks who pop out of bed with both guns blazing: Your gut is not *always* right! It can help, but you should make use of all of your resources, like your brain. Distracting my gut with a big bowl of ice cream while my brain works on the problem may or may not be my preferred method of handling this. I may really just like ice cream. Your brain needs to analyze the data to make sure the investment does match your goals. While your tendency may be to want to buy everything, try to focus on reasons to kill the deal. Balance with analysis is required. If you find something wrong, you can perhaps go back to the person selling the investment and negotiate the price.

Negotiation

*Let us never negotiate out of fear. But
let us never fear to negotiate.*

-JOHN FITZGERALD KENEDY

The art of negotiation is a skill you can develop only through practice. The good news, most, if not all, interactions between human beings can be looked at as some form of negotiation. Trying to decide with your friends where to eat tonight? As you sing the praises of the restaurant, you are currently salivating to go to, you are "selling"; and you are trying to get your friends to buy into your thinking. This can be seen everywhere in life. Now don't be fooled, because whether you're aware of it or not, we do negotiate these types of things all the time. And there are cultures that really do negotiate everything, including almost every financial transaction of any kind. They are great at it so learn from them. In the Middle East, for example, you might get yelled at, having it suggested that your mother was the offspring of a donkey and a swine, or be told how you are stealing food from the table of their seventeen children just for asking if the price they have listed is the best they can do. Big secret—it is not even close to the best they can do.

Some cultures have a leg up on us, but that doesn't mean we can't be just as good. It just means we need to practice. There are some great negotiation books out there as well as classes. I highly recommend them as a means of self-improvement. When they tell you the price for the class, always ask if its negotiable because how many chances do you really get to be a pain in the butt each day? There isn't the time to completely make you aware of all you should know when it comes to negotiation, but what I will do is give you some broad ideas.

There are two basic types of negotiation: **Competitive negotiation** where one party wins and one loses, and **collaborative negotiation,** where both parties win. Competitive negotiation is what is practiced by our Middle Eastern friends above. It consists of tactics, like flinching visibly when the price is first mentioned for an item you are trying to buy. This makes the other side feel like their price is way too high. Try it. Even if you know it is being done to you, it still causes a reaction in you. Anger can be another tactic, as are ultimatums, and threatening to walk away. Things like this can be learned, and with practice become second nature. Below is one of my favorite competitive negotiating quotes because of a. who said it and b. it's hilarious.

You can get more with a kind word and a gun
than you can with a kind word alone.

-AL CAPONE

Setting yourself up to invest

I prefer to save these kinds of bullying tactics for when they are attempted on me. My preference otherwise is to find a collaborative solution. This is one where I give up things that are not as important to me, but are more important to the other side. They do the same back. Both parties then receive a more valuable deal for themselves, while preserving good working relationships between the parties. Competitive deals often leave hurt feelings and burned bridges. Even if they don't, you are less likely to want to do business with the competitive negotiator again especially if there is an alternative out there. Learning to function with both negotiation skill sets should be part of your investment in yourself. Once you have it, it doesn't go away.

> *My Father said: "You must never try to make all the money that's in a deal. Let the other fellow make some money too, because if you have a reputation for always making all the money, you won't have many deals."*
>
> *-J. PAUL GETTY*

Chapter 20

Go get it! Achieving your American Dream

Action cures fear, inaction creates terror.

-Douglas Horton

We have looked at a lot of things to help us try and track down this elusive idea. I have laid out and described the critical tools and ideas in order to give you the skills to be a player in a field, which has recently been the largest growth sector (wealth wise) in the U.S. economy. Many of the folks reading this may be out of school working on how to at least get back to where their parents where financially, let alone do what every preceding generation has done and surpass them.

One of the things we looked at and learned with just about everything we did, was what a crucial part time plays. If I lend you $10 and you pay me back $20, is this a good deal? It depends. If I lent you the $10 today and you pay me the $20 tomorrow, it is a very good deal for me. If you pay me the $20 fifty years from now, then it is a bad deal for me. Time is a critical component in all things. It is fleeting. You are older now than when you started reading this book (you are probably thinking much older), but if I have done what I set out to do you have made an investment in yourself.

We all now know what investments are capable of doing over time, given a high enough interest rate. If you have the willingness to apply the tools presented here, and the will to find or create capital you need to work with, then the return you get will only be limited by the time you have left to invest. Time is now on your side. You have made the investment in yourself by reading this. Don't let that investment rot in a lousy savings account in your mind, earning no interest right next to the file with the lyrics to the Barney song. Put it to good use by supplementing it with more detailed information on a field of investment that appeals to you.

> *Whatever the dangers of the action we take, the dangers of inaction are far, far greater.*
>
> *—Tony Blair*

What about my day job

The big shift for this current generation is new technologies. It routinely steals formerly decent jobs from the market. If you are a person that has not graduated from college yet, then do not miss this. Invest in the best possible market skills with the education dollars you have. At a minimum, you should supplement whatever field you are going into with as many technology courses as you can. This is an industry routinely paying six figure salaries for entry level programmers. The technology that does exist is constantly spawning new technologies, which need to be designed and implemented. This is a market ripe with demand and desperate for a supply of good workers.

If the thought of being a keyboard jockey as your day job makes your soul cringe, then there are two ways to take that: Option one, this should motivate the crap out of you to invest early and often so you can retire early and tell your boss to shove the keyboard where the sun don't shine? Or option two, find something else. The other area of opportunity for our non-programmer types are skilled trades, that is, plumbers, electricians, and carpenters who not being rapidly being replaced by machines.

In fact, there is a tremendous call for people that can do this type of work. Unlike things you must go to college for, the trades actually pay you while you learn. So instead of racking up over $100,000 in college debt, you could be debt free, earning an income, and well toward becoming a master in your chosen trade. Masters in the trades are routinely earning more than six figures a year for only working a forty-hour week. Those that work more earn more.

When it comes to picking, if college is right for you, a part of that process should be analyzing the financial implications of the cost. You have lost the use of that money, or taken on debt that makes you lose the use of future dollars earned. Either way, you need to look at the demand for labor in the field where you are seeking a degree and the average income people with that degree earn in year one, two, and beyond. Don't just take the word of your guidance counselor. These guys look good based on how many kids they get to go to college. Do your own independent research. Something else to consider: What are going to be the payments on your student loans? This needs to be subtracted from the expected income of your chosen field's average starting wage. What is left is what you have to feed, shelter, and cloth yourself—oh yeah, and save (under consume) to invest.

If you are thinking of a degree in ancient Sanskrit that costs $100,000, you will have very little chance of this being a decent investment. In fact, you probably are going to spend a very long portion of your life saddled with that debt. Compare it with other degrees and include fields not requiring a degree. Do a time value of money investment analysis and follow where it leads. If you are passionate about a field that is an intangible, factor that in it needs to be weighed—the weight you give it is up to you. The question to ask is: Will you still love this field if you are never really financially out of the woods?

Next steps

Humans can do a thing called multi-tasking. Women would probably disagree, saying that men can't. I feel it may be more of a lack of will to expose men's true capabilities. If men were shown to have this ability, their multi-tasking skills could then reasonably be expected to be used for child care, home chores, or God forbid, listening to the summary of a significant other's day!

All kidding aside, the next step in this process is two simultaneous things:

* First, find an area you want to invest in and start studying it carefully. Ask folks in the industry questions, attend lectures, buy more books—and read them (a suggested reading list is located at the end of this book), and look for mentors.
* Second, at the same time, be saving money to invest. Figure out a plan to retire high interest debt and set a reasonable expected rate of return you want from your investments. If the interest rates you are paying on current debts are higher than your targeted investment rate, then you should pay off those debts before you invest.

You could also try to find a way to lower the interest payment amount on the higher interest payments. A reasonable rate to shoot for with a first investment is probably around 8 to10 percent. If you do your homework well, you can beat that, but it is always better to be conservative with your numbers because—as we all know—crap happens.

Once you have your capital and have chosen an investment type you want to proceed with, the next step is to invest. Have a clear plan of how and when you plan to get out of the investment before you invest as well as a contingency plan. If I buy a house to sell, I know the market sales price I can expect as well as how long it is taking for homes to sell in the area. In addition, I want to know the market rents, and how much I could finance it for so I can get most of my money back to reinvest while I rent it. All this information is just as a contingency if I am not able to sell. Better to have a plan and not need it, then to need a plan and not have one.

Conclusion

Inaction may be safe, but it builds nothing.

-DAVE FREUDENTHAL

The Roadmap to the American Dream

Okay, you've made it to through the final chapter. We started with where this idea of an American dream came from, tracked how it has changed, and what it looks like today. We looked at the tools you need to get it, and some moral objections you might have to the whole idea. We went over concepts that you need as groundwork for your education in thinking about money and investing. We spent a bunch of time giving you the math skills you need in order to analyze your various investment choices, and then told you some things to analyze about yourself to make sure you are prepared to invest. This book is not all you need. You will need more in depth resources on various topics, which is why I am including a suggested reading (or listening) list.

This book was written to preform like a pair of glasses. It provides the tools to see the world in a new way. Will this make you a millionaire overnight? No, that is for the investment books that should be in the fiction aisle. Opportunities are everywhere. We have given you the tools here that help provide you with the ability to discern a good deal from a bad one. Now stop wasting that ever-fleeting resource of time, and go make your American Dream an American Reality.

Suggested Reading List

Reading all of these books are not necessary to get started on your investment path. These are great books and they will give you a broader understand of business, history, economics, and government. An understanding of these things helps you to anticipate the market and patterns. I hope that you enjoy them as much as I did.

The Real-Life MBA: by Jack Welch, & Suzy Welch
How an Economy Grows and Why It Crashes: by Peter D. Schiff, & Andrew J. Schiff
A History of the American People: by Paul Johnson
Basic Economics: by Thomas Sowell
Rich Dad Poor Dad: by Robert T. Kiyosaki
American Entrepreneur: by Larry Schweikart, & Lynne Pierson Doti
MONEY Master the Game: by Tony Robbins
America Vol 1& 2: By William J. Bennet
Jack: Straight from the Gut: by Jack Welch, & John A. Byrne
The Quest: by Daniel Yergin
Developing the Qualities of Success: by Zig Ziglar
Free to Choose: by Milton Friedman, & Rose Friedman
Wealth and Poverty: by George F. Gilder

Suggested Reading List

The Intelligent Investor: by Benjamin Graham, & Jason Zweig
The Financial Crisis and the Free Market Cure: John Allison
All the Devils Are Here: by Bethany McLean & Joe Nocera
The Housing Boom and Bust: by Thomas Sowell
The Personal MBA: by Josh Kaufman
Trump: The Art of the Deal: by Donald J. Trump, & Tony Schwartz
The 7 Habits of Highly Effective People: by Stephen R. Covey
The Radicalism of the American Revolution: by Gordon S. Wood
No One Would Listen: by Harry Markopolos
The Millionaire Real Estate Investor: by Gary Keller, & Dave Jenks, & Jay Papasan
How to Win Friends & Influence People: by Dale Carnegie
The Mystery of Capital: by Hernando De Soto
Seven Events That Made America America: by Larry Schweikart
Naked Statistics: by Charles Wheelan
Wealth, Poverty, and Politics: by Thomas Sowell
The Virgin Way: by Richard Branson
The House of Morgan: by Ron Chernow
Charlie Munger: The Complete Investor: By Tren Griffin
The Boom: by Russel Gold
Energy for Future Presidents: by Richard A. Muller

Made in the USA
Columbia, SC
11 January 2020